Santa Clara
County
Free Library

REFERENCE

THE
ISSEI

THE 一世 ISSEI

PORTRAIT
OF A
PIONEER
An Oral History

EDITED BY
Eileen Sunada Sarasohn

Pacific Books, Publishers
Palo Alto, California

Library of Congress Cataloging in Publication Data

Main entry under title:

The Issei, portrait of a pioneer.

   Collection of 32 interviews conducted in
Japanese and translated into English.
   Includes index.
   1. Japanese Americans—History. 2. Japanese
Americans—Biography. 3. Oral history. I. Sarasohn,
Eileen Sunada, 1943–   .
E184.J3185 1983   973'.04956   82-22319
ISBN 0-87015-236-X

PACIFIC BOOKS, PUBLISHERS
P.O. Box 558, Palo Alto, California 94302-0558, U.S.A.

Introduction

Mention the word "pioneer" and most Americans envision someone who struggled across the Great Plains in a covered wagon to settle the West. This history tells the story of another group of pioneers who moved from the opposite direction—across the Pacific Ocean from Japan—to settle in the West and leave their imprint on the regional life of that area, as well as the entire country. Although these people arrived several decades after the 1849 Gold Rush, they consider themselves pioneers of the West too. They pioneered the fledgling agricultural industry in California, planting the first citrus orchards, establishing the rice industry, and helping to structure the marketing system for the state's fruit and vegetable crops. These immigrants also marked out new areas in small businesses all along the Pacific Coast. They call themselves "Issei," first-generation pioneer. They take great pride in this distinction, and they take great pride not only in having adapted their Japanese cultural traits to a new environment but also in having done it so effectively that the new land has come to value those traits.

This is an oral history that documents the collective experience of the Issei from early life in Japan and the formulation of their dream of coming to America to the reality of facing discrimination, finding work, weathering the Depression and the shock of World War II, coping with life in relocation camps, and finally, returning to pick up the pieces of their lives with the perseverance and dignity with which they began. Much of this experience has been documented in traditional history books, but this is the first major attempt to present the Issei experience from *their* perspective. The result is a very personal interpretation of certain historical events, one that is strongly colored by their Japanese beginnings. Other Japanese Americans, particularly those of the Nisei and Sansei generations, may differ in their interpretation of some events. It has become fashionable to present a much more militant appraisal of events concerning World War II and the relocation camps. However, it is important to remember that this portrait of the Issei is not an attempt to sell the Japanese American or his cause. It is an attempt to demolish old stereotypes, not to construct new ones; it is an attempt to reveal the Issei as they were and are. The Issei experience was not limited to the war years. Those years were only a part of a story that documents the hope, courage, sacrifice, and ultimately, the success of a people who not only endured but prevailed. Theirs is a story in which all Americans may take great pride. Their intent was to share their stories that we might learn about them and from them.

This history is composed of memories. There are facts and dates, true incidents, and an occasional statistic, but mainly there are feelings and impressions, the stuff that fashions the reality of a man.

Editor's Notes and Acknowledgments

All of the Issei whose interviews appear in this book have some knowledge of English but preferred to communicate in their native language; therefore, the interviews were conducted in Japanese and translated into English before the editing process began. Japanese is also the native language of the interviewer and the translators, who are not only bilingual but also have lived in both Japan and the United States. The editor is a Sansei, third-generation Japanese American. Out of some sixty available interviews, the thirty-two that are used in *The Issei: Portrait of a Pioneer* were chosen on the basis of their detailed recollection of events and their representation of the collective Issei experience.

One major editing problem was determining the speech patterns that should be retained in the story line of the interviews. There is a distinct difference between the modes of speech of the Japanese man and the Japanese woman. The men tend to speak in short, abrupt phrases, whereas the women use polite forms of speech and tend to use more fluid, descriptive phrases. These differences are most evident when the Issei reminisce about their early years in Japan. Some phrases in the interviews appear to be grammatically incorrect or awkward, but they are retained because they are common to the Issei style of speaking English. The editor has attempted to preserve these various speech characteristics in the interviews.

Throughout the text the words "relocation center" and, in particular, "camp" are used to denote the ten War Relocation Authority centers to which persons of Japanese descent were evacuated during World War II. Those terms were chosen because they are the references used by the Issei in their interviews. In recent years "concentration camp" has increased in usage, but this reference is not common to the Issei. It is interesting to note that in an attempt to reflect popular American terminology for a smoother translation, some of the translators used "concentration camp"; upon conferring with the interviewer, the editor learned that in no case was this term used in any of the interviews.

o o o o o o o o o o o o o o o

The interviews in the book were funded by the Issei Oral History Project, Inc., a nonprofit organization whose major purpose is to record the personal histories of the Issei before they are lost to time.

Although the academic community has made several attempts to sponsor oral history projects in the Japanese community, none of them have produced interviews with the candor and detail of those of the Issei Oral History Project. The success of the Project is probably due to the delicate balance achieved between accepting academic counsel and, at the same time, maintaining strict control of the project from within the Japanese community.

In 1969, when the Project had its modest beginnings, Dr. Thomas Swift, Dr. Dennis O'Brian, and Heihachiro Takarabe outlined a set of goals and a structure for the Project. Dr. O'Brian, an interviewer for the foreign affairs section of the Kennedy Library, also lent professional advice for the design of the questionnaire to be used during the interviews and the processing of the tapes.

The Project discovered through trial and error that ultimately the interviewer was the key to the success of any interview. The Issei tend to maintain a distance between themselves and interviewers from outside the Japanese community and interviewers who have not learned to observe the customs and forms that are still a significant bridge toward obtaining their confidence. The interviews completed by the Project's director, Heihachiro Takarabe, were judged to be the most successful by far.

Heihachiro Takarabe was born in Japan, is bilingual, has had an emigrational experience somewhat similar to that of the Issei, bridges a cultural and generational gap, and holds a place within the Japanese community as the minister of a Japanese church. To Issei of all religious backgrounds, his position, rather than his denomination, was significant. He was trusted—and asked—by almost every Issei interviewed not to misconstrue or abuse the information and confidences in the interviews. There are, of course, nuances in relationships that only persons of rare sensitivity can cultivate to elicit a memory and then a verbal confidence. This was a skill that Hei commanded as he guided the Issei through their old memories and taped the interviews. I am particularly indebted to him and also to the Issei Oral History Project's Board of Governors for permitting me to edit these unique interviews.

I acknowledge a lifelong debt of gratitude to the Issei who have shared their memories for this book and have given their life histories as a final contribution to the future generations of Japanese Americans and to all Americans. There are many Issei whose interviews do not appear in print here, but the momentum and spirit of their words and lives are in these pages as well.

My thanks go also to Laura Tanaka, who spent many hours typing and retyping each draft, and to Julie Mockler, Howard Sarasohn, and other friends who read the manuscript and offered many valuable suggestions as well as encouragement. And finally, to my family, many thanks for those precious hours to work on the manuscript.

EILEEN SUNADA SARASOHN

Contents

Prologue

In 1636 the Japanese government prohibited Japanese subjects and vessels from traveling abroad, and all foreigners, except a limited number of Dutch, from coming to Japan. For more than two hundred years, until the arrival of Commodore Matthew Perry in 1853, this state of affairs persisted. Had the Japanese government allowed free travel, the history and population of North America's West Coast would have been different indeed.

Following Commodore Perry's arrival in Japan, a number of dramatic changes in Japanese society began to accelerate immigration across the Pacific. Shortly after 1867, when Emperor Meiji was declared the supreme secular and spiritual ruler of Japan, the travel ban was lifted. Then the Japanese government took a number of steps to abolish the long-existing feudal system. By 1876 the essence of the feudal system, the maintenance of the samurai class, had been officially ended by a system of pensions, commutations, and the highly important establishment of national conscription. Because of these sweeping changes, economic disruptions were severe. Opportunities for many Japanese men remained limited as the practice of primogeniture continued whereby the eldest son inherited the family name, house, and usually most of the property. Therefore, by 1884 Japan had begun to allow immigrants to leave as contract laborers. Although it was possible for Japanese to emigrate to the territories of Hokkaido and Formosa, many found the climate and economic opportunities more favorable on the Pacific West Coast of the United States.

Finally, following the period of change from a feudal society to the institution of a parliamentary government, Japan undertook two major wars, one with China (1894–95) and one with Russia (1904–5). The effect of these wars on immigration was considerable, since many men of draft age chose to emigrate rather than be drafted.

These events accelerated the immigration of approximately 275,000 Japanese from a trickle in 1868 to its peak in 1907 and its abrupt halt by the Immigration Act of 1924. It is amongst these bits of historical data that the Issei story begins.

PART I:
THE DREAM

1

The Other Side of the Sea

NISUKE MITSUMORI

My name is Mitsumori, Nisuke in the Japanese way, but in English it should be Nisuke Mitsumori. I was born in Yamanashi Prefecture[1] on February 15, 1888. In the Japanese way I was born in the twenty-first year of Meiji. I am the second son in a family which had farmed for generations. My father was a serious country farmer, and my mother was the daughter of a farmer. I would say that she was a typical peasant's wife. She was a very stern mother and used to spank us immediately after we did something wrong.

In those days there were four years in elementary school and another four years for middle school.[2] I finished those eight years, but most chilaen did not go as far as I did. When I started going to school, there were about thirty students in each class. However, by the time I started middle school, there were only eight or so students left in the class. We studied everything that was required in those days: Japanese, arithmetic, calligraphy, reading, ethics, art, science, history, and geography. Since I liked to study very much, I was not satisfied with those subjects and attended a night school. There I learned Chinese history and Chinese classics. I went to a scholar of Chinese classics—famous in the village—and he taught me these subjects.

I do remember some of my teachers. Mr. Higuchi was a teacher in the elementary school. He was a priest and a very serious

[1]Japan is divided into forty-six local governing units called prefectures or *ken*.
[2]Primary education has been compulsory in Japan since 1870.

person. Mr. Kaneko was our principal. After Mr. Kaneko left, Mr. Shinohara came. He showed an interest in me as a student. According to the custom of our school, a scholarship award was given up to the third year in middle school, but no fourth-year graduating student was honored. The idea was that everyone at graduation should be equal. However, Mr. Shinohara decided to recognize me because he thought that I was an extraordinary student and would become a successful person in the future. (When I went back to Japan to visit last October, my nephew found that award—a certificate of achievement which my brother had kept somewhere in the house—and told me what a fine student I must have been.)

Since my family was poor in those days, I could not go on to a higher school, which is equivalent to senior high school today. It was rather costly to go on; however, I could go to a normal school, since it was prefectural and the tuition was free. But a person had to be eighteen years old to go to a normal school, and I was seventeen. In the meantime, the war between Japan and Russia had started. Since I did not want to be drafted, I decided to come to the United States and gave up the idea of going to a normal school.

Our neighbor's young son also went to the States; so I used to ask his family what the United States was like, how wealthy the people were, whether I could study over there and the like. I heard that the United States was a huge country—very rich—and that it was a country where one could act as he wished. I thought it must be a really nice place by what people said and by what I saw in pictures. I don't know the reason, but I longed to see this country.

In those days anybody who wished to come to the United States was considered an unpatriotic person. When a person became eighteen, he received a physical examination for conscription. From mid-March no one could leave the country, because the physicals were conducted from March 15 until July. The government said that every citizen should participate in the war between Japan and Russia, and all the eighteen-year-olds were hidden by their families. Therefore, I thought I had to leave as quickly as possible and applied for a passport immediately after New Year's Day. I must have received my passport in two or three weeks, because I left Japan in February. I did not have any particular idea of what I would do in the States. I had a vague idea that something would work out once I arrived.

SHIZUMA TAKESHITA

My name is Shizuma Takeshita, and I was born in Meiji 13—it was in 1880 on September 10—in Nagasaki Prefecture, Iki-gun, a small island. My father was a descendant of an old *shizoku* family (samurai clan) and a follower of Lord Matsuura. I had two sisters, and I was the only son. My father died when I was thirteen years old, and being the only son, I had to take over my father's estate. I was not allowed to leave. At that time there was no educational institution higher than the eighth grade on my island; so there was no way for me to receive a higher education there. That's why when I was seventeen years old, I sneaked out from home without telling my mother or grandmother and went to Nagasaki City to work in a lawyer's office and study law.

In those days, if doctors or lawyers passed an examination, they were able to get a license to practice. I worked in Mr. Kishihara's law office. Mr. Kishihara was very good to me. I went to court with him, heard arguments on cases, took notes, and helped him in other ways. One day he told me that he thought I was ready to become his successor and to apply for the licensing examination. About that time the requirements changed, and a university degree became necessary to become a lawyer. I was so disappointed that I felt like committing suicide. Mr. Kishihara sympathized with me. He suggested that I go to America, study English, and then come back to Japan and start a business or something. He gave me three hundred yen, and I took the lowest-class fare on the ship and came to America in 1902.

CHOICHI NITTA

My childhood dream was to become a navy officer—to go to college, then the Naval Academy, and become an admiral. My father was against the idea, because he had several acres of land and wanted me, the eldest son, to take over and farm the place. He thought I should not worry about making a living and that I didn't need more than an elementary school education. My father was educated in a private temple school. When he was sixteen, he cut his samurai hair-do.[3] He would not give me permission to go to college; so I decided to go to my uncle's place in Hawaii. I secretly

[3]In Japan hairstyles often denoted status and occupation for men as well as for women.

applied for a passport and received it. I needed money for the fare
to Hawaii, but my father was upset about my decision to leave
and would not give me anything. My mother also thought that I
should listen to my father, get married when I was twenty, and
maintain the home. I told my mother that the only way out for
me was to choose death. I wasn't that serious, but she was
shocked and did not want that to happen. She persuaded my
father to pay for my transportation to Hawaii, where my uncle,
my father's younger brother, had emigrated.

Minejiro Shibata

My name is Minejiro Shibata. I'm from Shimizu in Shizuoka. I
was born in 1905 or Meiji 35, so I'm seventy-one years old. We
were farmers in Japan; that is, farming was our main source of
income. Though we owned a boat, we didn't fish too much. Three
partners were co-owners of a boat for tuna fishing. We rushed to
the beach and fished whenever we saw fish; so we weren't real
fishermen.

Events in Japan. . . . Yes, I vaguely remember some things. I
remember the "rice riot" best. The wealthier families which had
a large crop of rice were all burned out. Some townsmen did it. In
those days the price of rice went sky-high, and the poor had a hard
time. The poor took their revenge on the rich and set the fire. I
went to see the ruins of the fire. We small farmers didn't suffer
too much, for we had yams, wheat, and rice on our own farms.
Those poor townsmen couldn't afford to buy enough rice. They
bought only one *sho* (3.8 pints) of rice at a time; so the term
"buying one *sho* of rice" was used as a pronoun for the poor.

When I was a boy, farmers had little cash. They ate the products
from their farms. My parents never bought a toy for me when I
was a child. I had a knife, so I made my toys with it. Even now I
make almost everything by myself. I was surprised that the children in this country couldn't make anything by themselves.

I graduated from high elementary school, which is a junior high
school here. There were no schools near my house, so I walked
three or four miles a day in order to get to school. I remember that
I didn't study very hard.

When I was fourteen or fifteen years old, I helped my parents
water the vegetables every morning in the summer season before
going to school. I felt so hungry before getting to school that I ate

my lunch on the way there. Since I didn't have anything to eat during lunch time, I bought some roasted sweet potatoes or dried persimmons at the cost of twenty or thirty sen. Even though I was sometimes hungry, I never stole anything from anybody. I was taught not to steal, and I have been impressed by that lesson since my childhood.

In May, 1919, when I was in my eighteenth calendar year, I came to the United States. My brother was here and he motivated me to come. He couldn't make a good life for himself in Japan; so he traveled to Venice, London, and finally to New York. He decided to remain in the United States. He then summoned my father and mother, and my mother summoned me here.

SHOICHI FUKUDA

Well, my father came over here alone. My mother died when I was very young, so I was raised by my relatives in Japan. I had to work when I was in the sixth grade in elementary school. When I was eleven years old, I entered the household of a Japanese pickle-maker as an apprentice. This happened on the same day that my classmates at school advanced to the sixth grade—all with new clothes. I still remember that day—April 1st. There were about twenty young apprentices in that household, but I was the youngest. The older boys were very arrogant when they felt good, and tyrants otherwise. I was beaten many times by them, for no one tried to take care of the young ones.

In my work I had to stick my hands into the cold salt solution even in the winter, and my hands became dry, chapped, and blistered. During the summer I had to deliver pickles to distant stores and had to pull a heavy cart to make the deliveries. The owner did not give me any spending money. At times I was so hungry that it would take me two to three hours to walk two miles home. It was a very difficult time in my life. I used to think that if only I had my parents, I would not have to go through this hardship. Hiding myself behind the big tubs of pickles, I would cry.

Then the pickle store went bankrupt, forcing me to become an apprentice in the household of a blacksmith. I also worked as a newspaper boy and at my uncle's pawnshop as well.

When I was sixteen years old, my father wrote to me. It was quite a rare happening. The reason I came to the United States was because my father sent for me. This is called "Yobiyose." I am not a pioneer Issei. People like me were called Yobiyose, because we were brought over here by these pioneers. But I call myself "Issei" because I did work with these pioneers. I think I have been here for fifty-two years, since I came here in 1917.

YOSHITO FUJII

My father came to the U.S. for the first time when his children were little. I hadn't been born yet. In 1884, the twenty-seventh year of the Meiji period, he came here with my elder brother Chajiro, who was sixteen years old then. My father stayed for two years to have a look at the United States. He traveled here and there in the northern (Pacific Northwest) part of the country with Chajiro. Then he returned to Japan and urged young people to go to America. According to the records, he was responsible for sending five hundred and thirty young people from Hiroshima to the U.S. It is one of the reasons why there were so many immigrants from Hiroshima.

My father was a farmer. Our family was an old one. My father represented the forty-second generation, and I represent the forty-third, according to the statistics. At that time the Japanese family system accorded the heir, usually the eldest son, to succeed to the family house, and the property was divided among all of the children. Though we had a pretty large piece of property, how little each would get! What can you do in the future with such a limited amount of property? So my father visited each village and canvassed for young people to go abroad. He left Chajiro in Seattle in order to have him take care of the young people coming from Japan.

My brother was an aggressive man and was active in the *kenjinkai* (prefectural association),[4] *nikkeijinkai* (the Japanese association), and in establishing the Buddhist church here. My brother started the Fujii Hotel at the age of twenty-one. He was the originator of the Japanese hotel business in Seattle. He built the hotel and opened it in 1899, and the young people from Japan—Hiroshima—stayed in the hotel. Later he became a paralytic.

By that time I had graduated from junior high school and was

[4]Prefectural associations were formed by immigrants who came from the same *ken* or prefecture.

planning to go to senior high school in Japan. My brother, who was back in Japan for the time being, asked me if I'd like to get a higher education. I asked him if I could go to the United States to study, and he agreed. So I graduated from junior high school in April and came here in June, 1919.

I imagined the United States would be a good country with a lot of future prospects. I didn't have any deep thoughts, for I didn't intend to stay here a long time. Everybody was planning to make money and return to Japan. I thought it would take at least five years to complete my education, though I felt as if five years would last forever. Elder sister said five years wouldn't be enough and I would need ten years, but I thought ten years would be unbearably long.[5]

○ ○ ○ ○ ○ ○ ○ ○ ○ ○ ○ ○ ○ ○ ○

SADAME INOUYE

My first name is Sadame. The Chinese character is one for *sadameru* (to decide, fix, determine). There is no special meaning for the character. At school, people used to call me Sadamu rather than Sadame. Sadame is usually a girl's name. I may be the only male whose name is Sadame. I did not feel ashamed of my name, for my parents chose it for me.

After the Russo-Japanese War, Japan was poor, and the government encouraged people to go abroad to make money. By going abroad I mean Hawaii. Those who could come to the mainland were either those who were invited to come or those who were specialists in certain fields and came here to do research.

The reason I came to this country was to make money. I had one brother and two sisters. I am the second child, but the oldest son. My family farmed and we had a stone-cutting business too. My father was in debt, so he sent me to this country to make money. I sacrificed myself for my father for the first ten years in the States. I paid back all his debts. At that time I took it for granted that a child would sacrifice himself for his family, although such a situation is almost inconceivable today.

[5]In Japan, family hierarchy is so important that the children often do not refer to one another by their names but by their position in the family line. The Nisei, children of the Issei, retain this custom, but the practice does not continue in successive generations.

Riichi Satow

We lived on a farm in Chiba Ken. Father was . . . I have to talk about our family shame which I have not even told to my children yet. My father lived a dissipated life when he was young . . . well, before he was married mostly. It had been the custom in rural Japan for the eldest son to become the head of the family by succeeding his father automatically after his death. My father, being the eldest of the brothers, became the head of his family at the age of eighteen; and all of a sudden he came to possess a lot of things: the family farm land, a little bit of mountain property, and other real estate. When young people made quick fortunes, there were a lot of temptations from outside in that people tried to make them spend their money. They got my father in gambling. He lost most of his property, even though he was married by then. People in Japan used to think that a marriage would be the best medicine to keep a dissipated son from being further spoiled. For this reason the family arranged to have my father married at a relatively young age, and it turned out that this strategy didn't work out with him as anticipated. That's why my mother suffered a lot, and the whole family was very poor. He did keep our house, for there were five of us children in all, three brothers and two sisters. One day my father came to his senses and realized what he was so far—a complete failure. Then he went to the United States to recover his losses.

Many Japanese at that time went to Hawaii under contracts to work on sugar cane plantations. For a commission, Japanese agents recruited young people as contract laborers throughout the rural areas of Japan. There were a number of people who came to Hawaii that way, usually with a three-year contract. Most of them were from the Hiroshima, Yamaguchi, and Kyushu areas. The thought of going overseas and making some money had long occupied my father's mind, for he caused unforgivable damage to the family—almost to the point where he could not possibly recover his losses. He first went to Hawaii. After six months there, Hawaii was annexed, and it became part of the United States. On that occasion, contract labor was banned, and everybody became free laborers. When this was done, there were some people who welcomed it and others who were stranded because of it. The laborers were free, but they had to find jobs to support themselves on their own. There was confusion for a while among the laborers. My father then decided to go to the mainland.

Father settled in Napa and worked hard. He was also a fairly smart man, and those characteristics of his eventually helped him a great deal. He became the foreman of a Japanese crew at a big fruit ranch and recruited more Japanese workers. He made quite a bit of money as foreman of the ranch. In the twelfth year after he left Japan, he came back home with some money. He bought back the farm land, the mountain property, and other items that were mortgaged. He was even able to increase his property holdings. That was around 1911, because in the following year my brother and I came over here.

Since most of the troubles with the family were all taken care of, my father decided to come to the States again. In those days two or three thousand dollars meant quite a lot to a Japanese person, and anybody coming back to Japan with that much money could do whatever he wanted to do—say, build a new house or buy some farm land. This was the dream that most Japanese emigrants had. Three years of hard work could bring a fortune for use back in Japan. I also had an increasing desire to come to the States, for I decided it wouldn't do any good to stay in the village. The only chance for me was to get out of there and go overseas. Japanese custom was such that the first son would succeed as the family head; consequently, the alternatives left for the second son and down were to marry into someone's family or to go someplace else to seek their own fortune—most likely to Tokyo or Osaka or to one of the other big cities. America was the first choice of places to go for almost everybody in Japan at that time. We thought lots of jobs were available and the wages were double because a dollar was worth twice as much as a yen. Our minds were filled with such dreams.

About that time I saw a minister walking down the street. He was walking around town one evening with his wife and baby. And do you know what? *He* was holding the baby, not his wife! They were strolling down the street like that. That kind of scene was very new and rare in Japan at that time. "Look, that's a minister. The husband is holding the baby, and his wife is walking free!" That's how unusual it looked to a lot of people. And everybody, I for one, used to go out of the house to take a look at them. We thought it was very modern, and very Western, and we figured ministers were Western-fashioned. To a lot of young people it seemed something to long for; yet at the same time it was something very strange. It was around that time that I began to think about coming over to the United States.

Right then my father came home, but he was to go back to the States again. I thought the opportunity for me was right. I asked him to invite me over later. One year after that, I landed in San Francisco as a Yobiyose. That's how I finally came to the U.S. and became an American.

KENGO TAJIMA

Well, it took 60 yen to cross the Pacific, and I had to carry 100 yen just to show that I didn't want to be on public charge. That money I borrowed from my uncle. Sometime later after I came here I, of course, returned the money. If you would like me to tell you what motivated most Japanese men to emigrate, there are two, maybe three, reasons. Of course, the Japanese people were mostly farming people . . . up to, well, the Taisho Era. The Japanese were of three classes: one small class of large landowners, whose land the tenants cultivated, and tenants. Between them there were farmers who held small farms and a little mountain property that varied according to the locality. Most immigrants came from the class of small landowners. How they came to own their land I don't know. In feudal Japan all the land belonged to the Daimyo and the people tilled the land, but they really didn't own it. After the Meiji Era came a class of small landowners.

They were sort of middle-class people. Now many of our immigrants came from this class. The economic situation at the time was not stable and there was constant fluctuation, and many small landowners had difficulty. Families were in danger of losing their land. In order to salvage the family situation, young men emigrated. They were mostly *chonan*, eldest sons in the family. They had that responsibility; so they emigrated. They came with the idea of staying in America for three years, saving money, and then returning to restore their family fortune. Still others came because they were the second and third sons in the family, and most of the family fortune would go to the eldest son. They could shift for themselves; so they came too. That's one class.

Then came another class of more educated young men to which I belonged. One group came over after they had finished *chu gakko* (grammar school) or maybe some *gakko* (school) above. They wanted to make more of their lives; so they came over. Some schools did not have the privilege of military service deferment. In order to avoid being drafted, some students came over to this country. Another reason for emigrating is that there would not be much chance for them if they stayed in Japan, because the future of most educated young men would be in government service. Tokyo University was especially built to produce government officials. Unless you went to the University of Tokyo and entered the law department and so forth, you did not have many opportunities. Those are some of the reasons why my contemporaries came over to this country.

Most of the early male immigrants were from the Japanese countryside rather than the city; most were above the lowest socioeconomic class; and most had a better than average Japanese education. Freed from some of the most binding economic and social barriers in Japan, these unusually energetic and ambitious people often achieved amazing economic success in the United States.

Unlike most immigrants to America, Japanese males did not bring spouses and children. They sent for families later on, or, in most cases, married much later in life. The female emigrant tended to be from a slightly higher socioeconomic class than her husband, was often ten or fifteen years younger than her husband, and was slightly better educated than the average Japanese woman.

Mrs. Kamechiyo Takahashi

I'm from Kokawa-mura, Naga-gun, Wakayama Ken. I was born in 1889. My father was a farmer. He had six *tan* (an outdated Japanese measure for land—0.25 acres) of land for rice and a mulberry field because he was raising silkworms. He died when I was four; so my mother raised us by herself. My older brother had already gone to the United States. He believed that a higher education was important but couldn't go on in school himself. He offered me the opportunity and wrote that he would send me money for school, but I didn't like studying. When it came to sewing, I could figure out how to cut material properly no matter how complicated the garment was. At school, math was all right, because I needed it for sewing. Geography and history weren't for me. As I didn't like studying too much, I went up to the sixth grade in elementary school.

Not being old enough, I couldn't attend a regular sewing school, but I found a place where I could learn only how to sew. As soon as I was of age, I entered a regular sewing school and completed a four-year curriculum. Then I served as a teacher's assistant for two years. I was at the school for six years altogether. I was always worried about examinations. But in sewing school I was usually the first to complete a project and to hand it to a teacher. I fully realized that it was important to develop your own interests. I had to prepare hard for the licensing examination. I took the examination after I got married to Takahashi.

I was nineteen years old when I got married. It was during a summer vacation. I met Takahashi when I was teaching school. He was also a schoolteacher. His house was two miles away from mine, which was pretty far to walk. After we had our first son, Takahashi was called to the United States by his brother to become a storeman. His brother owned a grocery store. Since I was pregnant again, my husband told me to follow him after my pregnancy was over. But then I didn't come here until our second child was three years old. It was in 1916.

Since my mother was alone, my children and I lived with her while Takahashi was in the States by himself. I wrote my brother to return to Japan to take care of my mother, but he didn't return. On the other hand, Takahashi warned me that my immigration visa would expire if I didn't leave Japan right away. My mother told me that I should go to my husband. She hoped my brother would return to her if I went ahead and left her. As soon as I arrived here, my brother closed down his bicycle store in Riverside and went back to Japan.

Mrs. Riyo Orite

My name is Orite, Riyo. I'm from Mita-mura, Takata-gun, Hiroshima Ken. I was born in 1895 in the twenty-eighth year of the Meiji period.

My uncle was the owner of a drapery shop and was the only male heir of my mother's family. When he died, my father decided to succeed to her family. Our original business was my uncle's drapery shop. My mother was too busy with her small children and family chores to help with the business; therefore, my parents closed the drapery shop and started farming. Not being very healthy, my father usually hired others to work on his farms. My grandfather was a doctor, and my father was good at doctoring too. After closing the drapery shop, my father became an acupuncturist in addition to his farming. His grown-up children were not fond of farming; so they lived separately. He was disappointed that none of his older children were willing to help with the farming; therefore, he later sold all of his property and went to a city—Hiroshima.

He opened an acupuncture business in the city. He also practiced herb medicine and moxa cautery.[6] He prescribed medicine which was a mixture of dry herbs and liver. I should have learned it. I remember he had a lot of patients all the time.

My father was good at doctoring. Before we moved to the city, all of us in the small village had planted rice together. I was fourteen or fifteen years old. One evening we returned home from the rice field to take a bath and eat dinner. It was around midnight when I felt some soreness in my leg. I didn't want to wake my father; so I just rubbed the leg. Finally, I called my father for help. My leg was red and swollen. Father wondered whether or not some poisonous bugs had bitten my leg. We used mosquito nets in Japan, and we wondered if there were some bugs in the net. We looked, but we found none. My father made a medicinal concoction for me, warmed my leg, cauterized it with moxa, and performed an acupuncture.

We went to a doctor as soon as day broke. The doctor said he would have to cut my leg off at the knee because the leg bone was inflamed. My father, shocked at the doctor's words, asked him to wait. He had been raising me to be a healthy child, and he didn't want me to become a cripple. He took me back home from the doctor by force. He cauterized my leg with moxa, rubbed it, and warmed it. Though he was busy in the midst of rice planting, he came back home three times a day to warm up my leg and that helped a lot. Then my leg was cured. The effectiveness of acupuncture and moxa cautery are said to be strong enough to burn away swellings. The symptoms never appeared after I came to the U.S.

My grandfather and grandmother lived with us in Japan. Let's see . . . how long? My grandmother was alive till I was eight years old. She was very old-fashioned and very strict. During my school

---

[6]Moxa cautery is the art of healing by gradually firing a substance, usually the down from leaves of the *Artemesia moxa*, on or near the skin as a cauterizing agent or counter irritant for the relief or cure of a disease.

days, the regular elementary school was extended to six years. It had formerly been for four years. Higher elementary school began after the sixth grade. My grandmother was stubborn. She said, "No matter how hard a farmer's daughter studies, she can never marry a cabinet minister." My mother insisted that I should be able to write my own name at least, and therefore she put me into a high elementary school. After graduation, I was taught sewing and weaving at home.

During my school days I played with my friends and had lots of fun. We went to the mountains to pick strawberries and brackens and often took our lunch with us, playing there all day long. During village festivals, I put on my best wardrobe, had my hair done at a beauty shop, and enjoyed *sumo* (traditional Japanese wrestling) games. A *mikoshi* (a palanquin-like shrine) carrying, a flute concert, and a drum percussion demonstration were held during the festival. Sometimes a slide show was held at a temple or a large home. The *naniwabushi* (recitation and chanting of various stories) had started when I was a child. The reciters stayed at the homes of villagers. I remember that I went to listen. Those were my pleasures.

When I was still a child in the countryside, a lady who was accomplished at sewing, flower arrangement, music, and many other things came to our village from Kure. She wanted to teach those things. As she couldn't find any other place, we invited her to stay with us. My strict grandmother believed that girls should be accomplished in such things, and she made me learn sewing, flower arrangement, *samisen* (a three-stringed Japanese musical instrument), and other things at home.

In those days, no music scores were available. I had to learn to play by ear. Being an old-fashioned lady, the teacher was very strict. I sat down before her, but I couldn't remember what I had learned in the previous lesson. Then she would hit me with the instrument pick. After having been hit, I was so frightened that I became worse. I cried, but I tried to learn, though I hated it. The teacher, because she was staying with us, saw whatever I was doing. I used to blow the fire with a blowpipe to cook rice. The teacher would come to me and say, "If you really want to learn *samisen*, you should hold the blowpipe as if it were a *samisen* and practice." When I cleaned our guest room, I wore a kimono with white sleeves. She would order me to hold the sleeve as a *samisen* and practice. I was scolded by her no matter where I was. Finally I quit instrument lessons because I really didn't like it.

At the age of ten I switched to sewing and flower arrangement. As the youngest one in the class, I was like a trainee. The first person who finished a flower arrangement put her work in an alcove. I had to observe it respectfully. Whenever you observe another person's flower arrangement, you are supposed to bow. Instead I sat by the flowers and touched them. The others, who were observing me from behind, laughed at my clumsiness, and I felt embarrassed.

Our family had been religious for generations. My father and uncle visited the temple often, and a priest stayed with us for five days during the spring and autumn equinox. Being a farm family, we observed religious rituals before harvesting rice, and people visited us from all over during the three-day Lantern Festival. There are many kinds of religious organizations today in the United States, but when I came, there were no temples or priests. White priests gave us funeral services. I felt lonely without any temples to attend after having come to America, but I remembered what I had heard in Japanese temples.

My father started his day after having offered flowers on the family altar and reciting a sutra. We couldn't eat breakfast till we worshipped at the altar. I still remember the sutras chanted by my father. I can't recite a sutra by myself, but I can follow a priest in reciting any sutra even now. What you learn during your childhood is valuable. I hear the same sutras here as I heard in Japan— the same sutras. You never forget what you learn during your childhood.

o o o o o o o o o o o o o o o

My husband had been living in the United States before his younger brother joined him. One family among my relatives wanted to adopt a child, but they couldn't find anybody.[7] Orite's elder brother was married to a lady who was a relative of mine. Thus, his younger brother was recommended and then called back from the United States. When the younger brother returned

[7]Often no child is involved in the adoption, but the phrase refers to an adult male who is willing to marry into an heirless family and assume the responsibilities and obligations, as well as the inheritance, of his wife's family. He also assumes the new family name.

to Japan, I met him briefly at a temple celebration. The younger brother said that his elder brother wanted to marry. He wondered if I would marry his brother. The proposal went smoothly. Since Orite's younger brother had been adopted by my aunt, we didn't have to trace Orite's lineage, for we knew his family background already. All agreed to our marriage, but I didn't get married immediately. I was engaged at the age of sixteen and didn't meet Orite until I was almost eighteen. I had seen him only in a picture at first. Ours was a picture marriage. Being young, I was unromantic. I just believed that girls should get married. I felt he was a little old, about thirty, but the people around me praised the match. I took a look at his picture and told myself that I was to marry him. His brother in Tokyo sent me a lot of beautiful pictures [taken in the U.S.]. I was more excited about visiting a lot of places than about getting married. My name was entered in the Orites' *koseki*.[8] Thus we were married.

Not having my husband with me, I lived off and on with both my parents and Orite's parents. Although my mother had decided to let me go to the States, she was worried about my going to a foreign country alone. She was willing to let me go if Orite returned to pick me up; otherwise, she was against the idea. She talked to the Orites, and they wrote him a letter. He returned in November, the following year. Everybody in his family was surprised, for he'd come back all of a sudden. I greeted him and gave him an address of welcome. Then he went straight into his father's bedroom. His father was eighty years old then. Being old, he just ate and stayed in bed. Not having seen each other for such a long time, the son and the father were all excited. My husband had brought bundles of bills, money which he had patiently earned for his father. He said, "Father, I have been working for a long time in order to make you happy. I'll give this to you." Both insisted that the other should keep the money. Then my husband asked his father if he could do something special for him.

The Orites were powerful farmers. Orite helped finish harvesting the rice and other crops. As I'd told you, he had returned to Japan after fifteen years. He was a fortunate man. No matter how long a person worked in the United States, fifteen or twenty years, he might not be able to return to Japan if he hadn't had good fortune.

[8]Each family had a *koseki* or family register in which every member's name was recorded.

With the money Orite had brought back, his father asked him to enlarge the storehouse where food was kept. Orite went to consult a carpenter on the matter at once. We had a flood once a year, every year, and the water came up to the roof. We would climb up to the roof and escape by boat. In order to prevent the storehouse from being flooded, young people in the village piled rocks up to their own height. Then they built a storehouse on the foundation. We simply went up the stairs to get to the new storehouse.

We held our wedding reception party in November and invited a lot of relatives. In Japan, those who were invited brought a straw-bag of rice. Looking at the straw-bags, Orite's father said with joy, "How lucky we are to be honored by so many people!" People also gave up *sake* (Japanese rice wine) barrels to commemorate the occasion. My father-in-law got up and said, "You've been given a lot in commemoration." Then he went back to bed. Orite asked his father if there was anything more he could do for him. His father wanted to get a new Buddhist altar for their home. When it was delivered, a priest came to our house and recited a sutra, and the matter was finished.

Orite had to leave Japan six months later. His father, being satisfied with the fine altar, didn't have any more requests. New Year's Day came two months after the altar was delivered. My husband and I made a New Year's visit to my family. We were to stay overnight, but my husband wanted to go. I decided to stay overnight because they were my parents, and he went back home ahead. He picked up his younger brother on the way, since they were planning a short trip the following day. When they got home, they found every door locked. Orite got in through his father's bedroom. There he saw his mother sitting by his father's bed. She was worried about his father, because he was breathing very heavily. Soon after Orite got back home, his father died. My husband was lucky. He was present at his father's deathbed. We came to the States after he'd concluded the funeral service and a forty-ninth day memorial service for his father. I said to him, "You'll have nothing to regret concerning Japan even if you die in America, for you have concluded your filial duty."

My husband and I left home the day following the memorial service. Our neighbors brought lunches with them and came to see us off. We went to an inn with the food and had a farewell party there. Then my husband and I got on a train. My father saw me off at the train station. My mother, who was still young then, had given birth to my younger brother right before I left and couldn't come, for it was too soon after the delivery.

My husband's eldest brother saw us off too. He said, "Don't stay in the States too long. Come back in five years and farm with us." My father said, "Are you kidding? They can't learn anything in five years. They'll even have a baby over there, for five years won't be enough time to do anything. Be patient for twenty years." Hearing those words, I was so shocked that I couldn't control my tears. My father told me to return to Japan if I wasn't able to adjust to things.

MRS. KANE KOZONO

I was born in Kokura, Fukuoka Ken, on September 11, 1880. My home was more in the country than in the city. There wasn't a school in the town where I was born, but I remember there was one in a big village that was next to ours. I didn't go to school that regularly. I had six older brothers, and since my mother was very busy, I used to help her. It was only after I grew up that schools were built in our village, so I don't know how to write. We were a Buddhist family of the Shinshu sect. I always had the impression that Christianity was a somewhat difficult religion to follow, but that there was no religion more gracious than Buddhism, which saves us without requiring us to learn any sophisticated matters.

I was married in Japan when I was twenty-two and had one child there. My husband was a farmer, as was my father. My husband came here to the States three years earlier than I did. When he didn't come back to Japan, his parents asked me to go and bring him back. They thought that two of us working for a few years would give us enough money to come home.

I had heard that the equivalent of a Japanese five sen was the smallest denomination used in America; so I thought I might be able to come back to Japan with a fortune; then with that money I would be able to help my mother visit the temple with offerings. I always thought of her, you know. Since I was the only daughter, she didn't want me to be away from the family, and she used to say that she would hate to see me marry a man from far away. When I married, my husband's family lived only about two and a half miles away from my home. Later on when I had to go the States, I told her not to worry about me, and also said, "Although

I'm going to go to America, please don't feel lonely when I leave you, Mama. Don't let loneliness make you ill. Don't die of it." She then replied, "Your husband is there waiting for you, so you'd better go. I'd probably worry about you even if you stayed here with us." Such was my mother. I wanted to send her money, you know, believing some of those stories, such as the five sen being the smallest denomination there was in America. My brother told me such stories too. He said everything was very expensive and that I had to work hard. I thought that I would be able to make a lot of money just so long as I worked hard.

Our child, a daughter, was three years old and my parents said that they would take care of her so that I could leave. At the same time my husband was thinking of having me come to the States because some of his friends were doing so with their families. So my parents looked after our daughter, and I came to help my husband.

Mrs. Hanayo Inouye

My father came to the U.S. about four times in all. He stayed here about five years each time. I grew up in a relatively comfortable, trouble-free family. My family could even afford a nurse for me until I was five years old, for wages were low in Japan. For various reasons, the Alien Land Law for one, my father came back to Japan.[9] He came back to build a new house, buy some land, and take care of other business. Mother was working on the farm with my grandfather. When my father came to the States for the first time, he became a schoolboy,[10] attending children of a rich, white family. He walked the children to and from their grammar school and learned to speak very good English. Since a lot of people from Japan in those days did not speak a word of English, his bilingual ability was especially useful in helping other people find jobs. My husband, now deceased, was one of those people who was helped by my father. My husband used to say that he never thought of marrying the daughter of the man who helped him find a job. He also used to tell us that my father was a very gentle, kind person.

American farmers don't have to work at quite such dirty tasks

[9]The California Alien Land Law of 1913 denied aliens who were ineligible for citizenship (the Japanese) the right to own property.

[10]A schoolboy was a domestic worker. Although this was a common job for the young male Japanese immigrant, it was difficult work, for in Japan men and boys never did domestic work.

as the Japanese farmers. You see, when I was still young, the farmers in Japan used to make rounds early in the morning in the nearby cities to collect human feces for fertilizer in their fields. Although my father was a village councilman, needless to say, he was not receiving enough salary for that to support the whole family. Farming was his main source of income. I still remember having a bull pull a cart—every farmer's family kept a bull in those days—with barrels of human feces on it. I used to wait for him to come around at the foot of a steep slope which we had to cross to get back to our village. When I remember that, I cannot but admire him for coming back to the village to be a farmer again.

My father had good penmanship and was asked by many people to write letters and notices for them and to record the names of guests at such occasions as funerals and wedding services. That made him well known in the village, and the people respected him for that, which was probably one of the reasons he was elected to the village council when he came back to Japan permanently.

He came back to Japan one time and was married then. After the first baby—that's my older sister—was born, he again went to the States and worked for about five years and then returned to Japan. He left again; but when he heard the news that the second baby was to be born, he had a plan of his own in mind. If it was a boy, he would invite him to the United States when he grew to a certain age, and then later he would come back to Japan together with his son. However, since the baby happened to be me, a girl, his plan did not work out. When my sister and I were still young, we spent only a few years with our father. I have one older sister, one younger sister, and two younger brothers.

My parents encouraged me to go to school. In fact, my family would have sent me to college, as in the case of one of my brothers, if I had wanted. Anyway, after six years in elementary school I went to high school for two years. There I learned lots of things that women at the time were supposed to know, such as sewing and flower arranging. I didn't like those very much, to tell you the truth. I liked to sing songs and play.

When I was still very small, my favorite pastime was to go into the woods of nearby mountains and collect *matsutake* mushrooms. I used to take my younger brother along with me and join my friends—usually six or seven of them altogether—from the neighborhood. Along a narrow path in the mountains there were a lot of *matsutake* mushrooms hidden under fallen leaves, twigs, and other things. My brother and I didn't tell anybody about it and kept the place as our secret spot. I would go out in the streets of nearby villages and say, *"Matsutake! Matsutake!"* and some people would buy them. They were really fresh and smelled very good. The money I made on mushrooms went straight into my savings.

Another way that I made money was selling eels. Every summer the water was drained out of our rice paddies. Then, when there was no water, it was easy to get in and catch eels. There were a lot of them in the rice paddies. They are very slippery, so I used to get some prickly cucumber leaves and grab them. I put them in a bucket, and went out selling them in a neighborhood town. The people would say, "They are big and fresh. I'll buy some." Then, again, the money was added to my savings in a trunk.

It happened very quickly that I was to leave my home and come to America. It certainly surprised my mother. By then I had saved quite a bit of money in that trunk, but I knew that I could not bring Japanese money to the United States with me. My husband told me that once before. So, when we were at the Hiroshima train station, I handed all my savings over to my mother and said, "Here's what I have saved up to now. Put it in the postal savings for my younger brother and sister. They can share it between them." With tears in her eyes, she then said, "Are you really giving it to them? I know you worked hard saving it. Well, then, I'll give it to them, and make sure to let them know it's from their older sister. Yes, I'll take care of it for you." She must have been very surprised, because as she said, she knew I had been saving it diligently and then all of a sudden I decided to give all of it to them. She cried.

When I was leaving the station, she said, "I am going to miss you very much when you leave, but I'll always be with you. We won't be separated even for a moment." At first I did not know what she was talking about. Later that night when I was undressing myself to go to sleep, I understood what she meant. I found a piece of the Buddhist altar ornament in the breast of my kimono. I was so sad when I left her at the station that I didn't know it was there. When I found it, I thought, "She is with me after all, my mother."

○ ○ ○ ○ ○ ○ ○ ○ ○ ○ ○ ○ ○ ○ ○

When I was a little girl, I was partly raised by my aunt, my father's younger sister. She had a son, but her husband and son were in the United States. They sent money to support her. Having raised me since I was very little, she didn't want me to marry a total stranger. She wanted to be close to me even after my marriage. That was not at all an unusual feeling for any parent in those days. Although her son was younger than I was by a year, her feelings for me were so deep that when I was seventeen, she announced that I was going to marry him. She and my parents so decided without really consulting me. Their plan was to bring her son back to Japan at the age of twenty, and after getting married, we were to go to the United States together. However, when he became twenty-one, he sent a letter to his mother, my aunt, and said that he was working at a salmon cannery with his father, but he could not follow his father's example because he hated that work. He said that he would be going to school, and, therefore, he would not be coming back to Japan for some time. Now, if I had to wait for him to come back but not know when he would, I had to worry about getting old. My aunt even thought about adopting someone to marry me so that she could keep me within her reach. The idea was soon discarded though.

In that year Mr. Inouye came back to Japan to look for a wife. Picture marriages had been practiced for some time; but they only produced a lot of troubles with those couples; so some time later they were banned.[11] It was all right, however, to come back to Japan, get married, and bring a bride to the States, and that's what Mr. Inouye had in mind. When he came home—both of us come from the same town—I learned that he was a very honest and serious man, and his family was doing very well. There were some people who suggested that I marry him, and I had always wanted to go to America; so we were married. I was twenty-one, and Mr. Inouye was forty-one. Because of this age difference, some of my relatives, along with my aunt, were opposed to our marriage. They said I was too young for him. My aunt naturally was the last one to agree to our marriage. She cried and cried, as

[11]In 1921 the Japanese government agreed to halt the emigration of picture brides. This "Ladies Agreement" resulted more from anti-Japanese attitudes in the United States than it did from the personal problems the practice caused for Japanese couples.

you can imagine, but a lot of people talked her into the agreement at last. She really couldn't insist on her idea of marrying me to her son, because she didn't know for sure when he was coming back.

Well, to me Mr. Inouye was a fine man, a man who had made his fortune on his own. As a matter of fact, the Inouyes are a very, very well-to-do family back in our hometown in Japan now, because of his hard work. Indeed, he was even able to build a house in Japan before our wedding.

Well, I was glad that a long-cherished dream of mine would finally come true, the dream of going to America. Our wedding ceremony was on July 28, and on August 15 we were already on our way to the United States.

MRS. TOSHIKO IGARASHI

I'm from Chiba Ken, and I was born in the twenty-seventh year in Meiji; that's 1894. Father was a physician. He was born in Tokyo when it was still called Yedo and was one of the first graduates of the Chiba Medical School.[12]

When father was still in Yedo, he found *Pilgrim's Progress* and the Bible, both in classic Japanese, at a bookstore. Freedom of faith was not yet recognized in Japan at the time. He talked to Yamaoka Tesshu, his *sensei* (teacher or mentor), about the books. And he told my father in reply, "It's good to have a faith, but don't tell anybody about it now." Such was the time. After graduating from the medical school in Chiba, he set up his practice in Kemigawa, now a part of Chiba City. But being a Christian practitioner, he started losing his clients gradually, for people were afraid of a *Yaso* (a Christian) to a point where they suspected that a *Yaso* doctor might give them poisonous drugs or do some harmful things to them. Anyway, no patients came to see him in the end.

In those days there were epidemics of dysentery and other illnesses in Japan. Yet there weren't many doctors around at that time. My father was one of the first few Western-trained doctors. He managed to make his living being assigned to those epidemic areas. Then later on he went to Kisarazu as a prison doctor and became a regular practitioner in the town as well. Technical skills

---

[12]This man was trained in the "Western school," as opposed to the "Chinese school," which was more common in those days.

are what count with a doctor, and by then people began to be educated. Gradually, whether the doctor was a *Yaso* or not made less difference to people, and they came to see my father. Because our family was Christian, we know very little of Japanese customs, that is, the customs that have to do with the Shinto shrine and the Buddhist temple.

When I was eleven or twelve, the Russo-Japanese War broke out. Russia was Greek Orthodox, and people at that time said the *Yaso* were no different from them; thus we were persecuted in Japan. In order to visit patients on the outskirts of the town, my father had to hire a *jinrikisha,* but other than that he went out on foot all over the town because he felt sorry for *jinrikisha* drivers who had to be seen with a *Yaso.*

At the times of town festivals, people carry a *mikoshi* (a palanquin-like shrine). Well, on such occasions, with the help of an overly exciting atmosphere, they knowingly knocked the *mikoshi* against the eaves of our house and broke the glass of the front doors. The townspeople who were in charge of the festival knew what was happening; to them we were only the *Yaso* also. Even so, they couldn't just pretend that they didn't know. Therefore, they came and stood in a line right in front of our house and told my father, "Very sorry. It was because of the lack of supervision on our part. Therefore, please let us pay for the repair." I still remember father sitting at the front door and replying to them by saying, "No, never mind. We will take care of it." Later a man from a glass shop in town came and fixed the glass. When we were about to pay him, he said, "They are going to give me a scolding if I accept payment from you," and he just ran away home. This is only one example of many.[13]

In my own case, stones were thrown at me while going to school. Even snakes, which I hate most, were thrown at me. After attending an elementary school in town, I studied at a women's school for four years before coming to Tokyo. Being a doctor, my father went to lots of different places and knew that—having seen some women's school graduates nursing their parents—those with a degree only in *kasei-ka* (home economics) were of little help in his field. So I took an exam to enter a hospital of obstetrics and gynecology, where I eventually obtained a certificate as a

[13]Although the townspeople in charge of the festival probably supported the action against the *Yaso,* their position of responsibility demanded that they complete their duties honorably.

midwife. Later I became a registered nurse. That's why I came to Tokyo. I became supervisor of the dormitory with around sixty to sixty-five students who were studying to be nurses and midwives. I attended the people of high class from Tokyo at the time of their childbirths, and in the case of operations, I was usually called to the important ones. Probably because of my father's influence, I knew more than the average student there.

Meanwhile, Igarashi, who was in the United States, and Koga, my sister's father-in-law, were making arrangements for my marriage. Through Koga my father apparently trusted Mr. Igarashi to marry me. Igarashi came to meet me in Japan. My elder sister was very reluctant to see me go away. She finally withdrew her objections since Mr. Igarashi had come all the way to Japan to meet me, and I came over here in 1920.

MRS. KAZUKO (MINEJIMA) HAYASHI

My name is Kazuko Hayashi. My ancestors a long time ago passed on to our family the same kind of writings for names. My mother showed me a family tree, and she said that each family chose a particular writing, a particular *kanji* (formal style of writing Japanese characters) for the name of their children. The name was particularly important for boys when it came time to state your full name. When men went to war or something like that, they had to have a good family name. These names were all written in the family book.[14]

My father was one of the survivors of Ako Hanshi. It's the Chushingura story.[15] Well, father was a samurai but after the fall of his lord, Ako, he had to become an unattached samurai. In the beginning, he did work for a Buddhist temple as a priest, and then after that, he found a job as a Shinto priest.

Later, father was the Shinto priest at the Kampei Taisha. He died of a heart attack when I was about eight years old. The Kampei Taisha, which is one of the most important shrines of the Shinto sect, was located in the mountains. There are rankings

[14]This is a reference to the *koseki* or family registration.

[15]Chushingura is one of the most famous stories in Japanese history. It concerns the heroic revenge of Lord Ako's death by forty-seven of his most devoted samurai retainers, who, in turn, were forced to commit suicide after the success of their revenge. Mrs. Hayashi's father was not one of the forty-seven who decided to join in the plot.

among the Shinto priests, and my father was called *"shogoi,"* the
fifth. That was his ranking when he died. The order to take certain positions used to come from the Emperor, and we called this
kind of official letter *"Jirei,"* and I still have one of them. Well,
this letter has the Emperor's sign, *"Kikunogomon,"* the sign of
the chrysanthemum, which is used as a water mark on the paper.
My family used to have lots of these papers, but they say they
were burned in Tokyo when Tokyo was bombed by the American
Air Force. When my father was sixteen, he was able to have his
picture taken with the Emperor. We come from an old and good
family, and father was a respectable man because he came from
such a good family; but our family name has fallen since his
death.

My mother was born in a place called Sakai. When she was
small, there was a plague and both of her parents died of cholera.
They say there was an enormous amount of wealth left for her.
Her family was in the sake-making business. Her grandfather was
called Asahi Ohachi, and he was a very famous man. He was
called a man's man, and he was able to present himself in front of
the Emperor. She was taught by this grandfather.

In any case, my mother had quite a bit of wealth, and she sent
Nakata Norinobu to school until he became an independent
lawyer. He became a prosecuting attorney and attained fame
when he prosecuted a national criminal, Omi Kentaro. This man,
Nakata Norinobu, was my father's good friend; in fact, he was
just like my father's little brother, and we used to call him uncle.

When my father died, there was no such thing as a pension, and
I suppose we did not have too much wealth left; so we sold old,
antique things that my father used to collect. I remember things
like that when I was small; so I imagine that was how my mother
raised money. My mother used to have a lot of nice-looking
glasses, cut glass. We had all these precious things, and little by
little we lost them. I suppose she had to sell them for us to be able
to live.

When my father died, the funeral ceremony was in the Kampei
Taisha. When my father first went up to Kampei Taisha, which
was up in the mountains, my mother sent the best maid, the maid
that she liked most, with him into the mountains as a second
wife, and she was at the funeral too. Well, they said if my mother
weren't there, they couldn't perform the funeral ceremony; therefore, she had to go there, although he had had his second wife

with him. We all went, though we were very small. The second wife had children too, and there was a girl who was the same age as I was. When we came back from the funeral, my mother shared some portion of our wealth with her. My mother gave to my half sister so that she could go to school. Because of that, she was able to graduate from the university for women, and she grew up in Osaka. She was well educated, but her mother's name was not a good name. I can't remember what it was. Well, she could not inherit the family name, you see. Even if a woman has education, if her mother is the second wife, they say, "Your mother is a second wife," and she is not accepted despite her education. Later I heard that she got married to a journalist. I don't know what happened to her though. I did not have any education; but because I had this family name, I was treated very well, I think.

Well, my father's lawyer friend, Nakata Norinobu, went to Tokyo when I was about fourteen years old. Because I was working around the house, he took me with him, for he liked me very much. He had a house, a mansion in Okubo, near Shinjuku, and there he had the job of tracing out family trees of the nobility. Instead of hiring a maid, I worked for him. He used to take me all over the place. At that time, I did not have a father anymore, although my mother was alive. I don't remember how old his son was; but when his son became an army lieutenant, he was transferred to Formosa with the army, and he wanted to take me with him. But my mother opposed this plan. She said, "My daughter has been working like a maid all this time, and she has to start as a maid in a strange land." Since she was very strongly opposed, I stayed with my mother. My mother was not able to hire a maid; so I did the housework. In school, I could not go to the more advanced stage; therefore, I finished elementary school and part of middle school. The rest of the time I worked at home.

As for coming to America, well. . . . A long time ago when Mr. Minejima was still in America, he had a good friend whose name was Kinezuka. Mr. Kinezuka came back to Japan and built a huge hotel. Mr. Kinezuka used to visit *Bayukyokai*, the Japanese-American Friendship Society, where my brother was executive secretary. He told my brother that there was such a man called Mr. Minejima who was looking for a wife. Mr. Kinezuka heard that I was staying with my brother and asked him to consider sending me to America with Mr. Minejima as his wife.

I told my brother, "I don't know anything about America, and I don't even know how to speak English," but he said, "Well, go to *miyai* anyway." That is the procedure for matchmaking. I went with him, pretending that I was his wife, but he introduced me as his sister. After that conversation, plans for the marriage advanced, and on June 15, 1909, we were married. You see, it was an old Japanese-style marriage, so we had a celebration and an *uino*, a dowry exchange. That was a kind of a sign for our marriage contract. Mr. Minejima's father's second wife brought a tremendous gift to me, and also she brought *montsuki* (a formal gown with the family emblem), which I wore at the wedding. His real mother could not come to the wedding. That's how we got married under Mr. Kinezuka's care.

MRS. AI MIYASAKI

My ideal of a husband was so high that I could not find a man to my liking; so I decided to come to America. I wanted to go to a big country where it was free. I wanted to find a husband whom I could help and work with. I had graduated from *jo gakko* (girl's high school) and had taught grammar school. The teachers would recommend policemen or people like that. I wanted to marry an officer or a doctor, someone like that. If a soldier came to seek my hand and he was a private, I refused.

When I told my parents about my desire to go to a foreign land, the story spread throughout the town. From here and there requests for marriage came pouring in just like rain! Still, I was particular and did not want to go as a common emigrant (laborer) and work. My father had a position in our town besides his business, and he was friends with the mayor. Miyasaki was the mayor's nephew. He came from America in search of a bride. At that time I was already promised to a man in Hawaii, who was a graduate from Waseda University. This man was educated, of a good family, and refined. This is why I decided on him. It was to have been a picture marriage, but. . . .

A friend came to visit me, and we went to another town to spend the day. On the way home, on the bridge, the mayor, another elderly man, and a young man approached us. I did not know this was to be a *miyai* (preliminary visit before marriage arrangements are negotiated); so I stood on the bridge and talked with the mayor. We did not talk for long. That evening I told my family about the mayor, the old man, and a young man whom I had met on the bridge. And then they came, the three. We served them sake and tea and talked. I was casual about looking at Miyasaki, and he looked me over. He was so quiet and did not say a word, that young man! I conversed with the mayor for he was kind to me, but did not talk with Miyasaki. He was a handsome man, but I did not think about whether I liked him or not, because I did not know that the purpose of their visit was a *miyai.*

Miyasaki did not drink, and the old man did not drink. The elderly man was Miyasaki's father, not his real father but a step-father. I was supposed to go to Hawaii; so I did not think any more about the visit. Then word came that he wanted to marry me. My father refused and explained that I was to go to Hawaii. But Miyasaki said that he just had to marry me. If he could not marry me, he was going back to America alone. The mayor approached my uncle and asked him to work out a plan to influence my father to change his mind. So my uncle came to persuade my father and said that the mayor came pleading. Miyasaki's home was good, and the mayor was very earnest about Miyasaki's request. The mayor could not let the man go back to America single. Couldn't something be done?

My uncle told my father to go and see Miyasaki once more. My father was moved. At least Miyasaki was here in person, he had brought money back with him, and he was a serious man, a good man. Would he not be better? The question was, who would go to break the promised marriage? My uncle said that he would. My father went alone to see Miyasaki on a pretense, for he could not say, "I came to look you over again." So Father went and said that he was looking for a woman teacher who lived nearby. "Do you know where she lives?" Miyasaki said that he did not know; so they talked. On the way home, Father went to visit a retired teacher. He talked about my situation and asked, "Were it your child, what would you do?" The teacher said that both men were of good families. "But if it were my child, I would give her to Miyasaki." So Father was persuaded and decided accordingly. Miyasaki was twenty-eight and I was twenty-three when we married. There was the situation about the army induction; so we hurried to America.

MRS. TAKAE WASHIZU

My name is Takae Washizu. The character for *"Taka"* means "high" and *"e"* means "a branch." I was born in Aichi Prefecture in January of 1900.

I only went through elementary school—for six years. I wasn't crazy about school and was absent so often that the teacher and the principal came over to my house. I hid myself while they were visiting my parents. I remember that once I picked up something from our farm and hid it in my kimono sleeve. When I ate it secretly in class, the teacher found me and scolded me. I also remember that two boys from my class and some of the upper-class students teased me in a nearby pine forest. That's why I hated school. Being poor, my parents couldn't speak up for me. My mother forced me to go to school and sent me off to school three times each morning. The children from poor families were never appointed as class leaders, no matter how bright they were. The children from rich families were treated well by the teachers and principal, because their parents often invited the teachers and the principal to banquets.

My father was a very quiet farmer. My mother was strict, which was only natural, for she had to take care of many children. There were nine of us. I helped my parents and my aunt on the farm.

A number of people in our village emigrated to America. Having been treated small in the village, I was rebellious against the village as a whole, and I wanted to get out of there. Besides that, a dollar at that time was worth two yen. I swore that I would never return to the village without having achieved great success. However, I missed my home village as time passed.

My cousin, who had succeeded in business in the United States, met Washizu at the Japanese association. My cousin told Washizu about me. Then Washizu borrowed money from a friend of his and returned to Japan to marry me. When we married, he was forty-three and I was twenty-one.

Mrs. Sadae Takizawa

My name is Sadae Takizawa. Once upon a time, Kiso Nakayoshi (a historical character) and his followers, being defeated in battle, ran into the mountains. They were in such a starved condition that they had to learn farming. Thus, my father's ancestor became a farmer. I remember arms and spears hanging on the far side of the room. Swords were placed in each box of armor. The boxes were something like long trunks. When I was a child, my grandmother showed me those things. Though we were farmers, we still treasured such things. It was in such a family that I was raised. My grandfather was somewhat different than most people. He didn't send his children to school as most parents did. Instead, he called a teacher to his home. The teacher stayed at my grandfather's place and went back home only once in a while. Therefore, my father didn't receive an ordinary school education. The children learned *Shiso Gogyo.* My father wanted to teach me, the oldest daughter, *Shiso Gogyo* even after we came to the United States. It's a book of strict moral lessons including the works of Confucius. My father had learned the book in his childhood and believed that it would be helpful for people—even for women—to lead a good life. I learned most of it by heart.

My father's brother had come to the States before my father. My uncle wrote to my father about what America was like, and my father decided to come. Father and his youngest brother came together. The three brothers worked and had a hard time. They sometimes regretted having left Japan. I'll bet they did regret it. Men could be bossy in Japan. In the meantime, my uncle (the second oldest one in the family), who had come to the United States first, graduated from the Theological School of the Episcopal Church in San Mateo and became a minister. I guess the three of them talked about how nice it would be if everybody came here from Japan. Since he had finished school, my uncle offered to go to Japan to bring us here if we wanted to come. Having his noodle business, my father couldn't go to Japan. He gave money to my uncle and sent him to Japan in order to bring us over. My father's mother, my grandmother, was still alive. When we asked her if she wanted to go with us, she said she would go. She would have her relatives here; moreover, all her three sons were here. She was afraid of not being able to see her grandchildren unless she came. In 1907 my grandmother, mother, myself, two younger sisters, and my younger brother came to the United States together.

2

The Crossing

CHOICHI NITTA

I got on the *America Maru,* one of three steamships that carried passengers to America. The sea was very rough, and it took us twelve days to reach Honolulu—usually it took only ten. I got seasick the first several days and couldn't eat at all, but later got used to it.

I arrived in October, 1903, and was sent to a quarantine station first. The physical examination wasn't particularly thorough. I passed it and went to the Haramoto Hotel and then arranged for a boat to Hilo. My uncle met me there and took me to his place by horse and buggy. I spent *Tencho-setsu* (the Emperor's birthday, November 3) and the next New Year's Day there. My uncle got me a job pulling weeds. I wanted to learn English; so I started to attend a night school after work.

My uncle had always understood me better than my father, and later, when I told him of my desire to go to mainland America, he said, "If you are going, I will go too." He paid my way, and we both came over. I remember on February 14 the Russo-Japanese War started. When we left Hawaii there was lots of commotion about the war on the plantation. We left Honolulu about that time and reached San Francisco on February 22. It was Washington's Birthday. Because of the holiday, we had to stay on the ship overnight in San Francisco. The next day, on the twenty-third, we went to Angel Island for our physical examination before we landed.[1]

[1]Angel Island in San Francisco Bay was the Ellis Island of the West Coast.

NISUKE MITSUMORI

I was surprised to find so many people aboard ship, but there were no women. I think the immigrants hadn't been financially successful enough to get wives from Japan yet. It was probably five or six years later that people started bringing their wives from Japan. A person had to work in the United States at least for three or four years to make money for the expense of going back to Japan. Those who made money went back to get their old lovers or to find a wife. There were a lot of people who could not go back to Japan to get their wives; thus, the system of picture brides was born. Men decided on their wives through the exchange of pictures.

SHIZUMA TAKESHITA

In 1902 when I came to America, I had to pay an entrance tax of three dollars. About ten years later a person brought suit against the government, and the tax was found illegal. Thereafter, immigrants entering this country did not have to pay the tax nor the two-dollar fee that we aliens were paying to stay in this country.

My first experience in this country was upsetting. Mrs. Uyeno, the wife of the Japanese consul, was the daughter of the largest hotel owner in Kumamoto. Her father wrote a letter of introduction for me to bring to Mr. Uyeno. When I arrived in San Francisco, I went to see him, but he was leaving for Sacramento and did not have time to see me. I thought he was avoiding me, and I was very upset. I left my gift for him, went back to the hotel where I was staying, and told my story to Mr. Takeuchi, a passenger on the same ship I had come on. Mr. Takeuchi said that I should not depend on people to help me, and he said that San Francisco was not a good place for me to stay because of the gambling and vice. He took me to Oakland and arranged for me to stay at the church dormitory for ten cents a night. Breakfast was doughnuts and coffee for five cents, and lunch and dinner were ten cents each. People can't believe it, but it was so in those days.

TOKUSHIGA KIZUKA

I was six years old when my father went to the United States. Eleven years later, at the age of seventeen, my father summoned me to work. My father came to meet me when I landed in San Francisco. Other than a picture, I had no idea how my father looked, and I did not recognize him—it was like we were strangers. At the immigration bureau, there was another passenger named Honda. His father thought I was his son, because his son was very big when he was young, and my father thought I was Honda, because I was small when I was a young boy.

San Francisco's Japanese town was located in the South Park suburb, so we went directly to South Park from the port. I did not see the main part of town. There were mostly Japanese in South Park—just a few white people. We spent a few days in San Francisco and a few days in Oakland before we came to Watsonville, where my father was in the apple business at that time. My stepmother's relatives were in Watsonville too. There were many Japanese laborers living in a camp in the area; so I didn't see white people other than the neighbors.

MINEJIRO SHIBATA

I think I came on the *Saibei Maru* in 1919. After stopping in Hawaii overnight, the ship went directly to San Francisco. Almost everybody on board was an immigrant. Eating was the only thing I did on the ship. The food served on board wasn't especially good, but I didn't mind. I didn't know anybody; so I had no friends or acquaintances to talk to and stayed on deck most of the time. With tears in my eyes, I watched other ships sailing in the distance. I also remember that lice bred in the ship because we couldn't take a bath too often. I can never forget that.

At first I thought the United States was a beautiful country. I arrived in March and stayed on Angel Island for three or four days in order to go through the immigration procedures. On Angel Island the wooden walls were covered with barbed wire. Chinese people drew letters and carved them on the walls. I was amazed at how delicate those letters were. They treated us neither too well nor too badly at the immigration office. I didn't care about the treatment, for I didn't have to pay for anything. The only thing I didn't like was the bathroom. There were a lot of toilet bowls side by side without any doors. I, being Japanese, couldn't stand it. They took our feces and examined it. They also examined us to see if we had a skin disease. I was released after that.

As the number of Japanese immigrants increased, so did the organized prejudice against them, particularly in California. By 1907 there were increasing reports of physical violence, and there were also attempts to segregate Japanese children in public schools. These problems were brought to the attention of the Japanese government, and the result was the gentlemen's agreement of 1908 whereby Japan agreed to restrict immigration in return for better treatment of Japanese already in the United States. The Japanese government believed that they maintained their part of the bargain by restricting passports to unskilled laborers and granting them mainly to children and wives of immigrants already settled in this country. In the years immediately following 1908, Japanese immigration to the United States decreased considerably, but then a curious increase took place. As single Japanese men began to establish themselves more or less permanently in the United States, the practice of "picture brides," arranged marriages with the exchange of photographs, began, temporarily, to increase immigration once again. The male immigrant's family in Japan would find what they considered a suitable bride, complete the marriage ceremony without the groom, and send the bride to the United States armed only with her new husband's picture and youthful hopes to meet her fate.

Mrs. Rikae Inouye

Most of the people on board were picture brides. I came with my husband. When the boat anchored, one girl took out a picture from her kimono sleeve and said to me, "Mrs. Inouye, will you let me know if you see this face?" She was darling. Putting the picture back into her kimono sleeve, she went out to the deck. The men who had come to pick up their brides were there. It was like that. I felt they were bold.

Riichi Satow

In 1912 I came on a big ship, the *Mongolia*. Of the Japanese, most of those on board were women who were picture brides, some forty to fifty of them. I don't remember anybody who was a Yobiyose among us. Actually I wonder if there were any of those except myself. I became acquainted with very few people on board.

There was an incident where one of the Japanese brides was molested by a sailor, and it created a big uproar on the ship. A meeting was called for by those who grew most indignant at the incident, and they had a discussion. The situation was never resolved, because the woman thought of her husband, who was waiting for her over here. She didn't want to make it appear that she was attacked, though she actually was. The final story that they came up with in her defense was that the sailor tried to molest her, but she defended herself well. A thousand and one different stories were told at the time, but it was settled that way in the end.

When the ship came into the San Francisco port, I felt, "Good, I finally made it!" I didn't think about the future, but I was simply glad to have arrived. One thing that caught my attention was the shape of the houses. They were all square and looked like boxes, really different from Japanese houses! The city itself was rather beautiful, despite the earthquake. Right from there I got on a train to go to the country, to Napa. Along the way I saw windmills, a lot of them. I remember wondering about those things. Then someone explained that they were to pump water.

MRS. KAMECHIYO TAKAHASHI

I left home in 1916 and got here on the ninth of February in 1917. It was a Friday night. Takahashi (my husband) and my brother came to see me at the harbor. They said, "Tomorrow is Saturday, the following day is Sunday, and then Monday is Lincoln's Birthday. . . ." I had left Japan in December of 1916, and was supposed to get here within the same month. But in Yokohama I was forced to delay my departure, because I had roundworms. After taking a lot of medicine and having another examination, I got on the next boat, so I didn't arrive here until February of 1917. Takahashi and my brother told me that no immigration officers would come till Tuesday because Monday was a holiday. Promising to pick me up on Tuesday, they left. I remained on board for a while. Then I went to the immigration office on Angel Island and stayed there for three days.

I had never seen such a prison-like place as Angel Island. There were threefold wire nets on the wall. There was a big wire net outside, a thick wire net in the middle, and a screen door inside. I wondered why I had to be kept in a prison after I'd arrived. My sister-in-law, who had experienced the same thing at the immigration office before, sent in *osushi* (a Japanese rice dish) to me. She meant to substitute it for the meals at the immigration station. Not knowing the situation, I shared it all with others before I got to Angel Island. No rice was as foul smelling as the kind I ate on Angel Island! I ate only a slice of toast with coffee for breakfast. I couldn't stand the rice for lunch and dinner, and I regretted not having kept the *osushi*.

I regretted having come, and I wondered what the place I was going to would be like. I trusted Takahashi because he had sent me a picture of a nice place where he had a store downstairs and lived upstairs. Later I was relieved to see that the business was prosperous.

Mrs. Tomi Osaki

When I came to San Francisco with my husband, we took a ship by way of Seattle. We paid thirty dollars to the captain for our passage. The ship was crowded. Most of the passengers were from Kagoshima and were coming to marry. At this time many marriages were arranged by exchanging pictures. Consequently, many girls married without much knowledge of their husbands. There was always danger for girls to decide to marry this way, because some boys lied about their pictures or professions. I know that some girls jumped overboard on the way.

Mrs. Hanayo Inouye

We came on the *Tenyo Maru*. On the way to Yokohama from Kobe the sea was very rough. I became so awfully seasick that I truly thought I was going to die. It was my first experience on such a big ship. Although I was all right after Yokohama, a lot of people suffered from severe cases of seasickness all the way. They threw up whatever they had eaten, and because of that they were having a hard time even standing up on their own. I can't forget how much I hated to go to the bathroom, for it was way upstairs. Everytime I had to climb up these steep stairs, I tried desperately not to fall off. Oh, it was really scary. Another thing that bothered everyone on board was the smell of paint. It was terrible on top of the seasickness.

Our beds were on racks. Men slept in one section, and women slept in another. We could spend the day together, but we were separated through the night. Well, one time a woman asked for a comb, so I let her use mine. Then, when I combed my hair with it later, my head became really itchy all over. There weren't good facilities to wash my hair on the ship. As soon as we landed, I rushed to a drugstore, and took care of it. It was lice from her hair! The sanitary situation on the ships in those days was very poor.

All I could see from the ship was just the blue sea, day after day. I kept wondering when in the world the voyage would be over, so I was truly relieved when I saw seagulls flying over us.

Mrs. Riyo Orite

We took the *Shizuoka Maru* and went to Kobe, where our passports were issued. We stayed there and had eye and duodenal examinations which were terribly strict. I had never had any problems with my eyes nor been sick in bed since my childhood. My eyes were all right, but there was a suspicion that I might have hookworms, and I was hospitalized. After having taken medicine to get rid of the worms, I had an examination, but I couldn't get rid of another type of worms. I was held back for three days more to undergo another examination, which I didn't expect to pass. By then my feelings had changed, and I didn't want to go to the United States. "If I don't pass the examination, I'll be lucky enough to go back home," I said to myself, but I was rechecked and had no problem. We got on the boat which departed for Kobe and then went to Yokohama for our departure to America.

Being newly constructed, the ship had the smell of paint. It gave me a headache, and I didn't have any appetite. The ocean became rough right after our departure, and I couldn't get up from bed. I was in bed from Kobe to Yokohama. My husband's younger brother came to meet us at Yokohama. Being sick, I remained on board. My husband went ashore with his brother, and they toured Tokyo and the surrounding area until early evening. . . . The boat anchored there overnight. Some passengers got on at Yokohama. For about five days after our departure I'd had such a severe headache that I couldn't eat any meals.

Then I started getting used to the ship and walked around a little. I had no friends on board except for one lady from my hometown. We were of the same age. I talked and walked with her on the deck and recovered gradually. I was completely well by the time we landed.

In June of 1914 we arrived in Seattle to have another physical examination. Then we went to the Fujii Hotel. The owner was from a town near mine in Hiroshima. I'm sure Orite spent quite a lot of money on the trip to and from Japan, but I was too young to be interested in how much he had earned or how much the sea fare had cost. I have an interesting story to tell you. Some Japanese ladies who had returned from the States decided not to go back, and they gave their Western clothing to the other Japanese ladies who were planning to go. There was underwear made of lace, but they didn't know how to wear it. I was in a black suit dress, which wasn't as beautiful as the lace underwear. I thought the dresses made of lace looked beautiful. They should have worn the lace wear under a dress, but they'd worn it on top! We found out after we got to the hotel. Hillbillies! The hotel owner's wife was surprised and laughed at those ladies when we got there. She was amazed, "How daring you are to have traveled in such a fashion!" Then we found out the truth. I was in a dress which I had bought in Kobe. One of my husband's cousins came to Seattle to meet us and told me that I had put on a blouse with the front side in back!

MRS. KO TAKAKOSHI

I was on the ship for over two weeks. I remember Mr. Tatsumi, who was on the ship. He later became a professor at the university here. There were some picture brides on the ship too. I missed my mother, and I was so lonely that I cried every night. After I reached here, my favorite aunts were here, and I wasn't lonely any longer. I passed through the immigration office easily; however, we got scolded when we took our bath there. We showered ourselves outside of the tub and then got in the tub like we do in Japan, so the water dripped downstairs into the office!

MRS. AI MIYASAKI

There were mostly picture brides on the ship—young girls, couples, men who came to Japan to find brides. Filipinos were on board also. The picture brides were full of ambition, expectation, and dreams. None knew what their husbands were like except by the photos. I wondered how many would be saddened and disillusioned. There were many. The grooms were not what the women thought they were. The men would say that they had businesses and send pictures which were taken when they were younger and deceived the brides. In reality, the men carried blanket rolls on their backs and were farm laborers. The men lied about their age and wrote they were fifteen years younger than they actually were.

The women were disillusioned and wanted to go back. There were many incidents of infidelity. Those women dressed fancy and worked in clubs and would find a man and run away with him. Then the husband would come with a pistol and shoot them. If children were born, the women had no choice but to bear the ordeal. Many Issei people were in that situation. They suffered. I heard from many Issei people about their tragic life. Many were not compatible. Their ideas were different. Not only material, but emotional hardships had to be borne. Many Issei mothers suffered much, but they could not afford to go back to Japan. Their expectations were great, so the disappointment was as great. I was fortunate because I had met my husband before I came here. So many imagined their prospective groom to be a certain type of great man. In our town in that era, the men all wore white clothes and dressed very nicely in the summer. Here in America, the men usually had only one dingy black suit, worn-down shoes, shaggy hair . . . and to have seen someone like that as you came off the ship must have been a great disappointment. It was only natural to feel that way.

PART II:
THE REALITY

3

On Being Japanese in America

NISUKE MITSUMORI

My first impression of San Francisco was bad. About the time when the Japanese started coming into this country, Japan won the war against Russia and took Port Arthur. Port Arthur was then considered the strongest military fortress in the Orient, and Japan took it with ease. Japan began to occupy a part of Russia in October. I think Americans started thinking that the Japanese were crazy. There was fear among Americans—particularly among government officials and the press—since such a small country as Japan successfully fought against a big country, Russia, and even took the impregnable Port Arthur. One Los Angeles paper used to write bad things about the Japanese and suggested that the United States should not let such dreadful people enter the country. This must have been the very beginning of the anti-Japanese movement.

It was March or April of 1905 when I landed in San Francisco. A man from a Japanese inn was at the port to meet me with a one-horse carriage. There was a gang of scoundrels who came to treat the immigrants roughly as soon as they heard that some Japanese had docked. They were like radical teenagers today. There were a group of fifteen to twenty youngsters who shouted, "Let's go! The Japs have come!" We rushed to the inn to avoid being hit. As we went along, we were bombarded with abuses such as "Japs," "lewd," et cetera. They even picked horse dung off the street and threw it at us. I was baptized with horse dung. This was my very first impression of America.

Some young people who were working for the *Nichi Bei Times* [a Japanese-American weekly newspaper] in San Francisco came to the inn to meet me. They suggested that I come to their newspaper office, because they thought there would be some work for me there. For three months my job was to set type for the paper. At that time American feeling toward the Japanese was already bad in general, and we were advised not to walk alone during the day and not to go out at night. It was particulaly dangerous after school was over. I never went out at night, and even during the day I tried to avoid the streets were American youngsters might be. I felt very insecure, not economically but physically. I remember those incidents in which young Japanese boys who worked for the paper came back to the office beaten up. It happened frequently. Sometimes we celebrated the fact that we were not hit that day. I began to think that San Francisco was not a good place to stay, and I went to Los Angeles . . . eventually Pasadena.

Kiyoshi Noji

I was at the Pacific School of Religion for three and a half years. I stayed at the dormitory in Berkeley and was treated well. I think there was some anti-Japanese feeling then. I remember a Miss Yukiko Furuta who achieved exceptionally good grades in high school, but she was not asked to speak as a valedictorian at the time of her graduation because she was Japanese. I read about it in a Japanese newspaper and was shocked. I heard there were other cases like this in California.

I don't remember personally encountering any ill feelings. I think it is because my contacts and associations were with Christians, and I attended Christian gatherings mainly. After World War II broke out, there were many shocking incidents.

I was twenty-seven years old when I came to America, and as a student I lived a simple life. Later on, I went to Princeton. During one summer vacation, some members of the Japanese Embassy staff from Washington, D.C., came to study at Princeton. Three of them decided to take a trip to the Southern states, and they made plans. One was to research the history, one was to study the geography, and the third was to study facilities.

The three went on the trip and after they returned from their vacation, we gathered at the dormitory to hear about it. They evidently visited the school that Booker T. Washington established. They told us that when the Negroes at the school heard that the three were Japanese Navy men, they organized a big welcome. They were taken to a room where pictures of two Japanese were hung. They were pictures of Prince Saionji and Count Makino, who were delegates to the Versailles Treaty after World War I. There Count Makino made a speech on equal human rights. The Negroes heard about this speech, and out of respect for these men, they hung their pictures at the school.

MINEJIRO SHIBATA

Since I'm short-tempered, I fought against the whites with a stick. I hated to be looked down on. Whenever the whites looked down on me, I got really mad. They called us "Japs." They must have thought of us as something like dogs.

After landing, I took a train from San Francisco to Los Angeles. Then I came to Terminal Island. Only Japanese people lived there; no English was heard or spoken. The whites working at the cannery came to Terminal Island only when there was a catch of fish during the daytime. Since the Japanese outnumbered the whites, the whites didn't say anything bad to us. They were quiet because they were afraid of being thrown into the ocean if we got mad. I felt good about that.

Talking about discrimination—there was the bill of anti-Japanese fishery in Sacramento.[1] That was a bill for banning the Japanese from fishing. We were all excited about it. The person who proposed the bill did that for money. I'm not sure that he hated us. Anyway, he proposed the bill every four years. Whenever the bill was passed, the fishermen from the Japanese Fishing Union went and paid money to revoke it. The bill was urged by the Slavic and Italian fishermen. There were quite a few Italians there. The Slavs were worse than the Italians, though. Those from Yugoslavia were the stowaways. We competed for fish with other white fishermen, you see. They called us "Japs," so we kicked them, and they ran away.

[1]Between 1919 and 1945 some twenty-six bills were introduced in the California legislature to prohibit Japanese aliens from engaging in commercial fishing. Most of these bills attempted to limit the issuance of licenses by using a citizenship requirement.

Sometimes gangsters threatened Japanese stowaways and robbed them. There were two large groups of gangsters in Los Angeles. The stowaways hid themselves whenever they saw an immigration officer. They were just like the Mexican aliens today. The stowaways on Terminal Island were from Kishu. They went to New York on ships and got off there. Not being able to feed themselves in New York, they came here. Some crossed the border from Mexico. As soon as they crossed the border, their relatives and friends picked them up. Immigration officers reminded me of a grampus. Whenever a grampus appears, all of the other fish disappear. Instead of a direct warning, we said, "A grampus is waiting." Then every stowaway went inside or hid himself. By the time the officer came in, everybody had gone.

ZENTASO YAMAMOTO

I was working way back in a remote, isolated site. It used to take a little more than an hour, since I was on foot, to get to San Mateo to shop. Then kids would come around saying, "Jap! Jap!" Sure, Jap, Jap. We were Jap in those days. Once in a while they would throw stones at me. Well, I would throw some back at them.

MRS. KO TAKAKOSHI

When we were farming in Rainier Valley, a parent was jealous because our son was an honor student. I heard him say, "Get the Jap out of here." However, later on they found out that my son could be trusted. One day, the mother came and asked my son to come and stay with her son while she went out shopping. That's the only incident I experienced. Our neighbors were all good to us. The neighbors competed in inviting my children to birthday parties.

MRS. AI MIYASAKI

We heard that everyone here was tall and pretty. We had just come from Japan and we were small. And yet, even to us women, the men tipped their hats and paid their respects. I thought America is certainly good. Japanese men would never do that. They take good care of us women here. Yes, I thought it was a good thing. The men, not now, but then, all wore hats; and they all tipped their hats to show the women respect, even to us Japanese. I thought, "America is free and democratic and respects women."

KENGO TAJIMA

Once in Riverside I went into a barbershop, sat there, and started to read a newspaper. While I was reading, the barber came and said, "We don't serve you." When I found out I wasn't wanted, I went out. I didn't know that Japanese were not wanted.

SHOICHI FUKUDA

There were prejudicial acts directed against individuals, and the whole society seemed to be against the Japanese people. We could not do anything. At that time anybody could open a drugstore with a learner's license, and a few years after working in the drugstore, one could take an examination to become a licensed pharmacist. I obtained a learner's license, but just about that time the regulations became tighter, and one could not become a pharmacist without citizenship.[2]

It was like that everywhere. In order to buy land or even to lease it, one had to be a citizen. We were disadvantaged by law; we could not even borrow land to farm. People who wanted to farm had to lease land in the name of someone with citizenship. It was very difficult. Those who had to borrow someone's name had to bring gifts to the name lender. Because we did not have citizenship, we always came out on the losing end when we were sued or when we sued someone. It did not happen to me personally, but it happened to many people. For example, when a Japanese person's car was hit by a white man, you could never win the case. You just had to cry and forget the loss. Even if the evidence was in our favor, it was quite certain that we would lose.

White people used to call us "Jap." When kids looked at us, they used to call us "Chink." That was a derogatory name for Chinese people, but they could not see the difference between

---

[2]According to the Naturalization Act of 1790, eligibility for naturalization was restricted to "free white persons." It was not until 1952 that citizenship for the Issei was made possible by an Act of Congress. Exclusion from citizenship became the focal point of most anti-Japanese legislation for many years.

Japanese and Chinese. I was not affected directly, but whites and Asians went to segregated schools. Places like Florin, Walnut Grove, and Courtland had segregated schools.[3] Things such as this were happening all the time; it was very bad then.

NISUKE MITSUMORI

In those days we had only the *Nihonjin Kai* (Japanese Club) in Pasadena. Their goals were mainly political. They may have supported a Japanese school. They celebrated the Emperor's birthday, showed Japanese movies, and collected some funds. When anti-Japanese feelings developed, the *Nihonjin Kai* took an initiative in creating a movement against this. However, when Americans started thinking that the *Nihonjin Kai* was an agent for the Japanese government, the church became a center instead for fighting against the anti-Japanese movement. The biggest problem we had was the Alien Land Act of 1920, which prohibited aliens from buying land.[4] Another big problem was the new immigration law of 1924 which stopped the immigration of the colored races. Pasadena was a Christian town, and churches had power then. In Pasadena this new law was not approved of.

CHOICHI NITTA

There was so much anti-Japanese feeling in those days! They called us "Japs" and threw things at us. When I made a trip to Marysville to look for land, someone threw rocks. It took strong determination to decide to buy land and live here permanently. Most of the Japanese thought they would work a while, make some money, and go back to Japan.

In 1913, the Alien Land Law prohibiting aliens from buying land came into effect. I bought my land before the Alien Land Law. I could have kept that property but sold it to buy this one. By

---

[3] These are small farming communities south of Sacramento, California.

[4] His reference is to the California Alien Land Law of 1920, which was designed to strengthen the California Alien Land Law of 1913. The 1913 law prohibited aliens ineligible for citizenship (Japanese) from owning land. The 1920 law prohibited the lease or purchase of land by corporations in which Japanese aliens held a majority of stock, prohibited the leasing of land by individual Japanese aliens, prohibited noncitizen Japanese parents from serving as guardians of property for their minor children, and prohibited purchase of land in the name of another person to avoid the intent of the Alien Land Law.

that time, the Alien Land Law was in effect. I was Sunday School superintendent and was teaching the youth class. A young Nisei (second generation, child of an Issei and a citizen by birth) man came from Hawaii. This young man came into my class, and we became acquainted with each other. I bought the property in his name. It was arranged as though I leased the land from him. I left it in his name, Yoshida, until I got my citizenship, which was after World War II. It wasn't changed over to my son's name when he became of age. Many people had trouble after they bought property this way, but Mr. Yoshida and I never had trouble. We still have close ties.

TOKUSHIGA KIZUKA

At that time in Watsonville it was getting better for the Japanese; but when we used to go to the movies on Sundays, they never ushered us to a seat in the center section, which was the best section. If we sat in the center, the usher came and told us to move to another section. Other than that, I did not feel any discrimination.

By 1929 my son was born, and I decided to live in the United States permanently. I thought that since I had no special education, it would be better for me and my children to remain in America. I decided to buy some land, but at that time there was a complicated law against Japanese becoming landowners; so I bought in my son's name with three witnesses. There was a judge named Sand; * he had always been very helpful to me, so I went to see him and told him about my circumstances. He told me to get witnesses and to go through the court procedure. I needed my son's signature, but he was only four years old. The judge said not to worry about it as long as he was alive. He told me to be sure to pay the taxes every year, and when my son became twenty-one years old, he would automatically become the owner. He was very helpful. Yes, I am very grateful.

When my children were older, they attended a small school on Riverside Road across the street from our property. That is where my son went until we were evacuated. They were very nice to Japanese in that school. There was an American who lived nearby and was a school counselor. He was very nice to us. When we

* A pseudonym.

were building our Japanese school,[5] he suggested that we use their school. But we didn't want to get the school in trouble; so we went ahead and built it on our land.

Mrs. Tome Takatsuki

In 1920, before I obtained my citizenship, we decided to buy a house. At that time a person named McClatchy, owner of *The Sacramento Bee*, was here. He was extremely prejudiced and did not like the Oriental people. When we bought a house, he severely criticized us, "A Jap bought a house! This family has twelve children. They must not live here!" He publicized these feelings in his newspaper, and we were scared. The real estate salesman was extremely afraid and came begging to us, "Please return this house. If you do not, I will lose my license and not be able to continue in the business." We did not know what to do. At that time my husband was working in the market business, and there was a person named Mrs. Nelson* who was nice to the Japanese people. She had thirty acres of land in the Oak Park area and had many Japanese farmers on her land, so she understood the feelings of the Japanese people. I went to her place to consult. When we explained our situation, she said, "Oh, you were the people who were attacked by the newspaper. Don't worry; we will go and see your place. Don't reveal our conversation to anyone." Mrs. Nelson and the real estate man came to see our place and looked at our property. She said, "Since this is a rundown house we will find another one for you." There was, on Sixteenth and "W" Streets, a two-block lot, and its owner suddenly had to go back East and wanted to sell the lot for cash. We did not have any money, but we arranged to buy it with easy payments. We built a new house on the lot. When the house was finally finished and we moved in, the neighbors discriminated against us. "If Japs move in, our property value will decrease," they said. Mrs. Nelson and her daughter Margaret* were wise people. They quickly responded, "These Japanese people have no children, are clean, quiet, and educated. If you don't want them, I will sell this place to a Negro family with seven or eight boys." The neighbors then

[5]Many Japanese communities supported "Japanese schools" which taught the reading and writing of Japanese and sometimes other cultural pursuits. These classes were conducted after public school hours and on weekends.

*A pseudonym.

said, "Please don't say any more, and let those Japanese people live here." We were then finally able to settle there.

Osuke Takizawa

At that time Americans thought Japanese were like slaves. All the men and women worked in the fields, even on Sundays; so whites thought that the Japanese were bad people. They thought of us as cows or horses. The discrimination was gaining much heat. We Issei had such a fearful time. When I was working on the farm, I received a check for payment. However, I could not cash the check, not even in a bank, because they did not trust the Japanese. Therefore, I had to go to a San Francisco bank to cash it. One day, I took a boat to San Francisco, and when I was waiting for a train, a big brick was thrown at me from a floor above by three whites. And they were laughing!

Juhei Kono

We were living in the countryside; therefore, we experienced less hostility than those in the cities. Once you were out in the cities, it was all different. Being called "Japs" was almost an everyday occurrence for us. Hardly anybody—maybe with the exception of women—called us "Japanese" as clearly as it should be said. Some people commented, "Please don't be offended if we say 'Jap.' It's only a word. It's almost an abbreviation by stopping at 'p' when we are supposed to say 'Japanese.' So just take it as such and don't be offended." But, of course, it is still distasteful to us anyway. So I used to tell them, "We don't hear it that way at all."

Anti-Japanese attitudes were gradually on the uprise. I heard that people even spit on Japanese in the streets. In fact, I myself, was spit upon more than a few times. Eventually this sort of thing caused us to think that it would be much better to go back to Japan. This is one of the reasons why so many people at that time wanted to go back to Japan as soon as they had saved enough money. Those who had never been insulted before in their life back in Japan had to take such insults, and the educated and uneducated alike were insulted indiscriminately in this country.

The period between 1920 till around 1925 was the worst time that America ever had. In 1919 this thing about picture brides was put under a ban, and then came the ban on immigration altogether.[6] You see, the Gentlemen's Agreement came to an end. Such was the time, and the exclusion movement against Japanese became more and more extensive each day. Look at the politicians of those days. They would say, "I am in favor of the exclusion of Japanese," and that became part of their campaign platform out of which they eventually gained more votes. There once was a Senator from California by the name of Hiram Johnson. He was one of those politicians. It was a time when you could only expect fewer votes if you were supportive of Japanese. The anti-Japanese movement by then had grown very important on the political level. Because of the social climate, what is called the "*beika*-movement" became very popular among the Japanese.

By *beika* I mean "Americanization." We gave up on the idea of naturalization, because we were told that we could not obtain citizenship. If that was the case, we thought, even if they don't give us citizenship, the Japanese had to become Americanized; so the churches of the time worked on Americanization and evangelism with the two combined. As for the Buddhist churches, they couldn't do the same. Buddhism at that time was, relatively speaking, less powerful. It was understandable in such circumstances for a conflict to arise with Buddhist people. An allegation that Christians had to cope with was that some were able to cooperate with Americans because they were Christians, whereas Buddhists could not do the same; therefore, the Christians were accused of taking advantage of the Americanization movement to strengthen our Christian evangelism. As you may know, it was after World War II that the Buddhists became as influential as they are today. Before the war in Tacoma, Washington, Christians were the majority within the Japanese community. Seventy percent were Christians then. Now it's reversed; only thirty percent are Christians and seventy percent are Buddhists. You will find a similar situation in Seattle too. Now the Buddhist people can freely enjoy their religious activities.

Becoming a Christian was one way of *beika*, but we also emphasized appreciation of American life. For example, people in this country used to take a day off on Sundays and go to church. We thought that we should do as Americans and adopted their custom of going to church on Sunday. Then, when the Prohibi-

[6]"Picture brides" were actually banned in 1921.

tion movement came about, we restrained ourselves from drinking. In short, we tried as much as possible to live as Americans live.

It's also against the American custom for parents to bring up their children with no regard to the children's own desires. We tried to adopt some aspects of American life to our own and to the education of our children. Japanese women in the past used to work in the fields with small children on their backs. Though nobody these days would say anything against it, it was thought at that time that Americans might be averse to such a practice. There can be actually two ways to interpret this habit of carrying a baby on the back while working. One is that Japanese people work with the baby on their back; therefore, they don't want to give their children much freedom. The second interpretation goes contrary to the first one: They take really good care of their children by keeping them close. The kind of message we got at the time was that Americans did not see it as we saw it—the latter interpretation. The social climate of the time was such that they would tell us, "Do you guys really have to make money even by working to that extent? If that is how the Japanese are, then we don't want any Japanese here."

Nowadays a lot of women in this country go out and work, but not in those days. Some people would say, "Japanese are no good. They make their women work." White women used these things against us. It may be useless to talk about it now, because it has to do with the differences of times. Times have changed, and the changes have been cruel to us. Another example is with the store business problems. We were always accused of working too long a time. White people used to say that they could not compete with their Japanese counterparts, for the whites worked for eight hours while we worked for ten or fifteen. We worked hard knowing that life is a precious thing, but they would slander us and say, "Money is all that they are concerned about. They work hard just to make more and more money." Unrestricted working hours caused one of the biggest problems among business people.

As you may well know, harsh discrimination towards Japanese increased right before the war . . . whether you were a college graduate or even a Phi Beta Kappa just didn't make any difference at all. As a result, even college graduates with excellent academic records became barbers or worked in laundries or on farms. A considerable number of Japanese went back to Japan then. Those of us who are still here today are the ones who put up with those experiences and decided to stay and fight against the anti-Japanese atmosphere of the time.

4

On Becoming an American

NISUKE MITSUMORI

I suffered a great deal, wondering whether fighting in the war (World War I) might be murdering and whether this behavior was in accord with God's teachings. I went to the draft board and told them that I was a Christian and believed that the love of God should be given equally to any human and that I did not agree with the act of human brothers and sisters fighting against each other. I told them that I would not be able to participate in such killing, but what I thought I could do was to provide some psychological help to those who fought in the war and those who were wounded in it. I asked them if they thought they needed me. They said that there were plenty of volunteers and that they would be able to put me in such a position. It was in April of 1917 that the United States declared war, and it was in July of that year that I finally volunteered for service after a great deal of consideration. However, I did not hear anything from the draft board afterwards. I thought that they might not take me since I was Japanese. Finally in November I received a notice to appear. I did not pass the physical examination the first time, but the second time I passed it, and I was ready to go.

In April 1918, I received my orders. There were about sixty people from Pasadena at Camp East, where I received basic training. Aliens who did not have citizenship needed to apply for it, so I did too. A clerk in the office where I applied for citizenship looked at my face and asked me whether I was Japanese. I said, "Yes." Then he said, "I am awfully sorry. You will be a good soldier, but under our present law we cannot accept your application." He tore up my papers and burned them. I returned to the barracks with the others. Other soldiers told me that I had better get out of the Army. They told me that I would be better off in Japan since I had to struggle with difficulties here. However, I told them that I did not come here to get citizenship but to serve the country and that I did not have any reason to go back. Some of them wondered about me and sort of suspected that I was a spy from the Japanese military.

After a while, people stopped talking to me. I felt strange. I guess they must have believed this spy business. I did not speak to them either and tried to behave as naturally as possible. After six weeks of basic training, we all were assigned to different military groups according to one's ability. Those who did not have any particular ability were all put in the infantry. I was also assigned to the infantry. After some training I asked our commanding officer if I was going to remain in that unit. He said, "Yes." I told our captain, Williams, who was very understanding, that I volunteered for the medical corps, since people at the draft board said that it would be possible for me to join a medical team as they had a lot of volunteers. I told him that to remain in the infantry corps was certainly different from my original purpose in volunteering for service. I made it clear that I joined the army to do service for those who were wounded in the war and for those who were in trouble psychologically or otherwise, and asked him if he could do something about this. The captain said, "I see."

Then he told me that I could ask to be transferred to a medical corps, but I would be assigned to the hospital on the base where we were, and I would not be able to serve those who were wounded in the war. He also added that those who were in the hospital on the base were sort of bad characters—some had venereal diseases, et cetera. He said that there were a lot of guys who caught venereal diseases on purpose so that they would not be sent to the war. He asked me if I would like to take care of those people or if I would like to go to war and take care of the wounded. I told him that I was interested in the latter. Then the captain said that I had better keep quiet and that he would do his best to put me in the position I requested once we got over to France. Thus, trusting what the captain told me, I kept quiet and completed training in the infantry corps. In June we received orders. On July 4, we left New York for England, and from England we went over to southern France, where we had to practice actual fighting. An officer came and trained us. About that time I put in a request to our captain and asked him if he remembered what he promised me back in the United States. He said that he still remembered and that he would take necessary procedures for me. He did. He was a very honest man.

Before I received orders for reassignment, we had to leave to fight in the war. It was the night before we actually participated in the war that I seriously thought about what I was going to do. We could see extensive smoke and flames coming out of the fighting area. The sky was red with flames. That night we were positioned in a sunken area, so I went up to the top of the hill and quietly thought about my faith and watched the war going on. I told myself that I really did not want to kill anybody, but I wanted so much to serve the wounded in the war. I did my best to pursue my original beliefs, but now I was in a situation where I could no longer escape. I realized that there were two aspects of not being able to escape. I had pride as a Japanese. I knew that a Japanese could not escape out of cowardice. On the other hand, if I went there, there was a good chance of being killed. This was my dilemma: I was a coward if I did not escape but I was also a coward if I escaped, and that, I thought, would be a disgrace to the Japanese. I was confused and did not know what I should do.

Later I thought that my position was a blessing. Ultimately we did not do any real shooting, although we did have machine guns. Our role was to protect an artillery corps which was right behind us. Their role was to fire guns. If the enemy attacked them, they would not be able to do their job. Therefore, those who actually fought in the front line were machine gun soldiers who were positioned about three hundred yards apart from each other, and the shooting was done with those soldiers as the core. It was seldom that we had to use our rifles. There were a lot of casualties. Soldiers in the medical corps ran back and forth to help the wounded, bandaging wounds and carrying the wounded to a sunken area so that they could take care of them. I thought it was a blessing that I ended up staying in an infantry corps. As I was small, I could not possibly have carried such big American soldiers. My job in the infantry corps was much easier, although I was wounded. After the war was over, I wanted to go back to the States immediately, so I told them I was all right. However, after I came back to the United States, I got worse. I had about five hundred dollars saved, but I used the money for getting medical treatment and recuperating.

Everybody was treated equally in the military. I was rather trusted. There was a sergeant who was in charge of the meals for our company and responsible for all the food hunting. The sergeant received some money to purchase necessary food for the company while we were in France, although we received some food from the military. This sergeant told me that I was the only person that he could trust and asked me to keep the money for him. I asked him what he would do if I died. He said that he could not help it. When the war was over, there were two million American soldiers in Europe. It took an awful lot of time to send those soldiers back to the States. We had to wait for our turn in France for seven months. I was treated rather well in France. Our company commander awarded me a medal for my conduct in the company, which he thought set an example for other soldiers.

Since I was small, it was very hard for me to participate in a long march and carry a gas mask which weighed four pounds and a gun which weighed seven pounds and one hundred and sixty bullets in addition to a heavy pair of shoes. Our section commander helped me with this heavy gun. I guess he sympathized with me because I was so small. I was the only Japanese among approximately three thousand soldiers there. I believed that all men were brothers and sisters; therefore, I did not feel unusual or different, even though I was the only Japanese in the group. I do not know how others felt though.

5

Work

In the 1920's anti-Japanese hysteria reached an all-time high and was climaxed by the Immigration Act of 1924, which effectively ended Japanese immigration to the United States. The intensity of this prejudice was totally out of proportion to the number of immigrants, for the entire population of both immigrants and native-born Japanese never comprised more than two and one-tenth percent of the population of California and only one-tenth of one percent of the entire population of the United States. Nonetheless, this intense prejudice existed, and the Issei dealt with it in their daily lives as best they could. But the immediate needs of simple survival, the demands of a new cultural environment, and a greater vision for the future always took precedence, and it is here that the Issei expended their energies.

JUHEI KONO

Back in those days, the situation was especially terrible for the Japanese, whether here in the United States or over there in Japan. The houses where they lived were just like chicken coops, narrow and small, and looked like remodeled stables. It was true in California too. I often used to visit Brawley in the Imperial Valley of California. Japanese people in that area lived just like that. Once their land lease expired, they had a horse pull their house and move it on to another field to work.

SADAME INOUYE

I was in Hawaii for two days. People at a Japanese inn on the island took care of the paper work necessary to come to the mainland. People from Kochi Ken, where I was from, seldom worked on the island. We got our passports stamped in Hawaii, and we came here.

I was not particularly surprised at anything when I first landed. I just thought that America was a huge country. Different kinds of food, clothes, language—it did not bother me so much. I thought San Francisco was a nice town; it was before the earthquake, which came six months later. Anti-Japanese feeling was prevalent at that time, and kids used to throw rocks at us. I had to run away. There was nothing else I could do. Other Japanese, too, had this experience. It was really vexing, but I could not have caught the kids.

I did not work in San Francisco. I just stayed overnight there at an inn, and the following day I took a boat down the river to an island near Stockton with another Japanese fellow.[1] A friend of mine had given me an address down there. We got to the place about midnight and spent the rest of the night in a warehouse. I remember it was still pretty cold; it was about the middle of March. The next morning we heard chickens, and we realized that people were around. We were pleased and waited until dawn, when we met an Italian to whom we showed the address. He did not understand English either but took us to a nearby Japanese labor camp, although this was not the one we were looking for. We talked to some Japanese people, and they sent a messenger ahead for us. We took another boat to get to the other camp. (Even within the island it was easier to go from place to place by boat.)

First we worked in the onion fields for a month or so. Then we went to a neighboring island to dig potatoes. It was about August when we finished the job and came up to Sacramento to work until the middle of September, when we went to pick grapes. While picking grapes, my friend and I both suffered from beriberi, and we were hospitalized for about a month in Sacramento. After we got well, we spent time at a camp where we had friends.

In the spring everybody went back to work, so I followed, although my legs were not strong. Our boss was kind and gave me

[1]Mr. Inouye is referring to an area known as the Sacramento Delta, which is honeycombed with small islands that are extensively cultivated.

an easy job. I scared birds from the field where the barley seeds were just sown. Then, about the end of March, water started covering the island. We waited at a warehouse for four or five days and hoped that the water would subside, but it never did; so we decided to look for other jobs and went to a Japanese camp in San Leandro. There we picked green peas and planted tomatoes. Though my legs were still weak, I managed to work somehow. About the end of June or July there was not much work left. My friend, myself, and one other guy tried chopping wood, which was rather unusual work in midsummer. We earned only fifty cents per tree after we chopped down the tree, dug the root up, cut the wood into certain sized pieces and piled them up. It was *quite* a job, and they paid just fifty cents a tree. Nobody would work like that today. I could earn a dollar and a half if I worked on three trees a day. That was equivalent to a regular wage in those days. This was not enough in the winter. In a regular camp we paid twenty cents for food. I guess we paid about twenty-five or thirty cents for our room per day. When I worked here and there, I carried my own blanket roll with me and slept where I could. Sometimes I stayed in boarding houses. In one house I remember that I paid fifty cents just for the room, although it was a really nice one. Even when I ate at restaurants, I did not spend more than twenty or twenty-five cents a day for food.

I chopped trees for a while and then came out to Sacramento in the fall, but there was no work. A friend of mine who was just goofing around used to come to my place for dinner. I could not help feeding him, though I did not like the idea. I asked him if he'd like to work with me. He said that he would, so we formed a labor group and went to Naples near Santa Barbara as a section gang for the railroad. There were between twelve and fifteen people in this gang. The weather was nice out there, and the work was not too hard; however, we soon found that it was really dangerous work. We asked our boss if he would pay us for the work we did on the first few days, but he refused, so we ran away. Two other young Japanese asked us if they could come along, and the four of us left camp together. The boss must have had trouble continuing the work after we left. Finally we went down to Los Angeles. We worked in the area between Huntington Beach and Santa Ana for about six months cutting celery. There were many Japanese in that area. We had a commission boss who called us up each night to tell us where we were going to work the next day.

After the celery season, we went to pick oranges and lemons. Later on I went to Gardena to help a friend. At that time there were strawberry fields in Gardena. When the strawberry season was over, I was asked to go to the mountain area in Venice. On a fairly large farm a Japanese was growing barley, potatoes, onions, and corn. I worked for this guy for about half a year.

Working in migratory labor camps was an experience common to many Japanese immigrants. Their situation was comparable to that of Mexican aliens who work as farm laborers today. However, the Japanese had the advantage of beginning in agriculture when it was still a fledgling industry. If a laborer saved his money, small farms were available for sharecropping, leasing, or even purchasing, albeit by surreptitious methods.

SHOICHI FUKUDA

When I came here, Japanese people could not buy land anywhere. I don't think Japanese people could even lease land. My father came to the United States and began a business. He brought canned goods and pickles from Japan and sold them in the Hayward area. The business did not work out very well; so he had to quit. Then he began to work as a sharecropper in Oakland raising tomatoes and cucumbers. I think the rate was on a fifty-fifty basis. When I came here, things were not going very well. In fact, my father even lost some money. He had to move around a lot, for everything depended on the availability of sharecropping lots. Sharecropping contracts were only signed on a yearly basis, so when I came to the States, my father was working at a cannery too. I became a schoolboy in the San Francisco area. That was the pattern of my life during the early years in this country.

When I was a schoolboy in San Francisco, my wages were very low. I was paid a dollar fifty a week. My work was to make breakfast for the family and then to clean up the kitchen. After that I went to an English school for Japanese people located at the Pine Methodist Church. I would get home about four P.M. and do some chores. Monday was washday. It was not like today, because we did not have washing machines. I had to boil tubfuls of water and wash clothes by hand.

Tuesday was ironing day. Baskets full of clothes were always waiting for me. Wednesday I cleaned the yard. The fourth day, I forgot now what I did. Anyway, I did all kinds of things like painting, cleaning house, and other odd jobs. On Saturday, at least for a half day, I had to clean the house. Sunday was my day off.

I don't recall making too many mistakes except for a few incidents. One day I found a box of cheese in the living room. Dairy products were not common to our Japanese diet, so to me it smelled so badly that I thought it was rotten. I brought it to the kitchen, and since my English was so limited, I could not even explain myself to my employer.

During the summer vacation, I went to a farm to work. I had to accumulate enough money to go to school for the next year. Most of the students used to do this. We used to look forward to this time, and I would go to the Oakland area to work. I also worked in a cannery in Monterey. I was able to accumulate a small amount of money and returned to San Francisco to go to school.

Because of personal reasons, I left the home where I was a schoolboy and went to San Diego and worked in a nursery for a while. It was owned by Japanese people, but I worked as a schoolboy. I went to elementary school there, although I must have been nineteen years old at that time. Later the owner of the nursery sold his property and went back to Japan, so I had to go back to San Francisco. There I found some housework. When summer came, I went to San Jose and worked for a nurseryman again. I spent several years doing these things.

Meanwhile, problems between Japan and the United States began to worsen. About that time I was planning to go back to Japan. Well, you see the situation here was not that good. We could not obtain citizenship, and we were ill treated. I wanted to go back to Japan, since I had not been back for a while. Just at that time I was injured, and I had to spend quite a bit of money on medical bills; so I missed the opportunity.

MASAO HIRATA

When I arrived in San Francisco, my father bought me a suit and a suitcase, and we stayed the night in that city. Though it was in August, the weather in San Francisco was cold. The next morning we traveled to Fresno, where I was surprised by the hot weather. It was over a hundred and five degrees! I will never forget that experience.

I started to work picking grapes. Dozens of people came into the camp to pick, but there were no houses for us to live in. We had to make our own beds. We piled up raisin boxes under a peach tree, put some hay on the boxes, and covered them with canvas. That was our bed. When we slept, we hung up mosquito netting. One side was slung from the branch of a peach tree and the other side over a stick we had driven into the ground. Picking grapes was my first job in America.

I worked very hard from early morning when it was still dark till late evening after dark. They paid us up to four cents per tray of grapes; so if we worked really hard, we got fifteen or sixteen dollars a day, since times were the best in 1920. This amount of money was worth twice as much in Japan. Just imagine! Working very hard in Japan, I only got paid thirty-six yen a year.

I worked so hard that I injured my right knee and became unable to bend it. Then I had a difficult time curing it and had an acupuncture.

I just worked like mad. I didn't know English or anything about America at all. Getting up early in the morning, I got lunch and a bagful of water. Then I went to a place where the trucks were parked. Sometimes the people from the vineyard came to pick me up, and I worked and worked. Work was everything. After the grape season was over, I asked my father to let me go to school. I was going to study and work as a schoolboy. But it was very difficult because I was unable to understand any English at all. Instead, I enrolled in a Buddhist society boarding school in Fresno. At that time it cost only two hundred and fifty dollars a year to go to school. Since I was eager to learn, I worked very hard during the summer vacation to save money for school.

The next summer my father found work in Arizona picking cucumbers, but he didn't come back though school was about to start. I didn't understand why because he didn't write to me. He usually came back to Fresno by the end of August when the grape-picking season started, but it was September and he hadn't returned. I was worried. Then I received news that father was ill and had no money to come back. I was shocked. He was my only parent. How could I go to school and leave my sick father alone? At once I sent the two hundred and fifty dollars, which was for my tuition, to my father in Arizona. He finally came back and thanked me with tears in his eyes.

We thought that it was not good for us to remain unsettled; so we started farming together. Then in 1923 anti-Japanese laws such as banning the inheritance of land and Japanese immigration were legislated. I decided not to farm against the law and came to Los Angeles in 1924.

First, I worked on the strawberry farm of a friend's elder brother in Torrance. Later I grew strawberries. In 1929 I got married and had my first daughter in 1930. Farming was really hard work. We could have a good year, but the next two years might be bad. I never got up later than five-thirty in the morning. The Japanese way of farming was just incredible. We worked and worked and worked desperately. You can never imagine how hard we worked by watching people work on a farm today.

Besides the hard work and legal discrimination, we had other problems. At that time there were very few Japanese women. One day a man bribed a married woman into having sexual activities in return for favors to her family. This man had even been the go-between in her marriage![2] Since her husband used to go out fishing often, she was probably lonesome too. The man told her that he would treat her family better if she obeyed him, and she did. But the man didn't keep his promise, so she finally told everything to her husband. At that time the law prohibited us to have our own land, so we got the land under the name of someone who was born in Hawaii [and was therefore a U.S. citizen] and was over twenty years old. By borrowing and using the name of this woman's husband, we had the land to work. We were afraid that we all might lose the land, because the man who bribed the wife was a member of our group.

We exerted a lot of effort to settle this trouble. We frequently visited the man whose name we borrowed to calm his anger. Finally we succeeded in settling this problem. We asked the accused man to live somewhere else and gave the right to work on the land to his son.

SHIZUMA TAKESHITA

I went to work as a schoolboy and received a dollar twenty-five per week with meals and lodging. I saved the money I earned, and whenever I accumulated five dollars, I took it to a Japanese bank and sent it to my mother and grandmother. In my first letter home, I mentioned that I was well and that I knew I had the

[2]In the traditional Japanese marriage, a trusted personal friend of both families negotiated the wedding arrangements.

responsibility of looking after the Takeshita family; so I sent the first five dollars I earned. Thereafter, I kept sending them money.

There was no adult education school then, and persons over twenty years old couldn't enter elementary school. I started to learn English privately but had a difficult time.

By 1904 I was working for a Japanese newspaper, but we had only thirty-seven subscribers, and they were paying only fifty cents a month. The next year I talked to the editor and suggested that we make a directory of all the Japanese living in the area. This is the origin of the directories the two San Francisco Japanese newspaper staffs put out bi-annually. Now we have many names, but in those days the directory was very small. I also did some research and wrote an article about the Japanese in the nursery business. Now we have many Japanese flower growers, but we only had a few then. And then I conducted a census of the Japanese population in Alameda and Contra Costa counties. I traveled by bicycle and got this information. There were a total of 2,546 Japanese; 2,298 were men and only 248 were women and children. I got advertisements to print in the book and paid for the cost of publishing the directory. Both the U.S. Constitution and the Constitution of Japan were included.

I also tried to help the Japanese business community. There were two Japanese-operated banks at that time, one a regular bank and the other a savings and loan association. The two were having financial difficulties, and I was instrumental in the merger of the two banks; however, later on the bank was closed. Although the Japanese bank started out with the same assets as the Bank of Italy, the Japanese bank went broke, but the Bank of Italy was a success, and it was the forerunner of the present Bank of America.

Sometimes I wrote articles in the *Nichi Bei News* trying to caution young Japanese men who were in this country against living an immoral life. In those days there were many gamblers and hoodlums. They went around and caused a lot of trouble by going into eating places and stirring up fights. I reported some incidents and got some of those trouble-makers arrested; therefore, my life was threatened. There were houses of prostitution too, and I criticized them in the newspaper. The trouble-makers came to me, threatened me at gunpoint, and tried to make me promise not to write about their businesses. I said to them, "Go ahead and kill me if you think you can continue your business by killing. I can't win by fighting with you—you can kill my body but you can't kill what's right. . . ." As they left, one person said, "Please don't make the articles too harsh." I didn't get killed, but there were incidents like this. At the risk of my life I wrote articles in the newspaper trying to warn young Japanese.

Mrs. Kane Kozono

Well, first of all, you see, I didn't understand English. Right after I joined my husband here, we rented a house in Alameda where my husband was a gardener. As the days went by, I decided that I needed to do something to better myself. I knew I couldn't do so unless I understood the language; therefore, I became a housemaid for a white family. Learning English was such a hard task for me. Oh, but I had a hard time because, you see, I can't even read Japanese. My husband would try to teach me how to read English at night, but by then I was exhausted and sleepy from working during the day.

My husband had come over here three years earlier than I and had a working knowledge of English. By the time I joined him here, he didn't have much trouble with the language, and fortunately he was willing to teach me what he knew. Despite the difficulty of those early days, I kept reminding myself that we had only three years or so to endure before going back to Japan with a fortune. So making money was constantly in our minds. I think I was lucky that the white people liked me.

I was getting used to life in this country by then and doing fine in Alameda. I was paid five dollars a week for the housework I was doing there. I sent all my salary to my parents in Japan, who had been taking care of our oldest daughter for us. By the time we left for Sacramento, I could understand a lot of what my employer said. When her husband would call from the garden, "What time is it?" I would think a little while and give him the time. He then would say, "Pretty good, pretty good."

I was settling into the life there fairly well, but we moved to Sacramento, where some of my husband's relatives were working on a farm. My husband started growing onions, and together with a friend of ours, I worked there digging onions, putting them in a sack, and so forth. I was young then and could do the hard work. From time to time, however, it was so difficult that I often thought I should have stayed in Japan. I had to cook for a lot of the field hands too. After I had babies, raising children was another big job. Whenever I went to work, I took them with me to the ranch, and I would leave them sleeping under a tree. Once in a while I had to make sure everything was all right with them there. And when the day's work was over, I would carry one of them on my back to our home. Men had to work only while they were out in the field, whereas I had to do all those things besides my share of work in the field. I did their laundry after work too. It was a really grueling, hard time for me.

RIICHI SATOW

I was in Napa with my younger brother for about five years altogether. My father stayed with us for two years, because with three of us working, it really made a big difference in his income. He kept all our cash and gave my brother and I some pocket money—enough for us to buy shoes, shirts, or things of that sort. However, every summer father always got sick; it was some sort of fever. When he got sick, it meant that he had to quit working for about forty days or so. Not working for such a long time during summer automatically meant a considerable economic disadvantage, for there was nothing to do during the winters in those days. My brother and I thought it best for him to go back to Japan as soon as possible, but he wanted to earn a lot more money to make his return to Japan a successful homecoming. We promised him that we would send him money, and he finally did go back. We were fearful that if he got sick again, that might be the end of him. We had given him our word that we would send him money, but it took a lot of pain and hard work to keep that promise in later days.

There used to be a big ranch on the outskirts of Napa. It was a ranch of about eighty-five acres of pears, peaches, cherries, apples, and other fruit. That's where I worked. Pruning in winter—you know, chopping off twigs—spraying and plowing in summer. I was to take complete care of the ranch, but it wasn't a year-round job; so it followed that I would continue working at nearby farms whenever work at the fruit ranch was over. That's how a lot of us Japanese used to work in those days.

Then my brother and I decided to go somewhere else, because in 1913 a bill prohibiting land ownership by aliens was passed in California. We had no hope of a good future in California, so we made up our minds to go to Oregon. Well, the situation was worse in Oregon. Sure, you could buy land up there if you wanted, but there was no work available in the winter. We ended up idle for almost a month. Then we decided to go to Sacramento.

We settled in Sacramento in 1919. There used to be a Japanese community in Oak Park and that's when I met Mrs. Nelson.* I worked for her for two or three months, so I knew her very well—even the way she thought. A lot of Japanese—I wasn't one of them though—got to be close to her with a kind of understanding that it might help them in some way. You know, it might be of advantage in one way or another in the future to have a white friend. They said that if someone were in trouble, she would help them. She did get to become friends with many Japanese, but it was all calculated. To her it was all a matter of interest. You see, we Japanese have a tendency to give big gifts as remuneration of someone's favor, a gift that is all out of proportion to the favor received. She knew this, and that was why she willingly gave a helping hand from time to time. She used to show me things and say, "So and so gave this to me, and so and so gave me that." A lot of people gave her gifts in return for her favors.

Anyway, the agreement between us was that I would receive a monthly salary of twenty-five dollars plus room and board. I also counted on her original promise that she was going to teach me English, which was one of the reasons I had decided to go there despite the low salary. I was a houseboy, but primarily I was to do yard work: weeding the vegetable garden, tilling the soil, and pruning and thinning the fruit trees. If that had been all that I was supposed to be doing, then I might have been satisfied with the work. At least I would have stayed there longer than I actually did. But Mr. Itano* had strawberries there in the vineyards leased from Mrs. Nelson. He was growing strawberries while taking care of the grapes at the same time. His grandchildren are still living there. Anyhow, I was soon expected to go and help him with the strawberries. The wages for my hoeing and other related work in his fields were to be pocketed by Mrs. Nelson. I didn't receive any of it. That sort of thing lasted some time, and I got fed up with it.

As for the English lessons, let me tell you about it! Mrs. Nelson had a daughter, Margaret,* who was around thirty-two years old. After supper Margaret used to give me books to read, you know, *The National Reader* or something. She just let me read those things for about half an hour each night, and that was it; I wasn't satisfied with the lessons at all.

*A pseudonym.

Mrs. Nelson had a lot of assets including property. Also a sister of Mrs. Nelson received an inheritance from her deceased husband, who was a banker. This sister was mentally disturbed, although she was not the kind of person who would harm others. Now Margaret knew how much her mother and her aunt owned, and she also knew that she was going to inherit it all sooner or later. She had a boyfriend somewhere—in San Francisco or someplace. Anyhow, she used to write him letters every day. Mrs. Nelson was suffering from some sort of lung disease and had to be treated all the time with a gadget, an oxygen bottle or something. She demanded that Margaret be there with her. She did not want Margaret, her only daughter, to be married and told her that if she married, she would have no inheritance. Margaret definitely wanted the inheritance; therefore, she had to keep the matter of her boyfriend an absolute secret. She used to tell me, "If a letter comes from my boyfriend, bring it to me. Don't let my mother ever know about it." And there she was, writing letters when she was supposedly teaching me English!

I was there for three months. Then I quit and took a trip to central and southern California. I traveled all over the place and hoped that there might be a better situation somewhere out there. Well, in the end there wasn't anything better. We, my brother and I, finally came back to the Sacramento area. In 1920 I brought my wife with me from Japan.

I leased some land, but besides paying rent for it, I had to dig a well and put in a motor for a water pump by myself. Then I planted strawberries. The harvest wasn't bad, but the expenses were quite high. I worked on that ranch for four years; then it was time to move on. I contemplated a move to San Francisco that would lead me to a more promising future.

There I got a job type picking at the *Nichi Bei Shimbun*.[3] At that time Mr. Abiko was still president of the company and Mr. Nakayama was the chief editor. He was a good editor, indeed. I stayed there for a year and a half. Oh, there I worked very, very hard. I made a great effort, and Mr. Abiko got to like me. Everything was going all right for me for some time, but then I got sick. I know I have to do my best with any kind of job, but at that time I believe that I just worked too hard. Besides my job during the day,

---

[3]The Issei make various references to a Japanese newspaper. The reference to the *Nichi Bei Shimbun,* the *Nichi Bei News,* and the *Nichi Bei Times* are all to the same newspaper.

I was going to night school to learn English four nights a week. I had three children by then, and my wife was working part-time—embroidery to help make our living. She did it for quite a while, and there were times when she had more income than I did. Both of us really did work hard, and finally my health broke down.

One day I couldn't get up after having a simple cold. Then I was hospitalized at Stanford University. The doctors there couldn't quite figure out what was wrong with me. They finally said it was pneumonia. They treated me free. Well, I had to pay for my meals. In exchange for that, I consented to let them use my case as study material for the student interns. After getting out of the hospital, I came back to Sacramento and started raising strawberries again. We went back to Oak Park, and I leased a ranch. The harvest for that year was just stupendous, and the harvest for the following year was again wonderful. The yield was something like two thousand two hundred crates, and we sold them at about two dollars and twenty-five cents per crate. We hired only two workers during the picking time, and my brother and I did all the rest of the work. With the money from the harvest, about three thousand dollars, I bought this place and moved in.

About that time I began to think of settling down in this country permanently. I was convinced that settling down here was a must. To do that, I had to buy a piece of land somewhere and live in my own house. I bought the land under the name of a corporation, because Issei couldn't buy land at that time.

The land registration was then switched from the corporation's into our children's names when they came of age. That's how we handled this matter. I continued growing strawberries and served as president of the Strawberry Growers' Association for some time before the war started. I had to work really hard as president.

The association didn't have much money, and most of us strawberry growers were poor and needed financing. The officers had to somehow come up with the money for that. Poor folks getting together don't yield any money simply by saying so, you know. There used to be a company called the Pacific Fruit Produce Exchange—maybe still is—to which our association sold all the strawberries we harvested. They marketed our Sacramento strawberries in Oregon and Washington. We borrowed the money in advance from them, and then gave the needy growers a loan. Later, when the crop was in, their balance was adjusted accordingly. That's how we operated our business in those days. Otherwise it was impossible not only to do business, but also to support the day-to-day life of many growers and their families.

In the course of our association's business, we naturally made some mistakes. For example, as long as we kept selling our strawberries to the Pacific Fruit Produce Exchange, everything was all right. Nonetheless, it is a characteristic of Japanese people that they are more likely to dwell on doubts—doubts that someone might be cheating or taking advantage of them. In reality, nobody was, you see. Nevertheless, some of them didn't know when to stop doubting. Whenever this happened, problems got complicated and confusing . . . often blown out of proportion because some people soon started saying this, and others arguing about that without any substantial grounds. From time to time it got to be just too much to handle. Once we switched to the Independence Produce for a year, and that was clearly a mistake on our part. We managed to get the Independence Produce to pay us, but then we had to accept a lower price for our strawberries. It was, after all, rather a small company in Washington and Oregon, and it was not able to compete on satisfactory terms. The association's executive committee, Mr. Sakuma, Mr. Abe, and I, took a study tour the following year to Oregon and Washington to see how the market was run up there. The tour was at the invitation of the Pacific Fruit Produce Exchange. They wanted to show us first-hand how they had the distribution network set up. In the previous year we had switched to the Independence Produce, and Pacific Fruit was quite concerned. Well, when it was all over, we realized that we shouldn't have changed our minds before. That was really a mistake, actually one of the big mistakes we had made.

KENGO TAJIMA

In southern Utah there were a number of mines where there were a half dozen or more work camps. The first thing I did when I arrived at a camp was to go to the kitchen to find the cook and greet him. He greeted all visitors—Christian pastors, Buddhists, entertainers, and peddlers—and he treated us to a good dinner. He used to give me a big steak. Unless I ate it up, he would say, "What's the matter! It's no good?" So I had to eat it all. Then the boys would come home from the mines and take a bath and eat dinner. They would come to a common room where there were pool tables and a number of round tables. Some would start drinking beer; some would sit around the table and play cards. At about eight P.M. someone would say, "A Christian pastor is going to speak to us." One table would be cleaned, the cards would be withdrawn, and I would sing a few hymns by myself and then preach. Within an hour and a half they would all go back to playing cards again.

The miners always had a place to sleep, had decent meals, and earned good money. Saturdays were paydays; so Saturday was a chance for the townspeople to bring out all their wares. Also big gamblers and prostitutes would come. In one town I remember a Japanese man who had a provisions store with a hotel upstairs where I would stay. The girl who took registrations was a prostitute. She would take my name down and say, "Don't you want me tonight?" I just laughed her away. That was one kind of prostitute. There were many others who would come out to hotels in the evenings, and there would be those who would go around, you know, to the section houses. There were all those women going from place to place selling flesh. That was a challenge to me. If they could do that, I must go round and sell my ware—the gospel.

Sometimes the men would come to speak of their own lives. One said, "I am such an unfortunate man—all my life's been one misfortune after another." I said, "How much are you earning now?" He said, "Three thousand dollars a year." I said, "Three thousand dollars a year is good money. Very few men in Japan make as much as you do, aren't you lucky?" They were just filling in their lot so to speak. They worked and spent their money. They had given up their original purpose for coming to the States, and they just lived from day to day.

Gambling was prevalent and caused quarrels and shootings. Quite often after one of those incidents the men would be taken to court. Sometimes I interpreted for them. Sometimes the attorney or maybe the judge didn't want to prolong the case because much time and money were needed. They decided the man was guilty, and they just shut him up. That was not fair! If a Japanese consented to go to jail for one year, they let him be after that. So consenting to go to jail for one year would be the best way. Sometimes there were more severe judgments. One Japanese fellow was sentenced to die and was taken to the state penitentiary in Provo. I visited him, and he was talking incoherently. I went back to the jailer and said, "This man is insane! Examine him and sentence him to the state mental hospital." That saved him from the death chamber. A number of years later he was working as a houseboy for the prison director. He worked in that family for quite a few years and became a forgotten man there. They lost his records, so he could have gone free. But he had lived there so many years that there was not much he could do on the outside. He just stayed in the prison director's house until he died. At least he was saved from hanging.

Another case occurred in Salt Lake City. Two men were working at a railroad station. One shot the other. The fellow that was killed was a good, quiet man very much liked by the community. The other man had a bad reputation, so he had no sympathy from the Salt Lake City Japanese community. He also was found guilty in a case involving liquor. He had a lawyer who helped him out of that case. This lawyer was a very poor one. In the first court the boy was sentenced to die. I knew the court was inadequate even for real criminals. It was a speedy judgment. I talked to the mine boys, saying, "I am going to see that this man gets a better lawyer. We need some money. Will you give some?" I think I got four or five hundred dollars. Then we wrote to his home in Japan. His family sold his holdings for fifteen hundred dollars and sent it to us. So we had about two thousand dollars. We got the best criminal lawyer in Salt Lake City. He took the case, and the court reconsidered. On the second day the judge found the evidence inadequate, so the case was dropped.

NISUKE MITSUMORI

When the strawberries were picked, my work was over. We decided to go to Fresno because we thought it was a good place to earn money. First I worked in a vineyard there. It was so hot that I could not even see things on the other side of the grapevine. We started working early in the morning and came back to our camp at night. We lived in a barrack—it was a terrible place. It is amazing to think how we could live there. One morning we got up early as usual, finished breakfast, and found that one of us was still sleeping. We tried to wake him up but found him dead. Nobody knew that he was dead. He had worked all day the day before, came back tired, and went to bed. He never woke up.

One of the things I remember even today is that we thought we would be really insecure if we did not have money. All the young immigrants thought that if we carried money with us all the time, we would not get sick. At that time we did not have any paper money but only coins. My friend suggested that I carry a five dollar coin with me always. What a silly superstition that was! But my friend was serious. I received a five dollar coin from him, and we parted. This young man who gave me the coin died about twenty days after that. He was working on a strawberry farm where he caught the fever. He was hospitalized but died a few days later. A messenger informed us of his death. We went to the hospital immediately. We found our friend lying on a bed and covered with a sheet. We took the sheet off and found he was dead. I was only eighteen at that time, and I was really shaken. These incidents made me realize a conflict in my life: Making money is fine, but it might be meaningless if I died in this struggle. I decided to become an accountant and took an entrance examination to enter a college. The result of the examination indicated that my scholarship was about the same as that of a high school graduate. Thus, I was admitted to a college. I finished four years of study in three years by attending summer school.

One had to have two years of practice in an established CPA (Certified Public Accountant) firm and a recommendation from the firm in order to take the CPA examination. The placement office at school tried to find a job for me when I was about to graduate, but they could not find a firm which was willing to hire a Japanese. It was 1926. They could not conceive of hiring a Japanese. Thus, I had to drop the idea of becoming a CPA. In those days, however, one could work as an accountant if he had a certificate from a school which indicated satisfactory completion of accounting courses. That's what I did.

Minejiro Shibata

The people on Terminal Island had lived in Portales up until three or four years before I came. They moved to Terminal Island because the canning company built houses for the employees. Those houses weren't made of plastered walls, but just wood. It wasn't too bad there, for we had a Japanese store, and we didn't hear any English. There were only Japanese and a few White Russians living there. After living among the Japanese for a long time, the Russian children learned to speak Japanese well.

I became a fisherman. I started to fish from May in the year that I came to the States. I earned some money during the summer season, but as fall wasn't a good season for fishing, I went to downtown Los Angeles and attended school. The American schools at that time had a system for non-English speakers without any grades. Not only foreigners, but also white students with low grades went there. I did my best to memorize the English, but when I got up in the morning, I couldn't remember anything. English is really hard. After listening to it for a while, I could learn it more easily. I went back to fishing the following summer and earned from a thousand to fifteen hundred dollars.

I went to Hollywood in the fall. Not being able to afford to stay in a hotel, I worked as a schoolboy. I washed dishes in exchange for meals and fifteen dollars a month. This way I was able to pay my way through school. I hear a schoolboy can get seventy-five or eighty dollars a month today. I was in Hollywood for a half a year and returned to Terminal Island after that. I wanted to attend high school, but I stopped studying along the way. Some of my friends graduated from the University of Southern California. They overworked themselves by studying and taking care of their parents and younger brothers and sisters. Many died of disease. Unless you are extremely healthy, it's impossible for you to go through college without any support.

When I returned to Terminal Island, I fished. Instead of spending money, I and a few others saved four or five thousand dollars to build a fishing boat together in 1924. Our boat was among the biggest in those days. We could heap eighty or ninety tons of tuna on the boat. There were fish everywhere then. After 1920 many Japanese fishermen made their living fishing for sardines. The canning companies would loan us money to buy fishing boats in those days. Then the company took the fish for canning. Canned fish in those days was delicious. Today it is old and lousy.

Before the war, there were about five thousand Japanese people on Terminal Island. We ate fairly well, but though our business was brisk, few fishermen became rich. (There isn't anybody on the island today except for the people working at the cannery. I'm sure those workers can get some food there, but I don't see any stores around there now. The only buildings are the warehouses for a cannery and a dock.) We earned more, for we built a bigger boat. I learned how to operate a bigger diesel engine. Since I couldn't get along with the co-owners, I sold the boat. In 1929 I went to Japan for ten months. After I returned, I was employed as an engineer. I earned about three thousand dollars a month—that was a large sum of money in those days. Finding a new continental shelf, I made three sailings a day. No one complained about it; no one could search for me, for we used no wireless radios at that time. I would catch a boat full of tuna, and right after I unloaded the fish, I would go out again. Nobody else did that.

Fishing might look easy when there aren't any fish around, because we just look for them. Once we start fishing, we often stay overnight—that's exhausting and dangerous. In 1928, while I was hanging the net, the end of it was accidentally cut by a rock, and I was caught under the net. I was told that I was unconscious for a half hour. The X-rays showed that I was fine. Some of the others got their legs or arms broken, but I was fine.

During a storm, I was often afraid that the boat wouldn't hold up, but I forgot the fear and hardship as soon as the storm passed. We never threw away fish because of a storm. We wouldn't have given them up even for our lives. Once some Japanese fishermen were fishing with us around an island. We warned them the night before that a storm was coming. We turned our boat to sea, but they anchored theirs. When the storm came, five people were thrown to their deaths on the rocks. We picked up seven others who were lucky enough to be thrown ashore by the waves.

I remember in 1924 a friend of mine came to me on the night before he was to sail. He shook my hand, left, and never came back.

Compared to farmers, fishermen are rough. They're foul-tongued, but they aren't ill-hearted. Mr. Matsuda from Fukui can vouch for that. Though he was a businessman he didn't stay with other businessmen in the evacuation camp. He stayed with us, for he believed that we, the fishermen from San Pedro, were good-hearted and honest in spite of our rough speech.

But I wouldn't ever want to be a fisherman again. Once you've lived in a town with a house and car, you can never go back to such a terrible life. It wasn't a human life. It was really rough.

Yoshito Fujii

I came here (Seattle) when I was nineteen years old and entered high school. Except for English, the classes were rather easy and fun. The teacher praised me, and I was popular in the class. I graduated in 1924 and entered the University of Washington.

My father was sick when I left Japan and died not long after.

Though my mother was healthy, she died suddenly of typhoid. I dreamed something strange one night; so did my elder brother. Then we got a telegram from Japan about our mother's death. My desire to return to Japan disappeared then. I had wanted to graduate from college as soon as possible in order to make my parents happy. The study was for them rather than for myself. I felt discouraged to have lost my parents, whose happiness had been mine. I thought about my position here and in Japan. A lot of Japanese people stowed away on boats bound for the United States in those days; yet here I was free to stay as long as I wanted to. Going back to Japan seemed a crime. I didn't want to succeed to any family property; so I decided to stay.

In 1928 I graduated from the University and then began a post-graduate program in sociology for a year after that. There was another Japanese student, Sugimatsu, who had graduated from Waseda University. He was a newspaper editor who had come here to study. Later he went to Los Angeles and established a Japanese language school. Sociology wasn't offered in Japanese colleges then, and we talked ambitiously about opening up a sociology department in Japanese colleges. The work was fun. I collected statistics and studied them. I love making records. I visited the police station in Seattle for half a year to get the records of past crimes.

As for crimes among the Japanese people, almost every case was one of drunkenness. Serious crimes were rare. I also studied the history of Japanese people in Seattle. For my graduate work, I studied the relationship between Japanese culture and trade. I compiled statistics on how Japanese people had been developing on the Pacific Coast of the United States. I found that the more trade developed, the more population increased. Then Japanese culture would be introduced. I made a map and showed the population distribution with different colors. I can't recall whether I left the original map at the University or not. I received praise for the map work and was offered an M.A. degree upon completion of my studies. I worked very hard. I studied trade on the Pacific Coast, in New York, and in South America. It was obvious that Japanese trade had been spreading from the Pacific Coast to other parts of the world every year. I worked on the paper till four A.M. every day. I couldn't have done it otherwise.

I was about to earn my M.A., but the professor in charge of my studies left for Chicago, and I couldn't follow him. I didn't feel it was too important to get an M.A. degree then and gave it up. I guess I should have finished my studies, but I was most anxious to take a job offered to me at that time.

I went to work for the Hanasaki Trading Company, which exported lumber to Japan. In the meantime, I got married. Not being satisfied with working for somebody, I made up my mind to open up my own business. I had the opportunity to get into the bottling industry. (There was a Japanese man who owned a bottling plant here.) I was president of the Junior Division of the Japanese Chamber of Commerce here in Seattle and organized a baseball tournament on the Fourth of July. I had to order soda for the players, so I went to the owner of the Japanese bottling company to order. He said he was out of stock. I said teasingly, "Don't crack a joke. Why can't you supply eighteen cases of soda? You own a bottling plant. What kind of monkey business do you have?" I needed soda from him by Sunday. My joke brought out something unexpected. I told him, "You're the only Japanese bottling dealer here. You're a monopoly among the Japanese people. You ought to hustle in business as hard as the Caucasians." Later on, he visited me and asked me if I would join him as a business partner. I told him I was too inexperienced. He insisted on leasing his plant to me at a reasonable price. He visited me on a Saturday and on Monday we concluded the deal. Though it started out as a joke, I couldn't back out of the deal. I had to be a man. I was surprised when I saw the plant. It looked as if it were a nominal operation and not well equipped. I hadn't had the slightest knowledge of the bottling business, but the owner, Mr. Kogitani, said he would help me for a month or so until I could learn the business. I went to Japanese town, where I found some workers to hire for my plant. I ran the business until the war broke out.

I worked hard, and it took five years to establish myself. There were about two hundred Japanese restaurants, cafes, and businesses here at that time, and everybody ordered soda from us. I paid up the loan completely in five years. I even thought about opening up the same business in Japan.

During these first five years of business I bought a building. It was an interesting arrangement. I still keep an account at that bank because of Mr. Kahkey,[4] a German banker who was kind to

[4]This is probably not the correct spelling, but is Mr. Fujii's pronunciation of the name.

us Japanese. An old winery building was put up for sale. There
were no buyers, for the price was high. One morning when I went
to the bank, Mr. Kahkey called me over. He said, "I have a building for you. Are you interested in buying it?" I said, "I'm interested in it, but where will I get the money? How can I buy it?"
He said, "What's a bank for?" He told me that banks wouldn't
have any business if there were no poor guys. He explained to me
about the price and down payment. He knew about the winery,
for he was the director. He set a high price for others. I just paid
twelve hundred down. Though the price was as high as thirty
thousand dollars for others, I paid a total of nine thousand. It was
a good deal. After he'd financed me, I collected forty dollars a
month rent from a hotel that opened in the building. That almost
made my loan payment. He said that a bank could run its business because people like me got loans from them. He also told me
that even if I didn't have cash, I should build up my credit. Having
credit is like having cash. No matter how much you buy, you
should make the payment at least a day before the due date. Then
you can get credit anywhere. I had six different payments at that
time; therefore, my savings account was empty, but I made all of
the payments on time.

I could have learned more from Mr. Kahkey, but he died during
the war. He taught me well. In those days everybody purchased
his property as a member of a corporation, because Japanese
people were prohibited from purchasing homes and land. The
hotel is still registered as a corporation. I own four corporations
now. The business lasted till the war. After the war started, I
leased a part of my plant to another company, and I was the
manager. A Caucasian leaseholder paid me. It was just rent, not a
business commission. He used my machinery, but what he really
wanted was my quota of sugar. I had one thousand sacks of sugar
as my allowance. Suppose each sack cost two dollars; I had a two
thousand dollar quota. It was quite a large sum of money at that
time. The leaseholder could pay the low rent easily. Finally we
had to close everything because of the evacuation.

SADAKUSU ENOMOTO

I was nineteen years old when I arrived in San Francisco. I
didn't have any experience as a schoolboy, and when I first

applied, I didn't get hired. But I got a job later and received only about a dollar fifty a week.

Once I was offered oatmeal mush in the morning, but I didn't know how to eat it; so I used my knife to cut it up into chunks and ate it with a fork. Someone told me I wasn't supposed to eat it that way. I didn't understand very well at that time but was told to put sugar and milk on the mush, break it up with a spoon, and eat it. It seems funny now.

I worked as a schoolboy for seven years. Then I decided I couldn't get anywhere and considered my future. There was some land for sale in Redwood City, and a friend said I could grow flowers there. The five acres was seventeen hundred and fifty dollars—two hundred down and fifteen dollars per month payment. I bought it in 1907 after the San Francisco earthquake. Later on, around 1910 the Alien Land Law came into effect and noncitizens were not able to buy land.[5]

I got married in Japan and brought my wife to America about that time. The law stated that if I died, the land would be taken by the state and could not be transferred to my wife. When my child was born, I changed my holdings into a corporation with myself, my wife, and my child. This was a loophole in the law. We made it into a joint stock company, the Enomoto Company, so the family could hold the land and expand. The land is very valuable now.

There was anti-Japanese feeling then, but we worked faithfully and our Japanese employees were all good workers. Neighbors liked us and we didn't have much difficulty. I employed about ten people. I grew flowers but when we were short of supply, I bought flowers from other growers and shipped them to all parts of the United States. I was also importing some things from Japan, especially fertilizer. Japan had good fertilizer—fish meal, oil cake, et cetera. I was investigated when the war broke out because I had quite a large import business. Federal investigators came and checked all my books. At that time, Japanese association presidents, businessmen, and men in import-export businesses were interned.[6] I was interned also in North Dakota. I worked up until the war but retired after that and have not been working since.

[5]The Alien Land Act was passed in 1913.

[6]Mr. Enomoto was imprisoned in a special camp for enemy aliens (Japanese, German, and Italian) who were considered potential spies because they had had recent business contacts with the enemy nations.

Mrs. Kamechiyo Takahashi

Takahashi wrote back to me in Japan to learn midwifery because Japanese pregnant women who lived in San Francisco didn't understand English and needed a Japanese midwife very badly. That's why I decided to study midwifery before leaving Japan.

I went to a nurse's training school for a year and then to a midwife's training school for two years. I studied only theories during the first year and practiced midwifery during the second year. Practice is the most important thing for a midwife; she needs a special technique that she can learn only through practice. The more deliveries a midwife experiences, the better she can be. These days doctors make deliveries quickly, but I believe in a natural, physiological delivery.

I practiced at a clinic of midwifery attached to the Wakayama prefectural hospital. I took both of my children with me when I went to school, and I rented a house for the three of us. It was tough for me to study with the little ones. My mother said how pitiful it was that in spite of my dislike for studying, I had to in order to join my husband in the United States.

I came to the States on the thirteenth of February; on the twenty-fourth, even before I opened up my business as a midwife, I helped my sister-in-law deliver a baby. It was the first time for me to cut a navel string here! A license wasn't required to become a midwife till June of 1917, when I had to take a licensing examination. Japanese people coming here today have a fundamental knowledge of English but not in those days. Not being able to understand English, I got help from an attorney named Okawara, who was a Nisei (child of an Issei and born in the United States). His father must have come here a long time before. He interpreted for me during the examination. After getting a license, I formally opened my business as the Takahashi Clinic of Midwifery.

At first I found a small house with some rooms. Later on, I moved to a bigger house located on Clement Street where Takahashi's store was. I had three beds at most. Today if you have a hospital delivery, you are discharged in a few days. At that time, you were supposed to stay in a clinic or a hospital for a few weeks. I kept mothers in my clinic for two weeks and provided Japanese food. Being a grocery store owner, Takahashi told me to cook good food for my patients. He didn't want me, a grocery owner's wife, to have a poor reputation in cooking. My patients from San Francisco and San Jose enjoyed staying in my clinic, for they didn't have to pay too much and also they could eat Japanese food. Having been interested in sewing, I didn't know cooking too well; so I had to study cooking very hard. Anyway, I tried to cook nutritious food which looked and tasted delicious.

I charged twenty-five dollars for labor and delivery. I charged two dollars a day for room and board. Later on, I raised the price to thirty dollars, and then forty dollars . . . as the standard charge was raised in San Francisco. Not like a hospital, I served tea when husbands visited wives in my clinic on Sundays. I was so busy that I had someone to work as a diaper-washer from eight o'clock in the morning.

I usually visited three patients a day. Before leaving home, I planned my visits according to the locations. It didn't take too much time to examine a patient. As her scheduled day drew near, I visited her twice a month. If a patient had some abnormality, I visited her more often. In such cases, I took her feces and had a doctor examine it. The doctor, a German, was kind enough to come to me whenever I needed him. I remember delivering twins for the first time. I and the mother had known for a long time that the fetus would be twins. At the delivery, the first baby came out all right; however, the second one didn't come out even after the placenta came out. The placenta shouldn't have come out before the baby because a fetus breathes through the placenta. I put the placenta back as soon as I could. I warned the father that the second baby might be dead. He said that he at least had one child all right.

I tried artificial respiration on the second baby; however, I couldn't bring him back to life. The baby was already dead before he came out. The first baby grew up to be a healthy man, and he's married now. A fetus whose heart doesn't beat inside a mother's stomach usually can't be revived no matter how hard you apply artificial respiration. If a baby is syncopic, he may be revived through artificial respiration. Two women with problem pregnancies left me and transferred to a hospital, where they had Caesarean operations. Both mothers and babies were fine. Takahashi's brother told me about one pregnant woman who killed herself by cutting out her tongue during delivery, for hers was disastrously hard. He said he couldn't help noticing pregnant women and wishing them good luck, because I was a midwife. Fortunately, I didn't have too many abnormal deliveries among my patients.

I ran the business until I got very sick in 1929. I had an assistant midwife who helped me whenever I needed her, but I myself took full responsibility, and called a doctor for only abnormal deliveries. My assistant told me to stop working and take it easy. Takahashi said that it was natural for him to work, but I shouldn't work that hard.

In the beginning, I had only mothers and babies; later on, mothers brought their big children too. The "picture marriage" was banned by the new immigration law in 1924, so a number of Issei males went back to Japan and brought their brides with them.[7] At that time I performed deliveries almost every day. I'm sure I've performed almost three hundred deliveries. I took patients to the hospital many times too. A midwife isn't supposed to heal sickness; however, she has to find it and consult doctors in time.

Some of my patients were so poor that they couldn't afford electricity. They used kerosene lamps instead. Being ignorant of sanitation, they didn't have any absorbent cotton, disinfectant, or ether. I couldn't believe this was actually happening in the United States. Japanese farmers here put their babies on a straw mat beside them while they worked on the farms. I had never seen such a thing in Japan. Farmers in Japan hired a babysitter for their babies; here they couldn't afford one. They ate rice and _miso_ (soybean paste) soup in the morning even in the States. No wonder the brides of "picture marriages" suffered a lot. They were terribly poor. I was lucky to have a businessman as my husband. In Japan, people never washed clothes in a kitchen sink. I was stunned to see people here washing their stockings in a kitchen sink.

There were three midwives in San Francisco and one in San Jose. I don't know about the Fresno area. After I began my clinic, one more midwife came to San Jose. She didn't stay there too long though. The country Japanese people in San Jose at that time didn't consult a midwife. Husbands did everything. It was unsanitary and dangerous. Getting nurse's training for a year in Japan, I was sensitive to such things. I told my patients to prepare the sanitary necessities by the eighth month. During the Depression days, some of my patients couldn't pay the fee of twenty-five dollars. It was believed in Japan that doctors were to serve people; therefore, I put up with my patients who couldn't pay the fee. Sickness attacks you unexpectedly, but childbirth is scheduled

[7]Picture marriages were actually banned in 1921.

for nine months and ten days. You should plan ahead and save little by little.

One couple had eleven children. I took care of seven of them. Though this couple couldn't afford the fee at the time of deliveries during the Depression days, they came and paid me after the war. Their sons went to the war and all came back home safely. They're fine adults now. Some people were honest like them, whereas others took advantage of me. Having sold on credit, Takahashi didn't get all the bills paid by his customers either. We were evacuated into a camp without having collected on all our bills.

MR. OSUKE TAKIZAWA

On April 28, 1906, I arrived in Victoria, Canada. I was going to San Francisco, but it is very difficult to enter from that port because of the rigorous health examination, so I went to Canada instead. They asked me where I was going from there. I said that I was going to San Francisco. They told me that there had been an earthquake; so I decided to stay in Canada for another year. My brother also came to Canada that year. In Canada people said there were a lot of jobs and that I could earn hundreds of dollars a month, but it was not true. My only choice was to work for the railroad company for a year. We repaired track for the railroad. Twenty people slept in one railcar and another car was the kitchen. We would go to places where rail repairs were needed or where snow had to be cleaned off the tracks. After that, I came to San Francisco by way of Seattle.

Mr. Machida met me at the seaport. He was the husband of one of my cousins and owned a celery farm. I was planning to help him. The farm was on Jersey Island.[8]

In those days we held the celery in our hands and walked on our knees to plant. It was hard labor. Today, it's done by machine. The machine digs out the soil, plants the celery, and covers it with soil. In our day laborers picked the celery too. They dug the soil, picked up celery one by one, and put them in a basket. Today, plows dig them out of the soil and laborers pick them up. Though the work was hard, I was young. I weighed between one hundred and forty and one hundred and fifty pounds, so that my thighs rubbed each other and got sore. Only the inner thigh part of

[8]Jersey Island is a farming area in the Sacramento Delta.

my pants got torn. Every Sunday, while other workers were playing *hana-fuda* (a Japanese card game) under the willow trees, I was
always mending the tears in my pants. A hundred and forty or
fifty pounds isn't too heavy, but I was short and chubby.

We didn't have any recreation at all. If you wanted to go to
town, you had to travel forty miles to Sacramento on a river boat.
You had to get on a boat to go to Stockton too. The river boat was
the only transportation we had. Our daily wage was less than a
dollar. The boss deducted twenty-five cents a day for meals. In
addition, he deducted a commission from our wage. Therefore, it
was almost impossible to save money. If you deduct twenty-five
cents and buy your daily commodities such as shoes, how much
of it do you have left? People who saved two hundred and fifty
dollars in three years drew others' attention at that time. Those
people went back to Japan with that money. When we didn't find
a job in one camp, we looked for another camp. We went to pick
grapes in Fresno. Whenever somebody moved to another camp
and left his torn shoes and pants, the others jumped in and got the
worn-out clothing. It was terribly hard to save two hundred and
fifty dollars in three years. The Issei had such hardships. The
Nisei (children of the Issei) can't imagine this though.

I worked on Mr. Machida's celery farm for three years. At that
time, we drank river water which flowed down from the sewers in
Sacramento and Stockton. Everybody suffered from typhoid fever.
I was taken to the Japanese hospital in San Francisco. I was the
patient accommodated in Room 4.[9] When I was put in that room,
I was afraid that it was all over for me. Right before leaving the
hospital, the doctor told me that he wasn't sure if I could be saved
in that room! While in bed, I would hear a milkman delivering a
lot of milk in the early morning, and I envied him. I wished I
could get well and drink milk again. I regained my strength
gradually, and after a while I wasn't satisfied with only milk. I
wanted more slices of toast, and I became greedy. Human beings
are something. Soseki Natsume[10] wrote: "Human beings are the
cleanest whenever they are sick." I thought it to be true.

TSUGUO NAGASAWA

My father had left Japan when he was twenty-four years old,
and I hadn't seen him for fifteen years; so I felt a little reserved

[9]The number four in Japanese is pronounced "shi" and is a homonym for death.
[10]Soseki Natsume was a Japanese writer of the Meiji period.

with him. When I was short of money, I asked my father for some, but I felt bad about it. I thought I should work and study as hard as possible. There were some fatherless working students over here, and I appreciated the fact that I had mine with me.

I worked as a schoolboy doing domestic work in the morning and in the evening. Since I had no school on Saturdays, I worked all day. Being a schoolboy wasn't easy, for the work was quite demanding. The job called for "room and board," which meant work in exchange for a place to sleep and food to eat. I also got paid five dollars a month.

In the beginning, I didn't know anything about cooking. That was understandable, because I had just come from Japan. At first I burned the potatoes. My employer's wife was a short-tempered music teacher. She took the pan off the stove and threw it at me. She had planned to fix mashed potatoes and was mad about the whole incident. I wasn't hurt, but such things occurred. White people . . . it's understandable, because they gave room and board to a man of a different race. People who didn't have any relationship or responsibility toward me sent me to school. It's understandable when I think about it in retrospect. I was to work for as much as I was given. The first family fired me after four months or so. They told me to go back home because my English wasn't good enough. Then I worked a year and a half with another family.

The white families—due to the racial differences—are strict. I had to work hard to satisfy them. I got up early in the morning to fix breakfast. After school and in the evening, I had to prepare the table and cook. They didn't like anything untidy, and I had to put on a pair of white overalls and an apron when I set the table and worked. I finished my duties at seven-thirty or eight o'clock at best. Then I ran back to my room and studied.

My father worked as a gardener in Los Angeles. Then his niece suggested he go to Seattle, Washington, where he got a job with the railroad company. He traveled along the Coast, and almost everyone knew Taizo Nagasawa, my father.

I got a job in Seattle working for Mr. Furuya. He had a lot of property with his banks and a store, but he eventually went bankrupt. It was a bad time. It was the time of the anti-Japanese movement in the government. The bank superintendent and other related people in Washington State caused the bankruptcy. Anyway, I worked for Mr. Furuya. Jobs for adults are easier than schoolboy jobs, which have more hardships. The job furnished me

a dormitory bed, and a cook fixed the meals. Mr. Furuya sent me
to a delivery line at the start. He told me that I had to carry one
hundred *kin* (sixty kilograms) of rice up to the third floor of a
hotel. I went out delivering all day long and learned the where-
abouts of things in the town. It was quite a tough job. Gradually, I
started working at the office which took orders. Then I trained
other store clerks in Portland, Oregon.

Mr. Furuya's main office was in Seattle. He had branches in
Portland, Tacoma, and Vancouver. He had offices in Yokohama
and Kobe, Japan, as well, and he owned two banks in Seattle. One
was on Second Avenue; the other was in Japanese town.

I was in Portland for about six years. After some thinking, my
father and I decided to try farming. We bought nearly one hundred
acres of land, and we began farming in Oregon. We only farmed
for four years. Since we had a lot of trees, we cut them down and
sold the wood, too. The landowner was a man named Black,* who
was a church minister. I don't know what church he was with,
but his policies were terrible. His way of handling the deal in the
end was awful. The accounting figures weren't correct, and we
didn't have enough to pay the taxes; so we quit. Arthur Black
foreclosed the mortgage, because we hadn't paid it off yet. He
confiscated everything. It was his underhanded way of doing
business that left me bitter. In 1941 when Japan attacked Pearl
Harbor, I converted from Christianity to Buddhism, and that
Christian minister was the reason I converted.

I went back to Portland and borrowed money from Mr. Furuya. I
thought of a way to start a wholesale florist business by transporting California flowers to Oregon, Washington, and Idaho. Mr.
Shibata and Mr. Shinohara of the Florists' Association in California had overproduced flowers, and they wanted somebody to sell
the flowers out of state. Everybody said my idea was excellent. In
the meantime, people in Oregon started boycotting me. The head
of the Florists' Association in Portland started saying that he had
no money to send out of state, and he influenced others. Then
other florists stopped buying from me. A white man named
Young cooperated with me in the same business, and he became
rich. He continued the business.

I relied on Mr. Furuya again and got a loan of fifteen thousand
dollars. There was a big grocery store which I bought and ran. I
had failed in the florist business, but I still had the truck left and

*A pseudonym.

used it for transporting goods. The store, located on a corner, was fairly prosperous. I ran the store for thirteen years, until I was hit by the war. I got up at three A.M. and went to buy farm products at an auction market where prices were reasonable. Selling the purchased products reasonably at my store, I could get more customers. The earlier I got to the auction market, the better products I could purchase. I was back home at five or five-thirty A.M., ate breakfast, and opened the store at about six-thirty. I worked till ten at night. My wife and I, we took turns staying up. I was married by then.

6

Life and Marriage

JUHEI KONO

The large numbers of men in proportion to women caused some community problems. The prostitution problem hit the worst stage before the picture brides came over. It was really awful—the biggest problem in the Spokane Japanese community was prostitution. There was a Methodist Women's Home in Seattle . . . it's not there any more . . . I'd seen many of "those" women around the Women's Home. They were not necessarily engaged in that type of work voluntarily, but rather they were forced into it. Those women would run away from it and go to the Women's Home for refuge. It was not a healthy situation for us Japanese; therefore, there was a strong feeling of wanting to go back to Japan as soon as we made enough money to do so.

In the meantime, the number of Japanese women increased, and with that trend the problem became less and less visible. By 1920 or 1925, it wasn't as bad, but that imbalance continued even after we saw a big influx of picture brides. The picture brides were supposed to solve some problems, but created others. Contrary to the expectations of the brides, some husbands were a little older than the brides had been led to believe, or some husbands were very ugly looking, and so on. These misunderstandings contributed to many family problems.

There was lots of gambling in those days. The men who played leadership roles in our Japanese community [Spokane, Washington] were mostly gamblers. There were moral dangers in the old days too.

YOSHITO FUJII

There were both successful and unsuccessful picture marriages. The brides were people who wanted to come to the United States. They achieved their first goal at any rate, and they seemed to be happy. Many stayed in my brother's Fujii Hotel in Seattle. A lot of young men came up from Sacramento to meet their brides. I couldn't tell who were farmers and who weren't, for all were dressed dandily. They even wore white gloves. Some couples had too much of a difference in their ages and might have had a problem. The impression you get from pictures could be quite different from reality. Anyway, they were happily married as a whole. The brides came here in their kimono. As soon as they got here, they were taken to the Abe Dress Shop, which was close to our hotel, to buy Western-style dresses. You can walk on the street in kimono without feeling embarrassed these days. At that time, it was too embarrassing to do so. The Japanese ladies looked different and beautiful in Western-style dresses. Some put their shoes on backwards and couldn't move well, for it was their first time to wear such clothing.

MINEJIRO SHIBATA

I'm not sure when the "picture marriages" started and ended. When I first came here, a lot of women came over as picture brides. One woman met her husband in San Francisco, and she claimed that the man was different from her husband in the picture. He looked more handsome in his retouched picture. I heard a lot of episodes related to those picture marriages. The pictures retouched by the photographer looked better than the actual brides and grooms, and they were disappointed with one another. As I recall, though, most couples got along all right anyway. There was no such thing as the "picture marriage" by the time I married. My wife was a Nisei raised in Japan.[1] I have three children, two sons and one daughter.

The majority of the Japanese were single at that time. They drank and gambled without saving any money. Few fishermen like me married or bought a house. Thinking back, I really pity them. These days, even a young couple makes a down payment

[1]Some Nisei, children of Issei, hold U.S. citizenship by birth, but were educated in Japan and then returned to the United States. The Japanese also refer to these Nisei educated in Japan as Kibei.

and buys a house. Young people today are wiser than at that time. Though the fishermen could have bought a house at a fair price, they didn't even think about buying. Living in company housing on Terminal Island, they didn't have to pay rent for a while. They were charged a little rent later. The only thing they needed was food. By eating their own fish, they could live quite reasonably. Though there were some women on the island, the single men outnumbered them. It was an awful life for those single men.

Mrs. Kamechiyo Takahashi

It took twenty-one days to get to San Francisco on the *Nihon Maru*. I met a picture bride from Hiroshima, who was looking at a photo of her husband and worried about her future. When we got to San Francisco, she didn't want to land. She cried and insisted on going back to Japan. One of the crew told her how much money her future husband had spent for her. He suggested that she should decide whether she would go back to Japan or not after discussing it with her husband-to-be. She never listened to the suggestion and went back to Japan on the same boat. I heard a lot about the picture marriages. That girl was the only one I had any direct experience with.

That girl had been told that her future husband owned a large farm, but she heard from somebody on board that he wasn't such a big man. Being from a well-to-do family, she didn't want to marry a poor peasant. In San Francisco I saw grooms with pictures in their hands announcing their names and addresses and calling out to their brides. The brides also had the pictures of their grooms and answered as their names were called out. But that girl never answered. Except for her, everybody on our boat was all right. After the new immigration law was passed, there weren't any tragedies like that.[2] Men went back to Japan and met their brides directly.

Having married Takahashi in Japan, my situation was different. Being a school teacher, Takahashi was a very strait-laced person in Japan. Reuniting with him after three years and four months, I was startled to see him drink. Moreover, he played cards and frequently came home late. I told my brother, who was here in the United States, that when he got to Japan, he shouldn't tell my

[2]Her reference is probably to a "Ladies Agreement" whereby the Japanese government agreed to end the immigration of "picture brides" in 1921.

mother how Takahashi had changed. My mother was fond of Takahashi, because he was well behaved. I didn't want my mother to worry about me. Takahashi's drastic change was a great shock to me. I missed my mother, who'd helped me a great deal with my children and other things.

The drinking caused Takahashi to have a serious stomach ailment. One doctor said that he had cancer and even if he underwent an operation, he would live only for a year and a half. I had only been here for two years, and we hadn't summoned our son to the States yet. My brother-in-law and I persuaded Takahashi to consult another doctor before we gave up. The second doctor said there would be a chance if he operated on Takahashi right away. The doctor found that the tumor was not cancerous. I was still working as a midwife at that time. While Takahashi was convalescing at home, I had to take care of him and work at the same time, but Takahashi began to recover steadily.

Choichi Nitta

I myself married a picture bride. I left Japan when I was sixteen and got married when I was thirty years old. Though I was from Yamaguchi, the wife of a Japanese pastor here [Loomis] suggested that I marry a girl she knew from Aomori, Japan; but my mother was against my marrying a girl from another area. Unless the marriage was recorded in Japan, a wife could not come to this country. It took quite a while to get my family's approval; so I was about thirty years old when I got married. My mother had suggested other persons, but by that time I had decided to live permanently in this country and had corresponded with this person in Aomori; so we understood each other quite well. My mother approved of the marriage with the understanding that the bride go to Yamaguchi to meet my mother. My mother met my bride and liked her. I understand that they had an elaborate wedding ceremony. My wife stayed in Yamaguchi Prefecture about three months and then went to Tokyo, where she had a younger brother in the Aoyama Institute. In Tokyo my wife prepared for her trip to America and came here on the *Shunyo Maru* from Yokohama in March 1917.

We had sent each other many pictures and my impression of her wasn't different than she actually was. She wore eyeglasses which didn't look very good; so I bought her a better pair in San Francisco.

WATARU ISHISAKA

All those picture brides would look at their future husbands'
pictures, and all those pictures were of good-looking young men.
But when they arrived in San Francisco, those young brides discovered that all those men who were waving at them were old and
baldheaded. When they discovered that those older men were, in
fact, their husbands, they cried and cried.

When I came to the United States, there was a very beautiful,
well-educated young woman who came from Kumamoto on the
same ship as I was. In fact, she came from the village right next to
ours. She was my age, about eighteen. When she saw her
husband-to-be, she was shocked to see such an old man. She
turned to me and said, "Would you please run away with me?" I
had come here to study and had no intention of marrying yet, and
it was a very difficult request. I told her, "It must be your fate.
You should go with him."

I was very young when I came to this country, and most of the
Issei men were middle-aged. They used to tell me, "You are very
young. You must learn how to speak in English." They taught me
some words which I already knew, but I just nodded and listened
to them. They told me how to gamble and how to find *joro* (prostitutes). They talked about those things every night. Well, I suppose those were the only things they could do to entertain themselves. Women were few; so many had no families.

It might sound unreal, but when I caught cold, these men said,
"Well, Ishisaka is very sick. He won't last much longer, so we had
better decide who's going to get his wife!" Things were that bad.
The only things they had were bars, gambling, and prostitution.
There were surprisingly few problems, though. The troublemak-
ers were those who did not get married. There were a few mur-
ders, and some wives were stolen.

There were some runaway wives; however, those women who
ran away or switched husbands were not happy. Those people
who built successful families were the ones who had the patience
and endurance to stick it out, even though they might have had
legitimate complaints. I knew people in both situations, but those
who ran away and went from man to man ended up tragically.
Human beings must have great strength to endure. Without that,
you can't be successful.

I was married in Florin. I knew my wife and used to bring flowers to her. I thought she had lots of good qualities; so I went to visit her often. I had a Model-T Ford at that time. There weren't very many people who had a car in those days, and I used to drive that car real fast so the engine would overheat. Then she got showered by the radiator water. One day my father's friend came over and said, "How long are you going to remain single? You'd better get married soon. I'll go for you and ask permission from her father so that you can marry her." So we got married.

My finances were limited, and I was looking after my parents all the time. When I finished one job in Sacramento, I went to Sebastopol, where I got a job drying apples. I didn't want to leave my wife at home, but it was a job for me and an economic necessity. My wife was pregnant, and while I was in Sebastopol, I received a letter from the midwife saying that my wife gave birth to two beautiful boys. Was I surprised! No matter how many times I read the letter, it said, *"soushi"* (twins). I thought, "Is she going to have a tough time ahead of her!" I asked my boss for a leave of absence to go home. I got as far as Napa, where I took the letter out and read it again, but it was the same letter with the same news. When I reached Sacramento, I went to the Third Street Pharmacy and asked if I had twin sons. The owners were Japanese, and they told me that it was true. That was the last time I asked that question. When I arrived at home, I saw two beautiful boys in bed. Well, I am very thankful for my parents, for they helped raise our sons; and I really respect my wife, for she took care of my parents as if they were her own.

Mrs. Ko Takakoshi

My sister's friend came as a bride. She was tricked into this marriage. This man returned to Japan, grew a mustache, put on a silk hat and frock coat, and rode around in a *jinrikishya* looking for a bride. My sister's friend married the man and came to this country, but found out that he didn't have anything. She couldn't even buy any clothes to change into. They stayed in a hotel room, because they didn't have a place to go. Finally, he went to work at a sawmill and meanwhile two children were born. They were so poor I felt sorry for them. I took rice and other food to them quite often. Later she took the two children and returned to Japan.

Zentaso Yamamoto

My wife, since I was going to America to work after all, had to be physically fit and hard working, you see. She had to be strong. I looked at two women, and my wife was better in that respect.

Mrs. Takae Washizu

We took the *Koya Maru* and landed in San Francisco. I stayed on Angel Island, and I'll never forget that place. I had to stay there to have a physical examination. My husband left me some money in case I should fail the physical and have to go back to Japan. I was released after several days. We went to Walnut Grove on Rally Island to work.[3] I'd imagined that the United States would be an advanced country. On the contrary, I was shocked by reality. There was no electricity around Rally Island, and the bathroom there was more primitive than the ones in Japan. Life in the countryside was very lonesome. We moved from one farm to another. We worked at the Fair Ranch for a month, picked grapes in Florin, and then went to another work camp. Some farms had separate rooms for couples; others didn't have any. Sometimes we slept in a barn with horses and cows. We led that kind of life until our children were born. Then we became tenant farmers and shared forty percent of our profits with the landowner. Later on, that kind of percentage was prohibited by law.

While I was raising the children, I took care of a lot of farm workers as well. I got up at four A.M. and fed the workers and my children by seven A.M. The workers had to be on the farm by seven. I went to work on the farm after washing dishes. I came back home an hour before lunch and dinner to cook meals. I always bathed last and washed clothes every night by hanging a lantern on a willow. I usually went to bed at midnight. I had to work as hard as the men. According to a newspaper article, Issei females died young. Men are to blame for that. Men didn't earn enough money for a whole family to survive; that's why women had to work and earn supplementary incomes. Men didn't fulfill their duty as the heads of families.

Many wives deserted their husbands in those days. There were many ads about finding wives in the newspapers at that time. I wanted to run away from my husband, for he was too old and too small-minded for me to communicate with, but I couldn't leave

---

[3]Walnut Grove is a farming area in the Sacramento Delta.

my children. I couldn't trust my husband to raise the children; besides I didn't have anyplace to go. I was just patient and dreamed about my children's bright future.

Issei mothers left their children at home and worked on farms. Nobody could take care of their children when they needed to go to the toilet or whatever. We couldn't ever afford anything fancy, and I didn't have too much fun. When my children were happy, I was happy too.

Issei men? I think it depended upon the individual. As for my husband, I daresay that he was a coward. Though I wanted to speak up and tell him what I felt about him, I didn't have an opportunity to do so. Since I didn't trust my husband, I couldn't hide my feelings very well. He got mad whenever he sensed my feelings in our conversation. I realized later that I should respect him as my husband no matter how unworthy he was. I read in a book that you should trust and listen to others, which I think is very true. A Japanese proverb says, "Be alert, everybody is a thief," but I don't think it is true. A wife must trust and respect her husband, and a husband must be responsible for his wife. He shouldn't misuse his power.

Women suffered other problems too. One man tried to make love to someone else's wife. Having been refused by her, he killed her child by pushing the child into a hole where there was a motor. Another man, who also tried to seduce one mother in vain, cut her daughter's hand. Mr. and Mrs. Toshiba's* child was kidnapped while they were working on a farm. Mrs. Toshiba had also rejected one man who tried to make love to her. The life we had here was sometimes almost unbearable.

RIICHI SATOW

In the beginning I was planning to go back to Japan after making some money. As the days went by, however, I started thinking of getting married. Picture marriages were very popular at that time, and everybody married a young woman from Japan that way. In my case it was not a picture marriage, but my parents and my wife's parents got together, as was the custom in Japan. Children didn't decide on marriage partners themselves; instead, parents would arrange everything, and the children obeyed their decision.

*A pseudonym.

Now when I went back to Japan, I had to leave quickly, because otherwise I would be drafted into the Japanese Army. I landed in Japan sometime in the middle of November, and on December 6, I was already on a ship leaving Yokohama with my newly married wife. We completed our wedding ceremony in a great hurry and got on a boat, the *Suwa Maru*, and headed for Seattle. There was an examination for hookworms in Seattle for those who were coming to the United States for the first time. In those days a lot of people from Japan had hookworms. They were stopped, and had to be treated there, which kept them at the immigration office for about a week. Like everybody else, my wife was temporarily held for that. I was staying at a hotel while I waited for her to be declared clear. Then we came to California. At that time I already had a strawberry ranch in Oak Park.

I had planted ten acres of strawberries, and when the harvest came, I went to Japan to bring my wife back. Therefore, she had to begin really hard work upon her arrival. Cooking and washing for the field workers was her job, among other things. No Japanese woman dreamed of doing such things. Once she got here, all of a sudden she found herself in the midst of an immigrant's life. It must have been a rather shocking experience for her, I . . . well, I don't know! At any rate, there was little room for her to enjoy honeymoon-like moments. Back in those days it was not like today. Everybody was really hard-working . . . simply had to be, otherwise we couldn't survive the times. My wife wasn't an exception.

○ ○ ○ ○ ○ ○ ○ ○ ○ ○ ○ ○ ○ ○ ○

Very few single Issei men are living at present. I think they were mostly failures. They failed because a lot of them succumbed to the loneliness of being single and eventually let themselves be trapped into the Magic 3. The Magic 3 for a man is made up of gambling, drinking, and prostitution. These are the three basic elements of man's dissipation and can really ruin your life. Some men would go to find a job somewhere, usually in the fields, whenever they were broke; but as soon as they got paid, they would go straight to the gambling houses, many of which were run by Chinese people. They went there to satisfy their gambling habits, but most of them wound up losing all the money they earned in the field. When they came out of those places, they would often look like they were going to die. I know a lot of cases like that, and some people ruined their lives completely because of their gambling habits.

One time I went to Dinuba[4] to pick grapes. Grape pickers were usually hired just for the summer, and we used to live in a big tent set up under a tree. I picked raisin grapes, and there were paper-type trays to put the grapes in as we picked. I think we were getting paid three to three and a half cents a tray. Wages were very low. We usually picked several hundred trays a day. Now there was a man whom everybody agreed was filling more trays than any other picker could. I don't remember his name, but anyhow just imagine a wild rabbit chasing something around trees. That's exactly how he looked in the vineyards. When the picking season was over, a horse-pulled wagon would come around and pick us up in the fields. There were trucks, but they were not as popular as wagons in those days. When the wagon would come, we would put all our blankets and other possessions in, get on it ourselves, and be taken to a nearby town. So on the last day of the summer's work, we would get ourselves ready to go home and wait for the wagon for a few hours at the most.

This man, who worked like a wild rabbit all summer long, just couldn't wait to be picked up, for his mind was already in a gambling house in town. He was dying to get there as soon as he was paid. I don't know how much he was paid, but some made more than two hundred dollars in those days, and he was certainly one of the best paid. I think I was making only half as much. We got on the wagon when it arrived and headed for Dinuba, where there was a Chinatown and a boarding house for Japanese. When we got to the town, we saw him walking out of a gambling house with his face absolutely dead pale. On our way to the boarding house, we said to each other, "Look over there! Look at him. He must have lost his last penny." That's one of the scenes that I can still recall very clearly even now.

I remember another incident. It's about a friend of my father's. He passed away a long time ago, but while he was still living, he was one of those men with the Magic 3. His whole life was like that, and because of it he was never able to settle down himself nor have his own home to go back to. He finally found his place at a convalescent home in Stockton, where he died. I think he was over eighty years old. Since he was one of my father's friends and I knew him personally, I used to visit him. Every time I visited

[4]Dinuba is a small grape-producing community south of Fresno, California.

him, I gave him twenty dollars or so for pocket money. However, no sooner than I was on my way back home, he would lose that money gambling. Someone later told me about it, saying, "There's no sense in giving him money. It's a waste. He loses it gambling in no time." Then I stopped giving him money. One day there came notice of his death. I asked Rev. Igarashi to attend his funeral with us—that's me, my brother, and Mr. Miyazaki, who was also one of the friends of the deceased. The four of us went to Stockton for his funeral and buried him at a graveyard in French Camp. I pay a visit to his grave there once in a while even now. A man is . . . when he is all alone, he is in fact a very weak creature. A woman is a lot stronger.

MRS. HANAYO INOUYE

We landed at San Francisco and then came to Elk Grove[5] in late September. When we got there, the whole place was nothing but vineyards. For some time I just kept wanting to go back home. Home is home . . . and I thought at the time that where I was born was the best place for me to be. I was lonely for my mother. She made me beautiful kimonos when I became of marriageable age, but I never got to put them on, not even once. She wanted me to wear them when I became a real bride, you see. Indeed, Japanese people, and the parents especially, had a certain discipline in those days. She made me kimonos and also beautiful *obi*-sashes but never allowed me to put them on. She used to tell me, "When you become a bride, neighbors will look forward to seeing you wear new kimonos every day. This one today, that one the next day. . . . You have to wait until then." Of course, as you can imagine, I was dying to put those beautiful kimonos on. Well, naturally she was not expecting me to leave home so quickly.

Later she wrote me a letter about it. "I am sorry that I didn't let you put the kimonos on while you were here. I know very well that you wanted to so much." You know, in Japan they have airings of kimonos and other clothes every midsummer. She said in the letter, "I was airing your kimonos today, and my tears stained parts of them. I'm very sorry." For quite a long time after I came here, I thought of my mother almost every moment. In fact, when I cut my finger as I was picking grapes, I called out, "Mother!" quite unconsciously. However, I think I began to like

---

[5]Elk Grove is a farming community south of Sacramento, California.

it here for its vastness of land and for the fact that a day's work meant a day's wages. Back in Japan I never had to work for a living myself, and therefore, working for money was kind of foreign to me.

When I arrived in Sacramento, we took a taxi to Elk Grove. My husband said, "We are going to the country. You'd better not put good clothes on." Anyway, when we got to the farm, Mr. Omaye showed me around and said, "Please make yourself comfortable in here." I couldn't be more surprised! He motioned to a corner of the barn where there was hay spread in a square shape with a partition! That was all there was! I certainly did not feel like taking off my clothes and napping there. I never felt more distressed in my whole life. My husband should have told me about such conditions before I left Japan. He had shown me some pictures off himself in suits and of nothing but the best scenery. Naturally, I thought I was coming to a really nice place when I left Japan. I might have taken it differently had I been raised in a less fortunate family. But as I told you earlier, I had lived an easy life since I was a little girl.

When I asked my husband where the toilet was, he pointed outside. It was out in the field. He then told me to hit the toilet with a stick before going in. I wondered why, you know. There were black spiders living in it, and that was why. As a matter of fact, many people were bitten by those black spiders, and I heard someone died of fever caused by the spider bites. I was quite scared of the place. I realized, however, that no matter how much I thought of my mother back in Japan or of anybody, it wouldn't do any good. I knew then I had to live with it and give it a try. But I told myself I was going back home as soon as I made some money here.

Well, that first night there was nothing I could do. There wasn't any other place to sleep. I spread a blanket over the hay. You know, in those days everyone had his own blanket with him wherever he went . . . rolled up, and with a rope tied around it. The whole place was so scary to me. There were potato sacks hanging down over the window. If it were a screen window instead, it would have been a little bit better. All of a sudden in the middle of the night I heard terrifying cries. I screamed, "My God! What's that? What happened?" The next thing I saw were two horses sticking their heads out right next to me. I was scared to death! My first night here was like that . . . coming all the way from Japan. Nothing could be done, however, and I just cried.

The next morning as I came into the vineyards to work, I was truly overwhelmed at the fine grapes, really beautiful, ripe, red tokay grapes. What came to my mind first was that it would be so wonderful if I could give some to my mother. Growing grapes was not popular where I came from, so I kept thinking how much she would appreciate them and how much my brother would love to taste them. My mind was not with what my hands were doing. Besides, I had no experience picking grapes. Pretty soon I cut my finger with the clippers by accident. I didn't know what to do. Then my husband came running to me and he squeezed fresh juice out of some grapes and rubbed it on my finger. It works very well, you know. Then I wrapped it with my handkerchief. Even after that I had to keep working. It couldn't be used as an excuse to stop. I kept telling my husband, "I want to go back. Let me go home." But he just said, "It's going to be all right."

He was a good worker. He had to work harder than usual that day to make up for my losses and also to be liked by our boss, so we made sure to keep pace with the other pairs. In the vineyards we all worked in pairs—even though I was just standing by his side and crying.

When the grape season was over that year, the boss said, "This is how much you earned," and he gave me a lot of money. I was frankly surprised, since I had never worked in my life before. Although there were times when I went out to sell *matsutake* mushrooms and eels, it was really more like fun. I helped my family during rice-planting seasons and harvest times, but again I was not working for money. So that year was a big surprise to me.

The food we had while working in the vineyards was rather good, at least better than what we had back in Japan. In Japan, we lived on wheat and a little bit of rice. I know that hardly anyone eats wheat any more these days. Also, we girls were instructed by our parents to get used to wheat so that we could endure possible hardships we might encounter upon marrying and living with a husband's family. Oh, I didn't like wheat at all. In fact, I hated it. Boys were treated differently, with a lot of love and care. That's Japan, you know. My younger brother was always served first at the meal table, and he always had rice only. After that, the rice was mixed with a lot of wheat, and then everyone else was to be served. My younger brother, the first son of the family, was given special attention and care. When I complained too much about wheat, my mother then switched to potatoes. Potatoes grew very well over there. Again, serving only rice to my brother, my mother then mixed potatoes and rice together to serve the rest of us. Over here I was served different meals each time, and I was even getting paid for my work. I was really surprised.

We were paid three dollars a day. That's ten hours a day, though. Everyone had to pay fifty cents for the meals. Since I did the dishes after every meal, they didn't charge me that fifty cents. I think I got paid as much as my husband, except that he was also in charge of horses when shipping out the grapes, and because of that he was making three-fifty a day. To feed and to take care of the horses he usually had to get up earlier than most of us. I thought to myself that as long as I worked hard in the United States and endured whatever hardships I might have to take, then it would be possible to save enough money and go back to Japan.

When all the work was over for the season, we went to a boarding house called the Hiroshima-ya, and waited for the next job. It was, in a sense, our home. Big trunks and other belongings of ours were all kept at the Hiroshima-ya. We had to stay there when there was no work for us; therefore, some people eventually suffered from accumulated meal expenses as the days of no work went by. Well, those people were referred to a job whenever there was one—given top priority.

It was winter already, the first winter for me here, and I can't forget how hard it was to live through that particular winter. There was work at a nursery in Newcastle; so we had to get up early in the morning. Although I knew that I had to eat something—we used to eat *miso* (soybean paste) soup for breakfast—so that I could work that day, that morning I didn't have much of an appetite, and I went to work without any breakfast. The boss told us to get in a line and to pull out some seedling trees. The roots of those trees were not completely cut, as they were supposed to be, and consequently they were very hard to pull from the ground. Whether you were a man or woman—it didn't make any difference—you had to do the job. Since I didn't have my breakfast, oh, I was so hungry. How I wished that there were some bread around on the ground! Or anything I could eat! I don't think I can ever forget how hard it was for me that day. My husband helped me so that we would not fall behind the rest of the crew. At any rate, truly I don't think that I can ever forget how hard that work was. There was a break at ten o'clock when you could go and get yourself some water. Other than that, the boss was constantly watching us—walking down the rows, back and forth. I was getting hungrier and hungrier, and it made me worry that I might not be able to eat lunch. You know when you get too hungry, somehow you lose all your appetite. I worried about becoming sick. I think I was getting pale, which made my husband worry too. Until then, I really had not done any hard work as such. Picking grapes wasn't that bad, but the work at the sapling ranch was really difficult and unfortunately just about all we could find during the winter.

I will never forget how hungry I was at the ranch. It makes me wonder sometimes how a human being is. When you have enough, you tend to waste it. When I have to throw away food, I feel guilty for not eating it all.

Then in March we worked on a hops ranch. We stayed there for quite a while and made a good amount of money. We took our earnings and savings to the Sumitomo Bank and sent it to Japan. I sent two thousand dollars. The exchange rate at that time was double, and so we were able to send four thousand yen. However, when I come to think of it, it drives me crazy. After all those hardships and difficulties, it was only double. I thought at the time it was quite a large amount of money. The money we sent was kept in the bank until this last time when I visited Japan. The cost of living was incredibly high. For example, just one set of kimono would cost around a hundred thousand yen.

The money that I saved after all the hard work—and cooking for a lot of people! How I hated that job! Inside my sash I kept the receipt which the bank gave me when I sent the money to Japan. I still remember the sweat stains on the receipt from the hot summer days. It was that kind of money, you see.

Later my husband became foreman at the Robinsons' ranch near Marysville. There he would get up around five-thirty to take care of the horses so that everyone could begin working at seven o'clock. We had about eight workers with us then; so I had to get up early. I cooked for all of them. When there were wives working together with their husbands, they would help me. We charged everybody fifty cents for the meals. I used to go out to work in the fields after all the kitchen work was done. I had to be back by four-thirty to prepare supper by six. I did the laundry for everyone too.

I was also in charge of preparing the bath every evening—a *goyemon* type that used wood to heat the water. I was required to keep the fire burning until the last person had bathed. In those days I never went to bed before eleven. All the men there went to bed early. When I was ready to go to sleep, my husband would wake up and say, "Oh, is it dawn already?" Then I would tell him, "No, no. I'm going to sleep now." I don't know how I did all those things, but I certainly did survive those days.

Mrs. Riyo Orite

We traveled from Seattle to Ogden, Utah, where all of our cousins got together, and we had a happy feast. Having stayed there for about a week, we started for Wyoming. I saw only sagebrush and cactus every day. No matter how far we went, we saw nothing but sagebrush. I don't remember how long it took to get there, but I felt lonely. Though I was with my husband, I felt helpless. I didn't know how far I was to go. Finally there was a small train depot where we stopped. It was Linear, Wyoming, where we lived for five years.

As a section foreman, my husband was given a two-story house with two bedrooms, a living room, and a kitchen. It was a fine house, for the previous tenants had taken good care of it. But I was really lonely. Our neighbors were four miles away. There was only a water pump and a depot around us. Even if we had closer neighbors, I didn't know how to greet people for I couldn't speak any English.

What Orite had told me about the United States all sounded exciting. Earlier in Japan I felt happy about being able to come to such a nice place. I was born in the countryside in Hiroshima, and I hadn't traveled much. I didn't question what kind of country this would be, for I was coming with Orite as his dependent, and the problem of language didn't sink into my mind. While I was in Japan, my parents treated me very well because I was to leave soon, and they had no idea when they'd see me again. My in-laws were kind to me too; therefore, I didn't feel lonely when I married.

My husband had said, "You won't have to do anything there. You'll just stay home to cook and clean. How lucky you are! You'll be a lady of leisure in the United States. You'll be happy." I didn't know American cooking, but I was told not to worry about it, for I would learn after getting here. It sounded great that all I would have to do was washing and cooking. I was sure that I would be able to do that. Orite should have told me that I was supposed to cook for the railroad laborers. He hadn't mentioned that at all. After Orite was given the position of section foreman, he had hired some Japanese workers. There were ten people altogether—Mexicans, Italians, and Japanese workers. There were seven Japanese people, including my husband and myself, for whom I cleaned and cooked.

On the first morning I got up an hour earlier than everybody else, because I had been told that I wouldn't be able to cook in time unless I woke up early; but I didn't know how to start a coal fire, though I tried. The time for the workers to get up was nearing. I asked my husband to get up and help me. I felt miserable and cried while he was teaching me to light the fire. If I had been in Japan, I wouldn't have felt that miserable. I had difficulty learning to adjust the heat on the stove; therefore, I sometimes burned the food, and at other times I didn't cook it well enough. Each time I goofed, I missed my home. I missed home day in and day out. After a month, I finally learned how to fix meals, and I made take-out lunches in the morning for the workers. After they went to work, I locked the door and stayed home alone. Because I couldn't understand the language, I was told, "Say 'no' to anybody at the door, always lock the screen door, and answer from behind the locked door when somebody knocks."

Being all by myself, I could finish chores quickly. I washed clothes and took them down off the line as soon as they got dry. Then I was bored. I should have studied, but I didn't feel like doing so. Our nearest neighbors told my husband to bring me to visit, but I didn't understand their language; therefore, I didn't want to visit them at all. Finally my husband was asked by the neighboring family why he didn't bring me to their place. They said that I must be mad at them because I had never visited. My husband suggested that I visit them briefly and took me there. I just followed him silently. Then he left by himself. I waited for him to return, but he had gone to work. I felt embarrassed. I didn't even know how to say "hello" or "good-by" in English. My husband should have taught me to say a few words.

I visited them all right, but I didn't know what I should say upon leaving, and I thought it impolite to leave without saying anything. I just sat there until my husband came back from work. He saw that dinner wasn't ready yet and found me still at the neighbor's house. He got mad at me, saying, "You've been playing and not cooking." I was surprised to hear that. Who was to blame?

He had left me alone, though he knew I couldn't understand English. I asked him where he had been. While he was talking to our neighbors, I sneaked out the back door. I started cooking as soon as I got back home.

Later the neighbor's wife told my husband to send me to her with a pencil and some writing tablets. I learned how to say "good-by" from my husband. The wife displayed a lot of canned food and taught me, "This is a can of tomatoes. This is a can of mushrooms." Since I couldn't speak English, I answered her in Japanese. I didn't want the same thing to happen as before, so I repeated, "Thank you," although I didn't understand her. I said, "Good-by," and came back home. I didn't feel like visiting her again.

Now I talk about the past and laugh, but then. . . . I remember the time I learned to bake biscuits for the workers' lunches because of the rice shortage. I was taught how to make them by one of the workers. I kneaded the batter and shaped it into balls. The oven at that time didn't have a temperature indicator, so I just put in my hand. If it felt hot, it was good enough. I opened the oven after ten minutes and found that the dumplings weren't done yet. I checked on them a few times before they were done. Then they got harder. I cracked one of them again and found it was well done. All right, so I wrapped them in a cloth, but I didn't serve them for dinner. I put them in a box for lunch on the following day. I also put in a can of sardines for each person, boiled eggs, and put butter and jam on the biscuits. The men took their lunches with them. When they came back in the evening, they teased me by saying, "Today's dog killers were delicious." I couldn't figure out what they meant by dog killers. I asked the oldest worker, "Did you get anything today? What's a dog killer?" He answered, "The biscuits you baked were hard enough to hit and kill dogs with. Therefore, we named the biscuits dog killers."

My husband said that he couldn't crack the biscuits unless he threw them at a telephone pole. Since I was the only woman, I was teased by everybody. I felt miserable. I couldn't do anything but cry. My husband . . . like other men in Japan, they are masters. They don't even hold brooms. My husband didn't want others to think that he was lenient towards a woman. He just scolded me. He didn't give me any understanding words. I thought he acted so because of other people. He never straightened even one room. He didn't teach me anything gently. He felt silly to support his wife before his friends. I cried whenever such things occurred, and I missed Japan.

I learned to bake bread too. The workers said, "It's nice to have bread rather than rice for a change." They sliced the bread and toasted it. I wondered if they toasted it because it wasn't done. I apologized to them, "I'm sorry. I did my best, but it was still undone?" They said, "No, it wasn't undone. In Japan people broil rice-cakes to improve the flavor. Toasting bread is the same thing."

In the meantime, one year passed. Hatsue, our daughter, was born in the second year. While I was pregnant, I missed my home even more. I wished my mother was with me. I was too busy working at home to go out. It took a whole day for me to cook and take care of my child. A young Japanese who spoke English wrote out some daily conversation in English and taught me how to pronounce the words. I was told to bring a pencil and some writing tablets to study with. I made up my mind to study English. Without English, I couldn't do anything. My husband asked me, "Aren't you going back to Japan?" I answered, "Yes, I will go back." He said, "If you learn English, you can't go back to Japan." Then I changed my mind about studying English, although no plan to return to Japan was discussed. When our child was four or five years old and began to attend a school opened by a company, I decided to study English no matter what my husband said. After finishing my housekeeping chores, I went to school for thirty minutes or so and learned the alphabet.

Eventually I could address the letters to my parents in English. I learned to speak English. It was broken English though, and my husband wasn't happy about it. He complained that I was behind in my housekeeping because of it. Gradually I got used to the life here. By the time our son George was born, I'd adjusted a little more. We lived in Linear for five years and then moved to Superior, Wyoming, for five years. We had five children in all.

The school was run by white people, and they didn't teach the Japanese language. Being Japanese, we felt our children had better learn Japanese. Around that time, a friend of ours was going to return to Japan. He suggested that we go to Sacramento. There was a Japanese school in Sacramento; so my husband went on a trial basis. He managed a boarding house, and he thought it was a good deal. I said, "Having five children, I can't cook for others. If you want to run a boarding house, do it by yourself." He said,

"Don't speak so. A woman has to cook." I had no choice, for he had already decided on it. I agreed with him reluctantly. It was in 1926 when we came up to Sacramento. Since we were running a boarding house, I had to cook starting the next day. I wasn't used to it. There were sixty bedrooms there. I couldn't fix breakfast for such a great number of people at one time, so I cooked breakfast twice. Our youngest child was born in 1928. We were all right, because we had a midwife here.

Around 1930 the Depression started. I'll never forget the Depression. One family couldn't afford shoes for their children to wear to school. Some people couldn't afford bread. The panic struck us. Running a boarding house, we couldn't inconvenience our customers in spite of the panic. We had a hard time getting necessary things in sufficient quantity to keep the business going. Economic conditions were getting better by 1936. Being older, our children were taking care of themselves more by that time. Around the time George graduated from high school, my husband died. It was in 1940. I was at a loss with my children. My children, who were only students, couldn't help me. It was hard for me as a woman to run the business alone. On the other hand, I didn't know any other way to make our living. If I hadn't run the business, I and my children would have starved. In 1941, the war broke out. I felt more uncertain then than at the time of my husband's death.

MRS. AI MIYASAKI

When we first came, Miyasaki had a restaurant near Reno in Sparks. I washed dishes. Restaurant dishes are heavy. In the beginning I didn't know any better and wore those high-heeled shoes. I suffered so much. "If it was going to be this way," I thought, "I should have stayed in Japan." Life there was so much better than this. Of course, I had insisted so strongly on coming here that I could not complain. I endured everything.

I could not carry on a conversation with the white people; so I was sad and lonely. The days were pleasant enough, but when I went shopping, no one could understand me. I didn't know how to wear dresses and shoes properly. Sometimes I wore my clothes oddly, and it was funny. Since I lived in a place where there were few Japanese, I had hysteria. I started to say that I wanted to go back to Japan. I was carrying my second child and the morning sickness was bad. All day I was unable to visit with any Japanese, for there were none. Miyasaki worked at night, and I was lonely. I started to think to myself how much I wanted to go home . . . the same as hysteria. Then, Miyasaki said, "All right, why don't you go back and give birth in Japan?" We went as far as San Francisco.

When we got to San Francisco, the ship I was to board malfunctioned, and the departure date was postponed one week. Friends in Sacramento heard about it and said, "It is bad for two young people to live separated. Do not stay where there are so few Japanese. Stay here. Sacramento has many Japanese and Japanese doctors. It is just like Japan. Do come and live in Sacramento." Miyasaki wanted me to stay, so he suggested, "Let us stay here awhile. If you still want to go back to Japan later, you may go." That was in 1918, maybe 1919. . . .

It was good that I did not go. When I came to Sacramento, it was like Japan, more so than now. The groceries, like in Japan, were displayed outside the store . . . *daikon* (a root vegetable similar to horseradish), carrots. . . . There were many Japanese. There was even a Japanese bathhouse and a few Japanese doctors, so we decided to stay awhile. We rented a house, and I gave birth to my second daughter. Miyasaki went back to Reno to bring our belongings. Now that we were settled here, we thought that we had better start a business. We bought a rooming house and we all moved in.

As long as I had decided to stay in this country and live here, I felt that it was necessary to learn the language and live the same as the Americans do. So I studied. In Sacramento at church there was an English class, and I took my child with me to study there. We did well in Sacramento.

Mrs. Kane Kozono

When I was having a baby, I couldn't go to a doctor because I didn't have the money to do so. My husband boiled the water for me, and I delivered the baby and cut the navel string by myself while my husband took up the baby and gave it the first bath. I did it all by myself like that with the help of my husband. When we were working on a hops ranch, the house where we lived was such a dirty place! I remember the dirty mattresses there. It was not a kind of place you want a doctor or a midwife to come to. The ranch boss lived close by, and just around the time I was expecting our son Ard, the boss's wife was also having a baby. About a week after their child was born, he told us that he was going to hire a nurse for one month and said she would be able to help me deliver my baby. That way I wouldn't have to worry about getting sick or anything during and after the delivery. He said that she was available for four or five dollars. Sure, I had the money, but as I said, the place was too dirty to ask a decent white nurse to come in to. Therefore, we did it all by ourselves. When my husband told the boss, "We had a boy last night," the boss said, "Oh, ya? So, you had a doctor come from town, then?" My husband said, "No. I was the doctor."

Wherever we worked in those days, the housing was just makeshift, because everyone stayed only for a year or two and then moved on. All the houses were patched up with pieces of board on the sides, so draft blew in through slits here and there. I couldn't possibly ask a doctor or a nurse to come to such a house. My husband learned how to help deliver babies somewhere by word of mouth, as did a lot of Issei women and men. Having seen me in pain, he used to tell me, "I am sure no man could endure such an experience. Only a woman could do it." My husband used to tell his boss, "My wife can do whatever a man can do. She goes anywhere with just a blanket roll on her back."

I used to think while in bed at night that I had never had such a hard time while back in Japan. My family had been working on a farm over there too, but the difference was that since I had older brothers who helped my father, I didn't have to go out and work in the fields. Such an experience was all new to me. Sometimes I am amazed that I am still living. I think I am somehow blessed to live on this earth, and I am totally grateful for that. Sometimes I think, looking back to what I have been through, that nobody else worked as hard as I did. I always remembered my daughter and my parents whom I left in Japan. My husband's father was paralyzed soon after I left for the States, and he used to write us letters saying that he was anxious to see me again and to eat some delicious food that he liked me to cook. My mother died the year after I left, and the following year my father passed away also. After working for fifteen years, we bought about twenty-five acres of land in West Sacramento. Then we had to work as hard as ever to establish ourselves there.

Mr. Osuke Takizawa and Mrs. Sadae Takizawa

Mrs.: The younger children in my family went through school in the United States. Then more children were born here. Only I . . . my father told me that I should learn English. I inquired about a grammar school, but I was seventeen and was too old to be accepted. At that time, there was a night school run by some Japanese, and I attended and learned English.

As I said before, my older uncle was a minister. The younger uncle was brighter and mastered English a lot faster than anybody in the family. My father and the minister, though both were college graduates, couldn't handle their youngest brother. They decided to send him to the Archdeacon's home as a houseboy. There he met the beautiful daughter. The Archdeacon was against their marriage, but her mother wasn't. The mother said that her husband was wrong. She believed if the two loved each other, they should marry. She told her husband, "Aren't you a Christian? In God's eyes, the Japanese, Americans, English, and all other people are the same. Your view is too narrow."

At that time Asians and Americans couldn't marry in California.[6] Therefore, my uncle and the daughter went to Seattle to marry and came back. I don't remember whether it was the *San Francisco Chronicle* or the *San Francisco Examiner*, but anyway they were followed by newsmen after their wedding, and an article appeared against the marriage. There was a big stir.

In the end the Archdeacon and his wife separated, because the Archdeacon couldn't accept his daughter's marriage. The mother lived with her daughter and my uncle. Five children were born. The Archdeacon didn't include his daughter in his will but did include his grandson. Although he couldn't forgive his daughter, he loved her in spite of everything. The Archdeacon lived by himself and died a lonely man. It was such a dramatic story! The Archdeacon's daughter is dead; my uncle is, of course, dead too.

When I was in Oakland raising our small children, the lady whom you [the interviewer] met here was around fourteen years old. She is the daughter of my uncle, the Archdeacon's granddaughter. Our house was next to my father's, so I knew whenever she visited my parents. She also stopped by our place. I just remember her as a child.

[6]The California anti-miscegenation statute was not declared unconstitutional by the state's Supreme Court until 1948 in *Perez v. Sharp.*

She visited us again after fifty years' absence. About three years ago, she called us on the phone and explained who she was. She wanted to see us and asked us if she could visit. I said that we had been wondering where she and the other children could be. We had lost contact with each other because of the war. She doesn't look like a Japanese, so she hid herself during the war, because she didn't want to be in the evacuation camp. Though we searched for her, we couldn't find her.

My uncle, the minister, felt responsible [for the family trouble] and gave up his ministry. He started helping with my father's noodle business in Oakland. I felt sorry to see my uncle with his degree in theology doing such simple work. In the meantime, he received an invitation from a Japanese church in Salt Lake City. The church needed a minister. He didn't know what to do and asked my father's opinion. He was so desperate that he even asked my opinion. I said, "Uncle, anybody can do this job here. But not everybody can be a minister. You've obtained your education. Why not make use of it?" He said, "Then I'll go." Finally, he went with his wife and children. My uncle believed that every child is a gift from God. Their children were born one after another. Not being able to support their eleven children, they became farmers. He struggled to make a living even after he became a farmer and asked my father for a loan.

The celery you see in stores today have long sections. The improvement of the breed was made by my uncle. His improvement was acknowledged, and the seedlings were starting to sell well. He could have made up for his past losses, but he died when he was about to sell the seeds for the better breeds of celery. When I go shopping and see the celery with longer sections, I remember him.

○ ○ ○ ○ ○ ○ ○ ○ ○ ○ ○ ○ ○ ○ ○

MR.: We married in 1919.

MRS.: We knew each other, but it wasn't a love match.

MR.: Her father owned a noodle factory and a grocery store in Oakland, and her mother was a bookkeeper for the grocery store. I was asked to help at the store by her father. There, I met my wife.

MRS.: It was a friend of Takizawa's who brought up the marriage proposal. He asked me what I thought about Takizawa. I answered that he seemed to be a sincere person. I couldn't remain at my parents' place forever, so I decided to marry. Takizawa was thinking of going back to Japan to find a wife if I didn't accept the proposal. The friend stopped Takizawa from going back to Japan till he got my answer. We knew each other, but it wasn't a love match. I remember I said Takizawa seemed to be a sincere person. My father asked Takizawa to keep the store for him after we got married. He had observed Takizawa's serious personality. He wouldn't have asked if he hadn't trusted Takizawa because the job required handling money and bookkeeping.

MR.: After we'd been married, I recognized a song my wife sang. I asked her who had taught her. She'd learned it from Miss Iida. Miss Iida was a graduate of a music college. She was too fine a musician to be an elementary school music teacher and instead taught by the hour. She taught both at the girls' school in Ueda and at our school in Akiwa. We were taught music by the same instructor.

MRS.: We met by God's providence.

MR.: Love matches weren't common at that time.

MRS.: On this topic, I remember I was shocked to see the ads in the Japanese paper. The ads were for catching eloped couples. The reward was twenty-five dollars or something. I saw such ads in the paper every day. I came to the United States at the end of the same year I had graduated from school. I was between childhood and adulthood. I thought Japanese society in the United States was frightening. Many single Japanese men came here, whereas not so many Japanese women did. Even married women ran away with other men. I don't know if men courted women. Anyway, different couples were in the Wanted section in the paper. I was upset by Japanese society in the United States, even though I was merely a child. In addition, I was scared of American burglars with guns, and black people. The black people didn't hurt me, but I just felt scared.

o o o o o o o o o o o o o o

MR.: I worked for my father-in-law at the noodle factory from 1921 to 1931. Then I entered Mr. Fujimoto's import-export business as a sales manager. Mr. Fujimoto was the leader of *Heimusha*. *Heimusha* was an organization of Japanese people who hadn't finished their military service in Japan. The members donated money and sent it to Japan in order to produce airplanes and other weapons. Some Japanese men, including myself, were delaying the military service. Mr. Fujimoto was one of our leaders. It was he who collected our donations and sent them to Japan. As soon as the war broke out, Mr. Fujimoto was sent to the camp for the heaviest crimes.[7] I ran the business in his place until the company was closed down.

In 1938, before the war, my wife and I went to Japan. I delivered about ten thousand yen donated by the members of the *Heimusha* to the Department of the Japanese Army. (Because I had delivered money, I was prepared to be arrested and taken to an internment camp by the FBI after Pearl Harbor was attacked, but I never was arrested.) After delivering the money, I asked if I could travel through Manchuria. I had been there just before the Manchurian incident, but later civilians weren't allowed to go into Manchuria. My wife and I went to Manchuria by train. All passengers except for ourselves were military personnel. We could have been killed if the anti-Japanese Manchurians had attacked our train. We viewed the Shinkyo area and saw the magnificent roads which had been completed.

MRS.: It was forced labor. It wasn't a nice thing to do.

MR.: Thinking back, I remember the open-air mining in Busen and a lot of soybeans piled up in the Tairen seaport. I wondered where the soybeans were supposed to go. What a magnificent place! Traveling by train, I saw how large it was. It was like the United States.

MRS.: Manchuria is spacious, whereas Japan has a lot of people in a limited space. I felt envious seeing how spacious China was. The Japanese should have treated the Chinese and the Koreans much better. The Japanese are apt to look down on them.

MR.: At a bus stop, I saw a Manchurian woman with a child. Some Japanese people stopped her and got in the bus first. She entered the bus last, and we made room for her. We were told by the bus conductor not to do such a thing. He said the Manchurian people would take advantage of our kindness.

[7]This is a reference to an internment camp for those suspected of possible war crimes or sabotage, as opposed to relocation camps where the general population of Issei and American-born Japanese were moved during World War II.

MRS.: He told us to let her sit down on the floor. I felt very uncomfortable.

MR.: Thinking back, I feel we did something terribly dangerous.

SHIZUMA TAKESHITA

When I started to work for the newspaper, I didn't know enough English to translate news from the English newspaper for the Japanese paper, but something wonderful happened in 1905. A Japanese lady who studied English under a missionary in Japan and who had taught English two years in a high school in Japan came to the United States as a bride, but her husband-to-be was already living with someone else, and they already had had a child. The lady could not marry the man; so she came to stay with her friends, Mr. and Mrs. Uyeyama [the landlords] in whose building I had my office for the newspaper and also the office for the Japanese association. Mr. and Mrs. Uyeyama thought she was the right person for me and suggested that I marry her. If she didn't get married, she would have been deported, for her passport was issued to her as entering this country to be a bride. We married—her name was Chiyono and she was a year older than I. She knew both English and Japanese well and was a great help to me in carrying out my duties as a correspondent for the newspaper. The main office was very happy about our work. We had no children.

In those days most of the Japanese brides who came from Japan couldn't speak English. Whenever they had to go to a doctor or needed help, my wife was their interpreter. She was of great service to the community.

In 1934, my first wife died from a heart attack. I was a widower for two years, but it was difficult to be in the insurance business without a helper. My friends, Mrs. Uyeyama and Mrs. Fujii, recommended a person to me. This lady had sons. The second son was in Oakland, and my first wife looked after him because his mother was doing domestic work for a family and couldn't be with him. She also invited the boy's mother over many times; so we were pretty well acquainted with each other. When the marriage matter with this person came up, I asked her son's feelings about it. He had no objections; so we got married.

MRS. RIKAE INOUYE

After landing in Seattle, I went to the immigration office for a few weeks because of the examination for hookworms. After I passed it, my husband picked me up.

I thought the United States was nice. We lived in the countryside. My husband went to work, and I stayed home. One day my husband said, "A ditch-tender is going to our house today." He discharges the water from the irrigation gate. My husband said, "When the ditch-tender comes over, tell him 'my husband is working over there.'" The ditch-tender came, and I said in English, "My husband is working over there." He understood me! The ditch-tender went to him right away. It was my very first conversation with a white man in English!

Most white people were kind, very kind. One old Indian lady also came over quite often. We were renting Indian property. Once I, my husband, and Mr. and Mrs. Akimoto, who were running a cleaner's, were invited to a white person's house, Mr. Novtoky's. Mrs. Novtoky told me to visit her so that she could teach me English. But I didn't intend to learn English at all, for I just stayed home.

The year following my arrival, we rented a different piece of property and moved there. I had a neighbor, Mrs. Morton, who was about my age and had children. I became close to her. When my husband went to work, I visited her and learned English and cooking. I appreciated her friendship. One day when I was visiting Mrs. Morton, something humorous happened. I believed that my husband knew English better than I, so I asked him, "How do you say '*kusai*' in English?" He said it was a "stink" in English. I meant every odor by "*kusai*." My husband didn't know any word but "stink" concerning odors. Mrs. Morton's son, Owen, who was three or four years old, brought me a perfume bottle. He said, "See, Mrs. Inouye." I said, "Oh, it's a nice stink." Mrs. Morton was suckling her baby in the next room. I heard her high-pitched laugh. Being surprised, I asked her, "Why are you laughing, Mrs. Morton?" By that time, I could speak to Mrs. Morton fairly well. Such humorous things happened. It was the first mistake I made in English. After that, my husband stopped teaching me English.

In the second year I had a miscarriage. Our next baby, Alice, was born in 1918. I had seven pregnancies with two miscarriages. One of our children, before turning two years old . . . there was a man-made ditch for irrigation, which was just like a large river. We had a home near there. Martha fell down in there and died. She would have been two years old within two months.

But I never felt homesick. My husband went bankrupt twice in the United States. He was stuck with unsold crops; yet he had to pay the workers. Everytime we went bankrupt, I remembered my grandmother's humble life. I neither cried nor complained about it. I took it for granted that such things would occur. My husband was always honest. When he went bankrupt, he was told by the bank to come and get a loan at any time.

The following year, we rented just a four-acre piece of property and grew onions, dry onions. We gave the tools, three horses, and machines to the owner for the mortgage. We just kept one horse. At that time the onions sold very well. The following year, we rented a forty-acre piece of property and could resume farming. It was nice to have the crops sold at a healthy price. We made money the year we were planning to move to California. It was in 1933 or 1934, during the Depression. We didn't face any real troubles then, but sometimes when I would ask my husband to buy me some necessities, he would say, "Oh, I forgot it." I assumed that he couldn't afford it and said, "All right. Next time is fine with me." I never complained because I understood his feelings. Nonetheless, he took care of me very well.

I'm lazy, but my husband was fastidious. When we married and came here, we knew that well. When I was going aboard the ship to come to America, my husband's sister-in-law said to me, "Rikae, Sadao is fastidious." My elder brother said to my husband, "Please be patient with Rikae because she's lazy." That was right after our marriage. We didn't talk about that then. After coming to the United States and we had enough time to talk, I said to my husband, "Your middle sister-in-law said you are fastidious." Then my husband said, "Your elder brother said you are lazy." My mother told my husband, "The lazy one and the fastidious one got married." My husband said, "Sometimes I want to hit you when you're lazy, but because your mother took care of you so well since childhood, I don't feel like beating you." So I got away with it. The merit of virtue is handed down to descendants.

We finally came to Brighton,[8] where we bought a home. My husband was good at growing crops. He knew the right timing. He timed it so well that he could grow cauliflower right before

[8]Brighton was a farming area outside of Sacramento.

Thanksgiving. Though my husband was good at farming, he was poor at business. Trusting others, he consigned the crops for sale to them. He couldn't make the sale any other way, for he couldn't hold on to the crops himself and wait for buyers. When the crops didn't sell, we didn't get any money. Three years after coming to Brighton, one Japanese friend said to me, "Mrs. Inouye, you have fine crops. Why don't you sell them at the Flea Market?" I listened to her. After coming and renting property here, I said to my husband, "I won't help you farm if you consign as you did. I want to go and sell at the Flea Market. If it's O.K. with you, I'll become a salesgirl on Wednesdays and Saturdays." He said, "Do whatever you want to do."

On the first day, my husband loaded the truck. In the beginning, I was told by the ladies there to bring this and that. You know the Flea Market, don't you? It's near the Libby Cannery. When I saw the market in the distance, I got nervous and my heart started beating fast. We got off at the given spot. The Japanese ladies there helped us set up tables and put the vegetables on them. Then my husband left. Well, I had talked big but I was silly. I didn't even face the front. The customers walked along the sidewalk where the tables were set up. Not having any customers, I turned my back and bent forward to touch my shoestrings. I pretended that I was tying my shoes. The lady next to me was kind and said, "Mrs. Inouye, a customer." Then I turned around and came out. The customers were happy about the fine cauliflower. They bought without any complaints. I said, "Thank you" and wrapped it. After the customers left, I turned my back and touched my shoestrings again. I couldn't face the customers at the front. The lady next to me said again, "Mrs. Inouye, a customer." I said, "Is that so?" and came out. I was like that for a few Saturdays. After getting used to selling, I started facing the customers. Watching the customer's eyes, I knew he wanted some of our goods if his eyes were fixed on our table. I faced the front directly and asked with a smile, "Do you like anything?" I became a good salesgirl.

We had turnips and everything, for we were truck farmers. I put one or two free vegetables in the sack. Going back home, the customer found the extra. Then the customer would bring a friend to us. It was like that. I was too busy to touch my shoestrings any longer. I learned that the cauliflower with cuts couldn't be number one quality, and they couldn't even be sold as number two. I cut out the good parts and piled them in strawberry baskets. I sold them for a very low price. The customers didn't have any trouble with them at home since I had cleaned them up beforehand. They sold well. I said to the lady next to me, "You should do this, too. They sell well without being labeled as number two." She said, "Oh, I see. That's a really good idea." She was happy too. I sold for a long time. Till the war . . . three, four years . . . up until the war broke out. Our business was prosperous then. After the Pearl Harbor attack, we couldn't go out to the market.

The Yamato colonies were a unique attempt to integrate the Japanese into American farming communities. Kyutaro Abiko, a San Francisco Japanese newspaper publisher, promoted the idea of Japanese Christian farm colonies in the area around Turlock, California. In 1907 the Livingston colony was started, and later in 1919 the Cortez colony was begun. A third colony was started in Merced but ultimately failed.

Mrs. Kazuko (Minejima) Hayashi

We arrived in San Francisco and stayed in the city for a week. After that we came to Livingston by train. To my surprise, Livingston was a wild, vast area; it was almost frightening to me. It was terrible! I had to begin by cleaning an old-style lamp. When I was in Tokyo, we had electricity and all other modern things including a telephone. We had two telephones—one in the house and one in the office. My brother told me, "If you go to America, they are building a Japanese village [Livingston] so you must work very hard." He also said, "It is quite an honor and privilege to be able to go abroad; so Kazuko, you'd better go and work hard."

At that time I did not have my mother anymore. The third brother was the one who was telling me these things. You see, I did not know how to work when I came to the U.S.A., but I was so overjoyed by the fact that I was able to have my own husband that I did not have time to think about the hardships which I must face in the near future.

The hardships? Well . . . whenever I had to go to the town, I had to walk about twenty miles, but there were all kinds of things there. There was a school in front of the store there, and every

Christmas season they had a party. I used to bring my kimonos and put them on these white people.

I remember once I went shopping, I wanted to buy a bottle of ink. I asked for ink, but the storekeeper gave me eggs. We used to have hundreds of chickens, and we had more than enough eggs at home. The storekeeper put them in a bucket and gave them to me. Well, I could not say "no," so I had to take home a bucketful of eggs!

Because my husband was the head of the village in Livingston, I had to accompany him to various places. Once I had to meet a judge's wife. I did not know anything about American customs, so when she stuck her hands out, I did mine in the same way and ended up shaking hands with her.

Mr. Minejima, my husband, had a lot of respect for Luther Burbank. He always wanted to name his own son, Ryuzo, after him. "Ryuzo," meaning to rise and stand.[9] They say if you write the character for "rise" three times, you will never go hungry. However, the resulting character looked very odd, so we had to compromise and decided on "money or gold" and "village."

My husband began to feel very ill; so he went to see a doctor in Turlock. We did not have a car; so he was brought to the doctor by horse and buggy. The results were not good. He could not sleep at night, and we thought we had to do something for him. The people in the village got together and collected some money for him, though they did not have too much. I remember it was over one hundred dollars they collected. They told us to take him to the University hospital in San Francisco. We brought him by train.

After Mr. Minejima entered the hospital, they took many X-rays and performed many tests on him. They thought it was cancer of the throat. Yes, they made an incision in his throat. At that time I was five months pregnant. It was the summer of 1911. I went to see my husband the night of July 3. At that time he could not see very well. He was trying to reach for a handkerchief, but he could not find it, though it was on the bed. His throat was swollen, and it was very hard.

Early the next morning Mr. Abiko and Mr. Saburo Nodaoto, who was famous for planting rice in Colusa for the first time, came to my room. Then they said, "Early this morning Mr.

[9]Luther and Ryuzo might sound quite different for English-speaking people, but for Japanese-speaking people, "L" and "R" sound almost the same, *Lu-Ryu.*

Minejima passed away." They took me out of the hotel and sent telegrams to important people. Those people whom Mr. Minejima had taken care of sent me lots of money—a hundred dollars, fifty, seventy. It was lots of money at that time.

We had to cremate him; then we took the ashes to Japan because there was no cemetery in Livingston. There was a bank called the Nichi Bei Ginko, and Mr. Umetaro Minake was president of the bank. He took me around to see people. It is a Japanese custom to do that. Its purpose was to greet people and thank them for the concern, care, and gifts that the family had received. Even after I went back to Livingston, he took care of me. Everyone said a woman should not live in a big house by herself; so neighbors' wives used to come and stay with me. They were very considerate.

Sadame Inouye

In 1917, eleven years after I left Japan, I received a telegram from my family saying that my father was very sick. I went back to Japan right away. However, my father had already passed away before I got there, since I had to go home by boat. While I was in Japan, I married my present wife. In Japan most of the marriages at that time were arranged by parents or relatives, and mine was too. My friend's father arranged it for me. We did not go to a shrine or a temple for the ceremony. I remember that our go-between acted as chairman at our wedding party. He gave a short speech, and my wife and I exchanged nuptial cups.

In 1919 we joined the Japanese settlement in Merced. The colony was started by Kyutaro Abiko of the *Nichi Bei* newspaper. The colony covered about twenty-five hundred acres, and we paid a hundred and seventy-five dollars per acre. With regard to the payment, we were supposed to put twenty percent down, which was thirty-five dollars, and pay the rest for the next eight years, which meant we made payments of seventeen dollars and fifty cents every month. Thus, it was rather easy to buy land. An American bank took charge of selling the land. It looked easy to start with, but the problem was that we could not get many people interested. The other Japanese colony in Cortez was very successful, for they had a good manager. About thirty families participated in that colony, while we barely gathered six families. The number was too small to organize any cooperative unit. We grew vegetables, but we could not find a good market for them. It was because our production was limited with only six families. If we had had at least twenty families, we could have made it. One by one, these six families gradually left, and finally we had to close the colony. I think that the failure was greatly due to mismanagement.

Our manager administered the colony with great difficulty. His manner of speaking sometimes even discouraged people from buying the land. Thus, we could not get many people, and the colony failed completely. Those who made down payments had to give up the money. If we paid all, we could have owned the land. Thirty-five dollars down payment was big money at that time, about equal to one's income for a month. We grudgingly stayed in Merced for six years, since we had built a house there. There were still a few people when we left. I do not know how much longer they stayed in the colony, but they, too, must have finally left.

After our failure in Merced, we moved to Riverside. I had to find a job somehow, since we had five children. A friend of mine had a grocery store and usually had several Filipino and Japanese employees. So I asked him if I could work for him. He hired me immediately and even let me build a temporary house by his store. I built a small two-bedroom house by myself. It cost me about three hundred dollars just for building material.

7

The San Francisco Earthquake

SHIZUMA TAKESHITA

Fire broke out during the San Francisco earthquake, and the town burned for two nights and three days. It was on a Wednesday night that Mr. Abiko, our newspaper editor, stopped by our place in Oakland on his way back from Sacramento. He, my wife, and I walked to the ferry and caught a boat to San Francisco. The newspaper plant wasn't on fire as yet, and Mr. Abiko wanted to get the Japanese type out; so we went to get a buggy to haul it. My wife and I put all the type we could in a sack and dragged it out to the sidewalk. When Mr. Abiko came back, he and I went down in the basement again to try and get more out, but a military policeman came and told us that he would shoot if we did not leave. Leaving all the type behind, my wife and I started back for Oakland. By that time it was morning.

There were many workers from the San Francisco printing plant already at my place and in the park across the street. My wife and I had only a few dishes, no large pots and pans, and only a one-burner gas stove without an oven. We didn't know how to cook for so many people. I washed a bucket, cooked rice in it and served rice and Japanese pickles and whatever we had. At night, we slept like sardines in a can.

Our pastor, Rev. Eiken Aibara, got together with the other churches and began helping the refugees with things that were donated. The landlord of the house we used as our church made us vacate the place, because he was afraid the building would be damaged with so many people going in and out. It was very difficult at the time, but we bought a house for nine thousand dollars. Before the earthquake, the property was valued at about three thousand. We bought other items and spent about ten thousand in total. The Board of Missions gave us a grant of five thousand dollars, but it was very difficult to raise the other half because the refugees were mostly students. You can see the list here—contributions were mostly two and three dollars . . . five was the most a person gave. We traveled all over California to raise the five thousand dollars.

8

The Depression

MINEJIRO SHIBATA

It was 1932—before the war—when we were seized by the Depression. The sardines . . . couldn't move them and all of a sudden the business fell apart. I gave up fishing and went to downtown Los Angeles. The Depression was there too. Some other people and I began to work in produce, vegetables. Cucumbers were twenty-five cents a box, grapes were also twenty-five cents a box, and turnips were twenty-five cents per . . . ah, but we couldn't make profits on anything because of the low wholesale price, so I returned to San Pedro. I had barely enough money to eat at that time. Some Japanese people couldn't even feed themselves.

There was a gambling house in Los Angeles where you could get a free lunch. I myself never ate there, for I didn't like eating at such a place. Lots of starving Japanese people ate lunch there, so no one in Los Angeles spoke ill of the gambling place.

Sometimes I gambled. The building we used to gamble in was beautiful at that time; it's dirty now. It was rumored that the Chief of Police was a stockholder. Whenever there was to be a raid, he phoned us to stop gambling for a while. We stopped and kept silent. Then a *Naniwa-jin*, a person from Naniwa, was murdered. After that the gambling place was watched so carefully that it went bankrupt.

SHOICHI FUKUDA

There was a huge S.P. (Southern Pacific Railroad) shop, and many people worked there. But with the Depression, the shop was closed. I did business with the shop workers on credit, but when the shop closed, we could not collect the money. White people were not like Japanese people, you know. When the shop was closed and they did not have an income, they did not even attempt to return the money they owed us.

Once the Depression was upon us and the price of goods began to get lower and lower, I could not continue my business any longer. I cashed in my life insurance and poured it into the store, but it was not enough to pull us through. The store lease was for five years, so we could not leave the business. People around us stole things from our store. It became so difficult that we even borrowed money from my wife's parents in order to continue.

Fortunately, the man who leased us the store also owned fifteen acres of land in the Florin area.[1] He offered to trade it for the store lease. The land still had a mortgage of about six hundred dollars, and I would have to take care of it. We did not know what to do. Every month we were losing about one hundred and fifty dollars on the store. It was very big money at that time. Even that bare land seemed to me a better deal; so we decided to take it and paid off the six hundred dollar mortgage. We did make an exchange, but now we did not know where to go, for we had no place to live. We used to live in a small room off the store.

My wife's parents and brother lived in Broderick at that time. (There were about ten Japanese families living there.) They were farmers and raised vegetables. We went to live with them and helped them to farm, but there was not enough space for us to live in their house, since my father-in-law's house had only one bedroom. They let us stay there for a week or so, but we could not live like that forever. My father-in-law said, "I will loan you fifty dollars in order to find used lumber to build a home."

I borrowed a truck and went out to look for used lumber. My father-in-law came with me. Someone told us that there was cheap, used lumber in a certain store. We went there and bought the lumber, but even in those days fifty dollars worth of lumber was not enough. Our problem was how to erect a house with this limited amount of lumber.

First, we built a twelve- by twenty-foot floor. Second, we had to have walls. If we built columns at four corners, we would not have enough lumber; so we had to build a house which did not have columns. We arranged the two-by-fours to make four walls and pushed the walls against each other. We nailed down the

[1]Florin is a farming community near Sacramento, California.

corners to stabilize them. That's how we made our house. It was enough to withstand the rain so that the three of us—my wife, my child, and myself—could sleep there.

It was very, very hot in the summer. We did not have a ceiling, and the roof was only a thin board. When the sun beat against it, the inside became very hot. We had a wood-burning stove made out of sheet metal. When we cooked, it added a terrific amount of heat to the house. The wall was full of holes through which the mosquitoes could come in. We had to paste newspapers on these holes not only to keep mosquitoes out but bees too.

In the winter it was very cold because of the thin walls. We used to put up blanketing to keep the heat inside. When it rained hard and the wind blew against the house, it shook violently. One night the wind was so strong that we wondered whether the house would be able to withstand the storm. My father-in-law told us to stay in his house. We brought out some beams and put them against our house to support it. Soon we heard a huge noise, and upon running outside, I saw a board ripped off a room and roof paper flying all over the place. We covered the inside of the house with canvas so that things would not get wet. That was our house at that time.

Wages were very low during the Depression. I used to work for ten cents an hour. Since we were at my in-laws' place, we did not have to buy vegetables. We just had to buy meat and other necessities. We did have enough to eat, though.

Our work began about five A.M. We worked hard all day, and after dinner we worked until eleven P.M. packing tomatoes during the season. We spent the summer like this; however, in the fall there was no work at father's place. Fortunately, a neighbor asked me to work for him. I was to handle a horse. Jobs were very scarce at that time, and I was very eager to work. Having never handled a horse before, I practiced with a horse for two days and then went to work. Many kinds of heavy equipment, such as a fertilizer spreader, were pulled by the horse. I piled up bags of fertilizer on a cart for the horse to pull. But since the horse was so thin, it did not have the strength to pull the cart. I had to lighten the load and do it little by little. I worked very hard for ten cents an hour.

There were no jobs after that; so I did not know what to do. With a small amount of money I bought dry goods to sell and deliver to families. I became a traveling salesman. A truck which belonged to my father-in-law was available for my use. I was able to sell things, but I did not know how long I would be able to continue, because I was worried about my health. If I became ill, that would be the end of my family. There would be no security at all; so I wanted to begin some kind of business again. Well, it so happened that there was a liquor store for sale. I made a down payment with what little money I had and began my business. It was rough going; it did not go well at all. We had our second child at that time. She was born in the house in Broderick.

SHIZUMA TAKESHITA

I was an insurance salesman during the Depression. In the Japanese community, we had a "Mutual Financing Club." Because of the Depression, some members couldn't pay up their share, and we had a terrible time. I suffered big losses because I signed security for many, and some of these people left town. I couldn't pay for everyone [those who defaulted on their payments] at once, so I asked for extensions on some. People criticized me. They said I lived well and even criticized my being a Christian and not following up on my obligations. In those days, most Japanese families didn't have rugs or a piano in their home, nor did members of the family have a bedroom of their own. I told them I would give up my house, sell everything I had except our bed and a few dishes, and I would give them all the money I had. There was a vacant space where my printing shop was, so I took our bed and dishes and moved in there. What we couldn't sell, we brought to the printing shop. I told them [the creditors] I would fulfill my responsibilities in five years. I think the debt was a little over four thousand dollars. I sold the printing shop to the shop manager for three thousand five hundred dollars, and I think I fulfilled my obligations in three years.

JUHEI KONO

The beginning of the Depression—it was really terrible! For example, a Furuya Bank and their store in Seattle—it was the biggest bank in the northwestern region, and the Furuyas were millionaires—went bankrupt in 1931. It was a severe blow to the Japanese community . . . very bad. You see, all those who put their money in the Furuya Bank, a Japanese bank, went bankrupt. It was in 1931, and at that time I was in California, where four or five banks closed down one after another in Sacramento. From 1929 through 1932, Japanese communities throughout the state of California were just miserably damaged.

It was during those days that a man by the name of Gentaro Kodashiro became known to many people. During the night he would leave several pounds of rice at the doorstep of a needy Japanese family and disappear into the night. Nobody knew who gave them those things. Much later they found out it was Mr. Kodashiro.

Kodashiro had some ninety acres of land in Winters, which is a little bit down the road from Vacaville. He was growing fruit there. Since he was a single man, he used to hire a lot of workers. But he couldn't make himself an exception to the Depression around 1929, and his business gradually withered away because of it. At last he sold all his land, and used that money in different ways. However, he never made a donation with a public announcement attached to it. He gave to the poor in a very quiet way; so we don't know the extent of what he did. The reason I know of him is that in 1932 I was in charge of churches in the Vacaville and Palo Alto areas and met some of those people who knew about him. It was seventeen miles between his house and the church. On Saturdays he left his house on foot and visited Japanese homes on the way. He would leave food for those who were especially poor. He used to walk the seventeen miles, which took him two days. On Sunday he would attend church services and then walk back home. On his way back, he visited different people again. Such was the man, Mr. Gentaro Kodashiro.

Later on, in 1933, I was assigned to a church in West Los Angeles. After that I really don't know much about what happened to him. After the war, he was in Oakland, so I heard, working in a church as a janitor. He was a great influence upon young people there. He was . . . what shall I say . . . a passionate man, a man of great passion. I always called him "The Saint of Northern California."

During the Depression the financial situation of the [Japanese Christian] churches was really bad. They couldn't even pay our salary; sometimes they gave me only three or four dollars a week. In the end, they somehow paid all, but . . . oh, that particular year we really suffered! I had to teach in a Japanese school in San Fernando, which is about thirty miles from West Los Angeles, where we lived. I had to borrow a hundred and fifty dollars when the fourth baby was born. That was our only debt. Out of that seventy dollars a month and sometimes only three or four dollars a week . . . I don't know how I paid it back! But anyway I did pay back the hundred and fifty dollars even then. That is the most difficult thing that I have ever done. I once told a minister that the Salvation Army and the Goodwill stores were my best friends. I told him that until I came to Seattle in 1954, I had never bought new shirts because I had to raise four children. During that time we didn't receive a children's living allowance as part of our salary, as we do today. But we gave the best education to our four children.

Mrs. Hanayo Inouye

It was the Depression time, and the price of grapes was pretty bad. Women were getting paid one fifty a day for ten hours of work. For men it was two dollars a day. It was especially hard in those days for those who were in business for themselves. For instance, a family that used to run a vegetable store said they had not had meals for days because of the high cost of rice. Some of us who weren't as badly off brought one cup of rice to the Japanese school. The teachers there collected rice from everyone that could afford to give and distributed the rice to needy families. This rice was distributed once a week on Saturdays. Besides rice, donations of canned goods were also asked for from time to time.

My husband used to work in the fields all day long until dark. One afternoon, however, he came back from work and picked up a newspaper. Then he said, "I'm going to the bank." The next day the bank closed. The very next day! He used to read the paper every night after work and was probably thinking about it while working in the fields. He withdrew everything we had in the bank. Then we wondered where to keep the money, for our house wasn't a good one. And besides it was obvious that we would lose everything if a fire should break out. We had one of those big tea cans—the Japanese students in those days used to peddle tea around the neighborhood—and put all our family valuables in it and decided to bury it underground. Well, one day, my children came home from school and said, "What's happening here?" The bills that we buried in the tea can got wet, so I was putting them side by side on the bed to dry.

Wataru Ishisaka

We did not go hungry, but it was very difficult. It was the same with everybody else. As you know, the Japanese are a proud people, and they will not accept charity from anyone. But we knew some people who were suffering greatly. They had lots of children and lived in shacks under the levee by the river. We used to take a sack of rice and other food and roll the goods down the levee. Then, you see, they wouldn't know who the donor was, and they could accept the food. The Depression time was a very difficult time for all people.

In Sacramento many people were picking things out of garbage cans. Well, so many Japanese were suffering that the Japanese association organized an emergency relief program and brought food to the needy during the night so that they, who needed the relief, wouldn't be embarrassed by it. I really give credit to Issei. Some aspects of their life might not have been so exemplary, but they were very sensitive in this way.

Riichi Satow

Oh, it was just that, really a great Depression. The labor force was more than abundant because of it, and that lowered the going wage at the time to a dollar fifty a day. Many Filipinos were available at that time. I, too, used to hire them at a dollar fifty a day.

The price of strawberries was only twenty-five cents a crate. I had to price them at least a dollar fifty a crate, or else there would be hardly any profit. But, you see, it went down to twenty-five cents or so when the worst came. Yet we had no choice other than giving in to whatever the going rate was. Gradually, however, the price rose from thirty-five cents to seventy-five cents.

Around the time when the price was seventy-five cents or so, the idea of a consolidation movement became popular. We would continue competing with each other for much lower prices if the growers and their groups were kept divided as they were then. Besides our Strawberry Growers' Association there were four or five organizations of a similar type. The disadvantage was obvious. We talked of uniting them into one and of setting up one system of distribution, as well as a sales network. Besides the low price and mutually disadvantageous competition, overproduction was another factor which came about because the total acreage of strawberries at that particular time had increased a lot. The consolidation movement was a success. We united and established the Strawberry . . . something . . . Exchange. And I was the president of that new organization. We used to ship seven carloads northbound for Oregon and Washington. That was the maximum they could consume up there. One time we picked eleven carloads to our surprise. Yes, it was a big harvest. Eleven freight cars lined up that day over at the Florin terminal. It was a gorgeous scene, but it was a big problem, as you might have guessed. We had to find markets for all we produced and ship out quickly. We sent the surplus to Los Angeles. Well, as far as the strawberry market was concerned, we were aware that Los Angeles was taken care of by its local growers; yet we did it anyway. We also shipped out one car to Salt Lake City. As the situation grew really desperate, even Texas became one of our emergency markets for that matter. San Francisco was counted out from the beginning, for it was sufficiently supplied by the Coast area growers. There was no room for us to cut in. Anyway, that's how we managed it. People now say that this valley used to be tops in strawberry production. But yet, there were times the industry had trouble like this. After we got together as one organization, we became a little bit better off than before. The gradually recovering economy helped too. Things like this lie in the history of the strawberry industry of the valley. And, at last, came the year right before the war. Every bit of the effort we had put in up till that day amounted to absolutely nothing.

PART III:
DECEMBER 7, 1941

9

Shock, Fear, and Confusion

Immediately after the bombing of Pearl Harbor, all Issei were declared "enemy aliens" and subject to FBI searches, arrests, and internment. By the evening of December 7, hundreds of Issei had been taken into custody and by February 16, some 2,192 Japanese aliens had been arrested. Most of those arrested were prominent leaders of the various Japanese communities on the West Coast, as well as large groups of Japanese fishermen who purportedly were spies for the Japanese Navy. Some of these Issei were eventually "interned" in prison camps and gradually released to join their families in relocation centers when investigations revealed that they were no threat to national security and had committed no acts of sabotage.

Mrs. Hanayo Inouye

It was on December 7, in the morning . . . my children had wanted a radio for a long time, and two days before December 7, we bought them one. They were so happy about the new radio that they got up early in the morning and were listening to it. At seven o'clock they came rushing to me and said, "Mom, it's a war!"[1] I asked, "What are you talking about?" I just couldn't believe it. All of us were really stunned by the news.

Restrictions were put on us, because our house was less than five miles from the Marysville airport. Those Japanese who lived

---

[1]Mrs. Inouye had forgotten about the time difference between California and Hawaii.

within the five-mile limit had to move out. A big family like ours—eight children—lots of belongings. . . . We certainly didn't want to move.

We used to send two of our sons to a *kendo* (Japanese fencing) school. My husband had bought each of them a brand new set of equipment, but when we learned that the FBI was coming to search our house, we thought that they might decide we were pro-Japan if they found the *kendo* equipment in our house. So one night my husband got up and dug a hole to bury anything the FBI might consider suspicious. We knew that even possession of the Emperor's photographs could be a cause for detention by the FBI. Helping the Japanese school was another probable cause for detention. Being bilingual, my husband naturally had been helping the school.

When the FBI did come to our house, Mr. Robinson, our boss, told them, "This Inouye family has been with us for many years. I will guarantee that they are not questionable people in any sense." Then the FBI left.

Living on the Robinsons' farm, we were somewhat in seclusion so to speak, and so relatively free from being directly subjected to such anti-Japanese sentiments of the time. The only problem we had was that five-mile limit which I talked about before. We moved to a new place which was about ten miles from the airport. All that time the Robinsons were very kind to us, as though we were real brothers and sisters. Then, soon after we moved to the new place, it was the time when all the Japanese people, Issei and Nisei, had to face the evacuation order. Meanwhile, the FBI visited us again and started searching the trunks we had.

My husband had had such a hard time back in Japan and borrowed a lot of money to come to the United States. His father's health had not been very good, and there were a lot of children in the family. At the age of sixteen my husband came over here to help out his family in Japan. Contrary to his hopes, he couldn't send any money back for quite a while, for he had attended a grammar school for about four years. After that, he started working in sugar beets and also worked on the railroad, among many other things. He said that at that time he was making one dollar a day, so that is thirty dollars a month. From that he sent twenty dollars back home. All of the receipts of the remittances he made were kept in a trunk, and the FBI found a lot of those receipts.

KIYOSHI NOJI

The feelings in the Salinas Valley weren't good at that time—especially when the war broke out. Japanese farmers in Salinas grew very good lettuce and carrots. . . .

On the day Pearl Harbor was attacked, I spoke to a women's group in San Mateo. After the meeting, the women started to talk about the bombing of Pearl Harbor which had occurred that morning. It was then that I first learned about it; so I went out to get a newspaper. It was already in the papers. I wanted to go to San Francisco, but my wife spoke against it, and we decided to return to Salinas. We passed by Moffett Field and noticed that the planes were gone that day. When we passed a gasoline tanker, the driver gave us a dirty look. In Salinas there was a lot of commotion already.

As you know, Fort Ord is near Salinas. I remember sending off soldiers to Bataan in the Philippines before the war broke out. When Japanese soldiers invaded Bataan, there were many casualties among our (U.S.) soldiers, which created additional anti-Japanese feelings.

There were many instances of hostile feelings. While I was discussing with Caucasian pastors whether there were possibilities of storing Japanese evacuees' belongings in their churches, someone in the telephone office cut us off. While we were having prayer meetings, someone threw a heavy object on the church roof to disturb us.

I remembered reading somewhere that General Araki of the Japanese Army once mentioned that if a war occurred between Japan and America, the Nisei (children of the Issei and American citizens by birth) should stay loyal to America, the country of their birth. I wrote about this in our church news on December 14, 1941, a week after the Pearl Harbor attack. I stated that by remaining loyal to the United States, the Japanese would gain honor for Japan. Our church lay leader showed the written article to the Chief of Police. Therefore, the Salinas police chief was very good to me and gave me permission to go wherever I wanted.

After the Pearl Harbor attack, the FBI men from San Francisco came to Salinas every day, and every day I went around to check on our church members to see if anyone had been taken in. In those days, we didn't know who would be taken in, so most of the

Issei men had a couple of small suitcases packed and ready. One of our important church elders, Mr. Yamaguchi, was taken in.

CHOICHI NITTA

It was on a Sunday, and on the way to church I heard about it over the radio in my car but couldn't believe it. When I got home, I turned on the radio, and the Pearl Harbor attack was broadcast extensively. I was shocked! Before long, the chairman of the Japanese association and several others were taken in for detention. I had served as the chairman of the Japanese association once, but I wasn't taken in, probably because it was over five years before.

MASAO ITANO

They arrested my wife and myself, but later on the same day she was allowed to go home. We were quite worried about leaving our children. The FBI went through our house and even picked up a toy pistol. I was taken to the County Courthouse and stayed in jail overnight before I was sent to San Francisco. We were limited to two meals a day. Our meals were black coffee and bread. On an empty stomach, they tasted good. People who were there before us used to hoard the bread for a night snack, but we newcomers didn't know that the evening meal was omitted.

We weren't prepared when they came to pick me up. My wife kept saying that we should be packed and ready, but I believed that there was no reason why I should be picked up, since I had committed no crime. We were totally unprepared when they came to take me in.

RIICHI SATOW

The Pearl Harbor attack . . . was absolutely a bolt out of the blue to many of us. From that point on, it was just a disaster. Whatever I thought the FBI might think incriminating, I burned. I kept the books I had. It was mainly in regard to correspondence and anything that would sound nationalistic, even a bit, that I burned. The FBI was running around searching houses and would arrest anybody if they found anything suspicious. They could find all kinds of excuses to do so. When I think back on it, I don't think

I had anything that would be considered subversive in the eyes of the authorities. However, I couldn't but over-worry, and I didn't want to take a chance.

As president of an industrial association, I was prepared to be arrested, but luckily they didn't do anything to me. Industrial associations were largely left untouched by the authorities. They were treated differently from the JACL (Japanese American Citizens' League) or any other similar organizations. There was one organization in the Japanese community which I thought might raise some questions. It was called *Heimusha-kai*, and I was one of its supporters. Through the organization we sent donations to the Japanese Red Cross Society, or some group like it. When things began to turn against us Japanese, we quickly decided to dissolve it. I guess the Sacramento chapter of *Heimusha-kai* was the first one to take that action. Tension was running high. Many of us felt extremely unsafe. But, when I come to think of it now, I believe it was after all divine Providence that nothing whatsoever happened to me. I was evacuated along with everybody else, and that was that. They never tried to come and arrest me.

Yoshito Fujii

Later at night I heard that the FBI had taken away some Japanese people for interrogation. I couldn't understand why. I didn't imagine that the same thing would happen to me. I just thought about my business. One Japanese after another was arrested, and they never returned home. They weren't criminals; so I was confused. Later, I learned that the government had taken emergency measures in order to prevent Japanese people from contacting Japan and from participating in acts of sabotage. My turn finally came later.

I was president of the Junior Division of the Japanese Chamber of Commerce. The FBI had it on record that I had taken a Japanese naval officer to the Boeing Company when he had visited the United States. Because of that incident, I was suspected of having some kind of contact with Japan. A couple of FBI men came over and told me that they had something to talk to me about. They said that I might stay overnight, and I should take my pajamas with me. When I got to the immigration office, I saw other people who had been arrested before, but I was confident that the government wouldn't do anything unreasonable.

I stayed at the immigration office for three weeks. My children visited me once in a while. We had no privacy, though. A guard was with us. My children, being small, couldn't understand why I was kept there. The bigger one was six or seven years old. The smaller one was about a year old. Then I was sent to North Dakota. I mingled with the fishermen from Terminal Island and the people from Sacramento.

About three months later I had a hearing. A paper which proved that I'd abandoned my property rights in Japan in order to establish my residence here for my children was presented at the hearing. Earlier I had written a letter to a local court in Japan, and the court had sent me the paper. The FBI picked it up at my place, because they thought it might be an important document. I told them to read the paper which stated that though I was Japanese, I had resolved to quit Japan and live in the United States for my children. An interpreter read it and translated it. I made the following statement to the hearing board: "Few people actually have documents to prove their resolution; however, most of the Issei immigrants are willing to live here for good. Whether or not they have documents to prove their status is irrelevant. The United States government is also to blame because we were refused the right to be naturalized. If you had allowed us, I would have been the first one to apply for citizenship. If so, I would have been a naturalized American and wouldn't have been kept here." I was released shortly after that and joined my family at the Puyallup Assembly Center.

After I was arrested, my bank account and other assets were frozen. However, my wife could get money for payments without any documents. She got money from the bank by submitting a report. The family was sent to the Puyallup Assembly Center in May. My wife closed up our business. She enclosed a part of the plant and locked up our valuables. She did everything. . . . We didn't know what would happen to us. My family welcomed me in Puyallup. Seeing their situation there, I couldn't help feeling miserable. Their quarters were worse than a cowshed. There was only one thin board between our room and the next family's room. We stayed in a tent dwelling in the camp. It wasn't a proper place to sleep. We had no bath, only a simple shower. The toilet wasn't bearable. We made beds for ourselves, five people including our three children.

Minejiro Shibata

On the very day that the war broke out, we left Terminal Island around midnight without knowing anything about the war. We went to an island located fifty miles off the coast, where we fished for sardines. Turning to look back, we didn't see the boats which were supposed to come after us. The only boats we saw were the ones far ahead of us. We thought something must be wrong. I turned on the radio about three A.M. and listened to the San Diego control tower broadcasting, "The Japanese airplanes are attacking Hawaii right now. This is neither a joke nor a lie." I said to the crew, "The radio said that the Japanese planes were attacking Hawaii," but nobody believed me. I stopped trying to convince the crew after a while. We started hauling in our catch of sardines about five A.M. We caught so many sardines that we had our net torn, but we saved about sixty tons. On the way back—it was before dawn—we saw the lighthouse was dark. Then the crew realized that what I had said before was true. The navy put a wire around the port, so we couldn't get in. As soon as day broke, the gate was opened.

It was a severely cold day. I saw Navy men all over the area, even around the canning company. The Japanese were worried, but they didn't know what to do. The Navy men came in one after another. They said they would take our Captain Hori with them, and told me to come with them too. Since I was waiting for the boat to be returned, I said to Oishi, "Oishi, if you go instead of me, you won't have to work on the boat today." He took my words with joy and left. He never came back after that.

We unloaded the fish, washed the boat, and dried the net. We weren't allowed to go out to sea after that. Though there was still enough fish for us to catch, we just stayed home every day. My wife started working at the cannery for the first time. The children and I stayed home together.

Right after the war started, a Korean doctor told the U.S. government that the fishermen in San Pedro were all spies; so a special investigating committee was formed. The committee reported to the government that the Japanese fishermen were all officers of the Japanese Navy. . . . Some fishermen were ex-Navy men, but none of us were spies. If we had been spies, we would have gone back to Japan before the war. I had been keeping a diary for a couple of years, but the FBI took it away. They returned it to me later. Once I went to Mexico and Central America—to Panama—for deep-sea fishing. When I was in Panama, I took a lot of pictures for no special reason. I burned them all in the basement when the war started. I could have been in real trouble if I had kept them.

The Filipinos in Los Angeles turned hostile against the Japanese, for the Japanese military forces had landed in the Philippines. The Filipinos sometimes tried to attack us. I always carried a screwdriver with me in case they pulled a knife. We weren't allowed to carry guns, but I was always ready to poke at their eyes with my screwdriver. The Filipinos didn't do anything to me, for I had some acquaintances among them.

The government announced the place where the residents of Terminal Island should go on the first of February. I was arrested on that day. It was about eight o'clock in the morning when the FBI agent came over. The agent said, "I'd like to ask you some questions. You must come with me." "I haven't had my breakfast yet; wait a while," I said. I served him a cup of coffee and changed my clothes. He took me to the immigration office. Every fisherman who had a license with a picture had been arrested. At first we were told that we'd be detained for only fifteen minutes or so, but the FBI didn't let us go. They should have told us the truth in the beginning. If they had told us, we could have been prepared. I would neither have escaped nor hidden. After staying there for several days, we were sent away by bus. Then we got on a train. Since the blinds were down, none of us knew where we got on or off the train.

We were sent to Bismarck on the Great Water. Being around the tenth of February, it was severely cold. The unprepared ones had only a shirt. I was cold and hungry all the time in the camp. I was afraid I might not be able to get out of there alive. The food was terrible for a while, and the rice was just like glue. We were given only a few spoonfuls of rice with a trace of meat in it. I was too hungry to sleep at night, but it didn't sound graceful to complain about our hunger all the time, so everybody clenched his teeth and bore the hunger like a warrior's son. Later on, a Japanese cook came, and the food improved.

Half of the people in the camp were German; also Italians were there. Each one of us was called and asked questions by the FBI. Some were hit and treated roughly. Though I was expecting to be hit at any time, I wasn't. They asked me, "If Japanese soldiers come here, what will you do? To which country will you pledge your loyalty?" I answered, "It's impossible for the Japanese to cross the Pacific Ocean. Don't ask me such silly questions." They were trying to test our loyalty. They also asked me, "Is anyone in your family in the active Japanese armed forces now?" I answered, "My brother used to serve in the Navy before this war." I thought I would be sent back to Japan eventually, but I was able to join my wife after seven months in Bismarck.

Sadakusu Enomoto

About one week after Pearl Harbor was attacked, the FBI came to my place. They let us carry on the business, but they investigated our books. I didn't do anything illegal; so I wasn't afraid at all. I had to close my business when they took me to an internment camp in North Dakota about one month later.

Rumors started that we would be put in camps, but I didn't think we would be killed. When we were traveling by train to North Dakota, the shades were always down; and whenever we stopped, there were machine guns. But there were so many of us together that I wasn't scared. I thought they did those things because of the war.

The government controlled the camp, and everything was orderly. I think the United States took good care of us. Food was plentiful. I don't know what Japan would have done under similar circumstances. I think there were about four hundred internees. The director of our trading company and many other well-known Japanese were there. There weren't any particular problems—it was wartime and I thought the Japanese government was probably doing the same.

When I was interned at the camp in North Dakota, my wife and five children moved to Denver, Colorado. When the evacuation order came, they moved on their own and did not go into WRA (War Relocation Authority) centers. After my hearing was over, I joined my family in Denver from North Dakota. We rented a house and stayed there until the war ended. I was around sixty years old then.

Tokushiga Kizuka

I was home for lunch after working in the field and had the radio on. When they announced the attack, I was so surprised I just could not believe it. I did not know what was going to happen to us, so I couldn't even work.

About one year after I bought my own land, I became a board member of a Japanese organization until World War II. I was in the *kendo* group, and the *Heimusha-kai,* which was established after the Manchurian War and later became a political issue before World War II began. I was also involved in the Japanese school, *Nihongo-gakuin,* which was built on my property. That was the reason I was imprisoned.

About one week after the war broke out, I was taken to Bismarck, North Dakota. I stayed there for about seven months. Then we were taken to Roseburg, New Mexico, which is located in the middle of the desert and is very hot, and spent the next two years and four months there. My family was in the Poston WRA (War Relocation Authority) Camp. After I was paroled, I went to join them, and I lived at Poston for about one year. By the time I joined them, they had a very nice school with many amusements such as flower arranging, recitation of Chinese poems, and movies once a week. It was a well-equipped camp.

Masao Hirata

I was worried and wondered what was going on. Banks refused to let me withdraw the money I had saved. We had lived there for ten years. My six children had been able to go to any shop they wanted without money and the stores would bill me later. But various rules were made after the outbreak of the war that prevented us from shopping. For example, we had to apologize before entering stores. A lot of news about the people arrested by the FBI began to be reported in newspapers. I was afraid of getting arrested, because I had a wife and six children to support. I had already planted seedlings on fifty acres of land, and all our money was invested in the farm. What could we do if I were arrested? So I started burying the things which might cause any trouble. Since I was practicing *kendo,* I had a lot of materials on it. I put those things together, dug a hole, and buried them. Then my wife suggested that burying was not safe enough and that we should burn them. So we started burning the things. Books were especially difficult to burn; so we had to tear pages piece by piece. We burned a lot of books. But on February 21, when I came home from work, the FBI was waiting to arrest me. I will never forget that day.

There was nothing for me to do. Two men from the FBI were waiting for me at my house and told me that they were arresting me as a foreign resident of an enemy country. They took me to jail in Indio. Then that same night around midnight I was moved to a jail in Riverside. The next morning I was taken to Pasadena and stayed there until they took me and others who were arrested to Santa Fe, New Mexico, for a hearing. After that, they divided us into groups such as the group to release, to parole, and to intern. They put a number on my clothes and took my picture as an internee. A card was written that I would be treated just as an internee. After the hearing, I told the people in the same group that we would be treated as internees according to the card. But they said, "No, how can we be internees since we are noncombatants?" But my guess was right. The others were mainly the leaders of various Japanese communities in America, such as investors in real estate and the president of the Central Japanese Association. Even though I had practiced *kendo* and also worked as a president of an association and as vice-president of an industrial union, I was not an important person for the Army.

On June 12, Army officers came, put each of us internees in a bathroom, and checked our bodies and our possessions. They put us on a train without telling us where we were being taken. Everyone on the train and those left in the camp cried because we didn't know where they would take us. The Army put a camp in the middle of the desert in Roseburg. There was a high watchtower and machine guns were set. They took away all of our possessions including money and locked us in a room. They told us that they would shoot us if we got closer than three feet of the fence. I stayed in that camp for one year, until 1943.

My wife sent two postcards to me. If they were written in Japanese it took one month to reach me because they were sent to New York to check the contents. Written in English, it took less time for them to be delivered because the Army checked them. At that time my eldest daughter was eleven or twelve years old, and she translated my letters in English for my wife and wrote letters to me for my wife.

I worried about my wife and my six little children whom I had left behind. I also worried about the land already planted with seedlings. You can't imagine how I felt at that time. I would have been happier if they had put my family together in a camp. Being separated from them made it unbearable.

In Roseburg they divided us into groups of thirty people and put each group in a shack. Beds were set up for us in it. They made us work a little bit. Every month we were given a three-dollar coupon. We spent ten cents each day, getting either a box of cigarettes or a beer. We talked about everything freely. We also listened to the radio news from Japan. We were not allowed to have a radio, but someone caught the broadcast by some means. I don't know how. Life in camp was not so strict. The only thing we had to do was to obey the rules.

Once we went on strike against their making us work. Then they ordered us not to go out of the shack except to go to the bathroom. Even when we went to the bathroom, a guard followed us. We younger people in our forties or fifties could stand it, but for the older people it was torture to be kept in an awfully hot room without a fan; so we gave up the strike.

I was angry at the way they treated families, separating us from our wives and children. Everybody else was mad too. When a family reunion became possible, they sent me to the camp in Poston, where my family was.

I was so happy to see my family again. The standard of living was much better than in Roseburg. A lot of things were furnished, even a golfing area, and we were allowed to go fishing.

JUHEI KONO

I was in Hawaii during the war. I had been sent to Lahaina to solve some church problems there. After the problems were solved, I was ready to come back to Honolulu. Then, boom! The war began, and I had to stay in Lahaina.

Immediately after Pearl Harbor was attacked, of course, all the Nisei people stood up and tried to defend Hawaii from a Japanese invasion. They took up guns and stood watch all night. They put barbed wire all along the coastline. After all this was done, people began to say that they didn't need the services of the Nisei. At that time the order for martial law came from the commander, and they took all arms away from the Nisei. The timing of events was really disappointing, for the Nisei wanted to do their best for America, and yet America did not allow them to do so. Wherever we went, anti-Japanese propaganda appeared. The Issei could speak only Japanese, and yet they were not allowed to speak Japanese in public. That kind of suffering is, in a sense, all right for the Issei, but the kind of suffering that the American-born

Japanese had to go through was special: They were not recognized as American citizens.

Nisei students at the University of Hawaii decided that the best thing to do was for them to die for America;[1] so they drafted a resolution, "We will stand up and die for America, give our lives to America." With that spirit they appealed to the commander in Honolulu. [Lieutenant-General Delos C.] Emmons was the commander at that time. In a petition they stated: "We are American citizens, yet the American government refuses our service. If the government decides to use us not as soldiers but as workers in a labor battalion, we will give our services to America as laborers. We don't ask for any salary as long as you provide us with a place to live and food to eat. If there is a dangerous task, we are prepared to give our lives." After Commander Emmons read this petition, he said, "I really cried. We didn't know the spirit of these people." Emmons gave this letter to the Honolulu newspapers, and the newspapers in turn wrote about this appeal. That marked the beginning of a change in the Hawaiian people's attitude toward the Japanese in Hawaii. They used to think the Japanese were dangerous. They called us "Jap" and said, "A Jap is a Jap," when, in fact, they were American citizens. But after this support from Emmons appeared in the newspapers, people began to think differently.

This idea of a labor battalion was adopted, and the Nisei students began working for the Army, or wherever they were wanted. They called the labor force the Varsity Victory Volunteer Corps. There were seventy or eighty people, and later it increased to a hundred and fifty or so. Finally, they had to reject volunteers because there were just too many. The Varsity Victory Volunteer Corps was visible throughout Hawaii. The commander and everybody else kept close watch on them to see how they were doing, and they did fine work. The newspapers began to write about the beautiful things they were doing. Almost every week stories of the VVV appeared in the newspapers. Now, this changed the minds of the Hawaiian people, and they gradually began to think, "Japanese are after all—even though they are of the enemy's race—trustworthy." Later, because of the VVV, the 442nd Volunteer Corps [the 442nd Regimental Combat Team] was formed. The VVV was proof of Japanese-American loyalty.

[1]The phrase "to die for America" underscores the belief that Japanese do not go to war with the idea that they will personally survive.

Behind the story of the 442nd we should not forget the VVV's great spirit of sacrifice.[2] So few people remember the VVV, but I was really impressed.

MRS. TAKAE WASHIZU

Masaki heard about it and told us the news. My husband and I didn't believe it in the beginning. Then a next-door neighbor's wife said the same thing, and I knew Masaki was right. The president of the Japanese association told us that the Japanese military forces had attacked Pearl Harbor and that we should be careful when we had to go out. I was mad at Japan for having done such a foolish thing. We had been told before that the Japanese forces would come to the United States on a number of military boats and save us whenever war broke out. On the contrary, Japan created the worst problem ever for the Japanese people in the United States.

In the meantime, the Japanese people on the West Coast were notified to move out by May. Several weeks before May, soldiers came around and posted notices on telephone poles. It was sad for me to leave the place where I had been living for such a long time. Staring at the ceiling in bed at night, I wondered who would take care of my cherry tree and my house after we moved out. I also thought about my mother in Japan. I regretted not having returned to Japan earlier. Soldiers came, and I was moved with the other Japanese people from Sacramento. In my childhood a number of soldiers passed through our village once in a while. All of the villagers welcomed the soldiers. The soldiers encouraged children to become brave men. My image of Japanese soldiers was good. However, the American soldiers who attended the evacuation were mean. Whenever I did something wrong, they put the muzzle of their rifle on my long hair. Other soldiers sent from the WRA (War Relocation Authority) also had rifles. They checked to see if we had cameras or weapons. The evacuation started around noon. We were given sandwiches, oranges, and milk for lunch. Each family was given a number. The bill for the evacuation camp had been passed, so that the camp was legal.

---

[2]With the exception of high-ranking officers, the 442nd Combat Regiment was composed of only Japanese Americans and was recognized as the most decorated unit of its size and length of service in American military history.

10

Possessions

In addition to the five-mile travel restriction that was imposed immediately, the Japanese community learned on December 19 that the United States Treasury Department had frozen bank accounts bearing Japanese names. This government restriction was later modified to allow withdrawals of up to one hundred dollars per month. Plans for evacuating all West Coast Japanese were discussed, and on February 19, 1942, President Franklin D. Roosevelt signed Executive Order No. 9066, which authorized the secretary of war to undertake a massive evacuation of all persons of Japanese descent on the West Coast.

Evacuation dates posted in Japanese communities permitted only a few months, and in some instances only a few days, to make decisions about whether or not to sell property; therefore, the sale and storage of goods were completed at a huge economic disadvantage. The evacuees had the additional restriction of being allowed to take only what they could carry in their own two hands; so the problem of liquidating assets and personal belongings was even more burdensome.

Most evacuees were first transported to assembly centers for a few months to await the completion of the more permanent relocation centers to which they were eventually moved.

Tsuguo Nagasawa

Here in Portland there was a grocery store owned by a Chinese man four or five blocks away from my store. He put up a sign: "This is not a Japanese store." The Japanese people were discriminated against that much. There was nothing I could do about it. The customers, who had been dealing with me for over ten years, changed their attitude abruptly and shopped at another store. No violence was done to me, but they didn't shop at my store.

The white people knew that the Japanese people had to be evacuated to assembly centers by a certain date. We had two and a half months. In the meantime, Mr. Furuya, who had loaned me the money for the business, went bankrupt, and a state bank superintendent came down to Portland. The bank superintendent sat at the counter and told me that he'd close down the store unless I made a payment. It was such a cruel thing to do, but I obeyed him.

A big businessman came to ask if I wanted to sell my store. I felt miserable. I had to experience such a thing only because I was Japanese. Although wholesale stores bought back some items, the market price of the goods had gone up by then. However, they bought back the goods at the original price in the invoice. That was highly irregular, but I was in a weak position. Selling goods individually wouldn't help me pay off the loan. Returning them to the wholesalers brought in a larger sum of money; therefore, I put up with returning the goods to the wholesalers at the original price because I was Japanese and the times were bad.

MRS. RIYO ORITE

Hearing a lot of rumors from my customers every day, I felt uneasy. They tried to encourage me, but I felt helpless about the boarding house and procrastinated about closing this business. My husband had died the year before, and it was a difficult time. Then the evacuation came along. It was awful. Because of racial prejudice, people threw rocks at us, and I was scared and worried. Most of the Japanese stores had closed down; therefore, I had to shop at a Chinese store in order to feed my customers. I had to start packing my things, but I was unable to do much as long as the customers remained. As the evacuation day drew near, I asked the customers to move out ten days ahead so that I could set things right. My children weren't much help, for they were young. The boarding house was large, with sixty rooms which I had to clean. Each bedroom was equipped with a bed, dresser, chair, bedspread, quilt, and so on. I requested the government to pay five dollars for each room. They didn't pay me that much. I left the boarding house to them almost free of charge. It couldn't be helped. I only got paid one hundred and fifty dollars for a sixty-room building. I had no choice in the matter.

MINEJIRO SHIBATA

During the war we went completely broke. The government didn't take away our fishing boats but kept them and let others with citizenship use them. The users never paid the rent. Moreover, every owner found that some of the tools stored in his boat were missing. Everybody suffered loss.

My wife remained on Terminal Island when I was arrested by the FBI. The Japanese there were only given two days notice before they had to evacuate sometime in February. Not knowing what to do, my wife piled up all of our things on my car and sold everything for seventy-five dollars. The government claims that they have compensated us for our loss, but the compensation wasn't enough for us to regain our property.

RIICHI SATOW

We were told to take only as much as we could carry in our two hands. How much could you carry in your two hands? One big suitcase . . . well, how can you really manage with a big stuffed suitcase? Knives were not allowed, nor household cutlery, nor guns, of course. We left our possessions in one of the rooms of our house which we arranged to be rented out when we left for the camp. We asked someone to watch it for us. Then, with whatever we could carry in our hands as instructed, we got on a train. Books were impossible. . . . The possibility of being sent to a cold place made me worry because I had many children to take care of, so we took as much clothing as possible. Whether they were rags or not, it didn't matter. It turned out, though, that the weather that welcomed us in the camp was very hot, and we didn't need any heavy clothing.

MRS. TOME TAKATSUKI

When we were evacuated, the Japanese home owners were not able to use their names to purchase a house, so they had used their children's names or names of their friends who had American citizenship. They were at a loss as to what to do with their property. There was a real estate establishment in Sacramento named Avis and Cox.* The person named Avis was a bad man. I heard from many people that they lost their homes due to his dishonest transactions.

Mrs. Rikae Inouye

We hadn't purchased the property yet and were still renting. We had many sets of tools, and we were asked to sell them for almost nothing. Thieves also came in those days, for we didn't lock anything up. We put new tractor tires in the barn, and thieves took them. We evacuated after having sold the tools for almost nothing. It was awful.

Shoichi Fukuda

I was in the hospital for sixty days, and I was so sick I could not see anything for forty days. The day the war broke out, December 7, 1941, was the day when I got out of bed and walked for the first time. I had to walk along the wall because I was so weak.

We could not travel further than five miles from our house. Our church was in Sacramento, beyond the distance that we were permitted to travel; so we could not go to church. Although we lived in Florin, our business was in Sacramento; we did not know what to do. All the banks were closed to us; we could not take anything out. The accounts were reopened for us later in the camps, and the money was returned to us there. I was not able to go to the bank in Sacramento, because it was located more than five miles away from my home; so I had to transfer my account to the bank in Elk Grove.

As for my business, the materials (bolts of cloth and other dry goods) that I bought to sell were stacked to the ceiling in my wife's room. I wanted to sell these things to the people in the Lodi area after the grape season was over. Well, I had to sell all these materials to pay my doctors and the hospital. I was still weak; so I stayed in the car and my wife went out to do the selling. I could sell only the things which I had at home, because I did not know when we would have to evacuate. We sold our goods at half price because once we were evacuated, we would have to leave every-

*A pseudonym.

thing behind. We had to limit our sales to the houses which were within that five-mile radius. Even under such conditions, we were able to sell all the items we had.

While I was sick, I could not work; so I could not pay the wholesale stores. The owner of the wholesale store trusted me and said, "Bring the money anytime you are able to do so." I usually did business on a cash basis and was a very good buyer from this wholesale store. I just *had* to make enough money and pay them back. I was very glad when I was able to repay that debt.

The people in San Pedro were evacuated first. We were evacuated just about last—sometime in May. We did not receive any personal notice of evacuation. The notices were posted on the telephone poles by the highway on a Thursday. I suppose the government put them up in the morning, but I did not know about it until evening. The next day, representatives from the Florin JACL (Japanese American Citizens' League) chapter came to see us, and told us that we would be evacuated on Sunday morning. We had only two days to prepare. We were told that we were leaving at seven in the morning from the Florin train station. We were to gather there and would be transported by bus. We were told to take only as much as we could carry in our hands. We were not to carry anything with a blade or anything which might be dangerous, such as guns.

On Friday, I went to the bank in Elk Grove and withdrew all the money we had there and bought coats and other clothing worth one hundred dollars. Everybody told us to buy many things to keep white people happy, so we bought lots of things, especially clothing. Our children had some savings, but as we had no assurance as to what might happen to the money, we drew out the money and bought overcoats for each.

Before the evacuation orders came, I had made an arrangement with a white man to sell our truck. We had just purchased a good stove, a piano, and a radio. We had to sell these things we owned very cheaply. Many white people came into homes and asked the occupants to leave their things for them. They knew that the Japanese people had to evacuate and sell whatever they owned at a loss. When the evacuating Japanese quoted a price for their household goods, they were told that the price was too much and were forced to sell them on the buyer's terms. For instance, the stove for which we paid two hundred dollars was sold for fifteen. It was the same with the radio, washing machine, and all other tools and appliances. We had to sell everything so cheaply that it was just like throwing things away, but when we came back, we could not even buy a washing machine. One person came in and asked us to leave everything—curtains and all. I guess he did not have anything in his own home. The day we moved, I called up this person, but he did not come, so we had to close the house and leave.

I had no choice but to sell our panel truck, which I had bought a year before for four hundred dollars. I made an agreement with the purchaser that I could use the truck until the day of evacuation. However, this man did not show up on the day of evacuation either. I did not know what to do, so I loaded it up with our luggage and went to the gathering place. When I left town, I asked a friend, a garage owner, to keep the truck for me. He later sold it for us for one hundred dollars. We had asked people in the Christian Center to take care of our home, so we called them up and confirmed the arrangement. Even to say "good-by" we had to ask a friend to come within the five-mile area allowed us. We packed strawberries, had a picnic, and promised to see each other again.

PART IV:
THE CAMPS

11

Feelings

TSUGUO NAGASAWA

On the 7th of December in 1941, the Pearl Harbor attack came. Such a catastrophe had actually occurred! Asleep or awake, I felt as if I were losing the color in my face. In such an emergency, material losses or gains were beyond my concern. A big war had broken out! I knew that our lives as well as our property were at stake. I wondered what would happen to us . . . after all, being put into a camp. Some people said we would be put into a camp and an airplane would be crashed on us to kill us. Many people were worried about that.

MRS. RIYO ORITE

I felt that we were being protected in the camp. The reason I felt so is that I had been treated terribly before I moved to the camp. People threw rocks at me and did all kinds of other bad things to me, though the government had issued an ordinance to prevent such misdemeanors. I didn't feel like living outside of the camp. I wanted to go as soon as possible.

We arrived at the Tule Lake Camp by the end of 1942. We stayed there for less than two years, and then were moved to the Topaz Camp. There were only Japanese people in the camp, and many were skilled people who started classes to teach various things. There were English classes, sewing classes, and some others. You were free to choose any according to your interests. One highly educated married lady came to the camp. She said, "You'd better learn English because you won't stay here for good. When you have your own job, you'll need English." I decided to attend an English class. The more I began to understand, the more things I felt interested in.

I and Mrs. Mizobe were good friends in Topaz. We had fun together climbing mountains and collecting shells. We didn't have to worry about cooking or buying food in the camp. Some people complained about the camp. It may not be good that I express my positive feelings, but the war is over now.

Topaz is located on reclaimed land and used to be a lake; so we found a lot of shells. We picked up shells and worked with them making artificial flowers and pins for our dresses in one class. Before coming to the camp, I had to plan menus, cook, and work hard for the others in a sixty-room boarding house. In camp I didn't have to cook breakfast after getting up in the morning; a bath was made for us, meals were served, and we didn't have to wash dishes. It was as if we were millionaires. I enjoyed camp life. If it hadn't been wartime, life there could have been a paradise. I had no idea what would happen to the Japanese. However, I appreciated being able to lead such a life in spite of the war.

MRS. RIKAE INOUYE

Hearing the news, I became discouraged and very saddened. I couldn't go to the market and sell. Our eldest son, Minoru, came home from school—he was a junior in high school.[1] I told him, "Minoru, Japan has lodged an attack." Minoru hadn't heard the news yet. He threw his notebooks on the sofa and said, "The Japanese have lost face." I felt sorry for him. He had been getting along well with his white friends. I didn't know what to say. I felt Japan was thoughtless. I didn't think Japan understood.

About the evacuation? Some people complained about the evacuation, for those with United States citizenship were also evacuated. I feel that the Japanese people were put in there [camps] to avoid danger. There were a lot of bad people. You couldn't tell who had citizenship. I didn't complain even a little bit, for I thought we were put in there for the sake of safety. Others complained harshly that even the United States citizens

[1]Mrs. Inouye has probably mistaken the time sequence of her conversation. Hawaii was attacked on a Sunday, which is not a school day.

were put in the camps. I didn't agree with them at all. We were put in there for the sake of safety. I didn't complain.

Nisuke Mitsumori

Though a lot of people objected to the relocation, I myself believed it was good for the Japanese. After the war started, all the Japanese leaders were taken away and detained. I was the only person who still maintained an office in Los Angeles, and a lot of Japanese came to my office to consult me. All Japanese were considered the enemy once the war started, and people felt that Japanese should not be hired. Such an order never came, but it was the general mood during that time.[2] Approximately ten Japanese who were working for a government office felt they could no longer work for the department, because they were considered enemy aliens, and their representative came to see me and ask for help. They were really in trouble, for they were unable to find any other jobs and didn't have enough savings. I told them not to worry. I thought America was a Christian country and she would not let her people starve to death. I knew that in World War I enemy soldiers were well fed, clothed, and sheltered when they surrendered. I believed that the United States government would not let the Japanese suffer. I told them not to worry and that a new way would be opened for them, and they went back.

Those who managed hotels came to me and complained that they could no longer collect charges. People who had grocery stores could not collect on charge accounts from customers. Everybody was worried and uneasy about what would happen in the future. From early in the morning to late at night I was overwhelmed by people's complaints, inquiries, and worries. Some woman's husband was taken away by the FBI, and she could no longer pay rent for her place. She asked me when her husband would come back, but I had no idea when he would be released. A lot of women and children were in trouble after their husbands were taken away. With five or six children, these women did not know what to do in the absence of their husbands. They could not draw more than one hundred dollars at a time from a bank. Assets

[2]Many persons of Japanese ancestry were discharged by both public and private employers, evicted from residences, and suffered economic boycotts. In February 1942, the California State Personnel Board voted to bar all "descendants of nationals with whom the United States is at war" from future civil service positions.

were frozen, there were no jobs, but still we had to make payments.

When I heard about the evacuation, I really thought that the Japanese would be rescued. Our worries and uneasiness would be solved by this. A lot of people say that it was inhuman, but I feel that war changes the psychology of people. In such abnormal circumstances as a war, the duties, obligations, reason, and justice we normally possess become paralyzed. There was nobody to help us when we got hurt under these circumstances, so the only thing I hoped was that something could be done to save our lives. I was delighted to hear news of the evacuation, for I had listened to so many people's worries. Not really understanding the circumstances under which we lived then, a lot of people say that it was inhuman, undemocratic, and un-Christian. Neither reason nor common sense would work in such an emergency situation like the war. People were frantic then. So if you ask me what I think of the evacuation, I still think it was good for the Japanese. At least it provided us some stability.

MASAO ITANO

My eldest son Harvey finished U.C., but he was not able to take the final examination due to the evacuation. Since he had maintained straight A's all through college, they allowed him an A grade without having the final test. He was the first person in the history of the University who maintained straight A's all through his academic years, and he received a gold medal for it. It was sent to him in the Tule Lake Camp. He was in Berkeley attending school at the time of the outbreak of the war, but he joined the family in Sacramento and went to Walerga Assembly Center near Sacramento and then to Tule Lake in northern California.

RIICHI SATOW

How would it be possible to make a living? . . . that was the biggest question that came to my mind. I had a large family, and the children were still small. The eldest was then going to a junior college and was able to work if she would quit school, which she did eventually. The problem still remained: How were we going to live in this country as enemy aliens? Would it really be possible to stay here and make a decent and reasonable living? When the news came that we were going to be put in a camp, it in fact eased my mind, because in it I saw the possibility of getting our life stabilized. And at least the fear that the government was going to let us starve was gone. You see, some people were actively stating that the government was going to make us all starve to death. There were thousands of wild rumors going around, and some sounded as if they were true, authentic stories. One other rumor had it that they were going to machine-gun all of us down. Besides those rumors, there were very irresponsible articles in some papers. Once in a Sacramento paper someone wrote that we Japanese must be evacuated—you see, we were branded as a public nuisance by this editor—although it would be a waste of money, and that the authorities should send the Japanese to remote places to let us starve. Such an article was actually written by one of the editorial staff and printed. I read one myself. Under such circumstances you can't blame people for spreading the kinds of rumors I told you about. It turned out that our lives were not endangered in the camp after all. I sensed it after a few days there. I thought that although there were lots of rumors told, nothing like that would actually happen, and that the U.S. government would assume its responsibility of looking after us.

Kengo Tajima

Well, my primary idea was that I was a pastor and should do the best thing for the people to be reconciled to their situation and to do their best under the circumstances. I always tried to see the good side, the light side of things. Not *"shikata ga nai,"* (it can't be helped, it's fate), but that I should do the best under the circumstances and see the good side, even though there were soldiers guarding the camp.

One of the boys, a mischievous child, would run out of the wire fence to the store across the street to buy things. A soldier who was there to prevent such things just took the child and carried him across the street to the store. It was a beautiful thing for him to do.

Tokushiga Kizuka

It is rather hard to say, but when a person is imprisoned in a camp surrounded with barbed wire—if he has no freedom, he

loses all hope and gets to where he doesn't care anymore. That is
how I felt. For someone who had his own business, worked hard,
suddenly lost everything and was imprisoned, it was very hard,
particularly after what the government did to the American-born
Japanese. The government deprived them of the rights of American citizens; yet they imposed the duties of American citizenship. That I did not like. Of course, I was Japanese-born, so I could
not become a naturalized citizen. But the Nisei were born and
educated in America; they are true Americans. Knowing that
other Americans, who were supposed to be the believers of Christianity, did things like this—it was hard to take.

Yoshito Fujii

We were at the Puyallup Assembly Center about a month or
two. In the meantime, a crew was sent to Idaho to construct a
camp there. Everybody gave up and accepted the situation as a
wartime misery. Japanese people cooperate in times of hardship.
Everybody was considerate enough not to cause any inconvenience. The assembly center was fairly well organized, I wasn't in
the mood to complain about anything. The young people there
took care of things very well. After we moved to the Minidoka
Relocation Center, I wanted to take it easy and not work. The
headquarters asked me to apply for a job. I was leading a lazy life
without work. Even if you work hard, you never know what
might happen to your life, and I had given up life to a certain
degree. I just hoped that my children would lead a happy life. I
said that I'd rather make my best efforts toward my children's
education.

Mrs. Ai Miyasaki

Japan did such a terrible thing, and we were immigrants of the
enemy country. It was reasonable that we would be put in camp.
Very often people complained about the living conditions. They
would say, "When we were outside, we never ate such things." I
felt that people ought not to complain. If this was Japan, would
we be treated as well? Although we were put in camp and felt
miserable, we were aliens. We should be grateful to receive things
in sufficient quantity and have decent treatment. People were
wasteful like with the hot water for baths or milk, which people
were throwing away. I thought that this is group living; so people

should not be selfish. All should be considered, and everything done for the benefit of the group. People who said that they lived so good outside really did not.

But American-born Nisei were put in camp too. When I thought about it, it brought tears to my eyes. That was a big mistake. Even now the nation admits it. Since Nisei were not recognized as American citizens, they were put in camps. And yet, America drafted the Nisei into the army. America was in error.

SADAME INOUYE

According to my diary, I seemed to have enjoyed life in the camp. Since I did not need to work for a living, I had time to read or to do things I liked. Being put in camp? I thought it could not be helped since we were foreigners of the enemy country. However, I thought it was not fair to put Nisei in the camp. My oldest son was just the age to be drafted at that time. However, he had a problem and was put back in camp after a physical examination. To our surprise, as soon as my son became better, the military people came and took him away. I thought it was very unfair that all the young Nisei men were taken for military service while all the Japanese were kept in the camps. I saw a great contradiction there. When my son left the camp in 1944 or 1945, Germany was still fighting strongly. I remember that I was so relieved when I heard from my son a few days later.

MRS. KO TAKAKOSHI

After we got into the camp, some of our friends' sons went in to serve in the U.S. Army, and some were killed in action. Because of illness, one family returned to Japan, leaving their two sons. The elder boy didn't have to serve, but the younger boy went and was killed in action. I still remember the warm handshake with him when he left. That was one of the saddest occasions I remember. Because his parents weren't around, they gave me his flag. I later gave it to his elder brother. Then my best friend's son, who had a young wife and a little baby, was killed in action. It was very, very sad.

MRS. KAMECHIYO TAKAHASHI

We had bought a house and my husband had been happy just to smell the trees in the garden up until we were evacuated. We lived there only for a year and four months. It was great to own a house of our own. Even mowing weeds gave us pleasure. In the meantime, the war started and Takahashi regretted having bought a house.

My husband was president of the San Mateo Japanese association and also chairman of the Japanese school. There was a list of Japanese people to be arrested in those days. We heard that Takahashi was on the list. Meanwhile, his brother, who was treasurer of the Japanese school, was arrested. Having seen his brother being arrested, Takahashi was so worried that when he came back home on that day, he vomited blood. As this was during the war, he couldn't enter a certain hospital. I had given up midwifery and was working as a dressmaker for a white family; the husband was the chairman of this particular hospital. Though the man liked me and wanted to help my husband, he couldn't arrange special accommodations for my husband due to the objection of others; therefore, my husband entered a county hospital. Being shaken on the stretcher, he vomited blood again on the way to the hospital. I packed two suitcases in case Takahashi should be arrested, but he never needed them.

Takahashi was fine for a while in the camp. Being exhausted, I got very ill and was hospitalized. I guess Takahashi got high blood pressure being worried about my illness. He usually visited me in the hospital at three in the afternoon. One day, he told me that he would visit me again in the evening and asked me if I wanted him to bring me anything. That was our last conversation.

I was wondering why he hadn't shown up when our son came and told me that Takahashi had had a fit of apoplexy and been carried to a hospital. He didn't intend to tell me if my husband had recovered. Takahashi never got well. Being weak myself, I almost couldn't bear my husband's death. My husband, having suffered from a serious illness, lived till our sons grew up, at least. But my life in Topaz Camp was miserable. I made a desperate effort to endure the hardship, but I wished I had been sent for by the Lord with my husband.

Minejiro Shibata

My wife and children remained on Terminal Island for a few months, until the Navy ordered her to move out within forty-eight hours. She sold my car and other belongings to the junk shop for a low price. She moved to another place and stayed there for about ten months until she was sent to the Santa Anita race track. After staying in Bismarck (internment camp) for seven months, I was able to join my wife at Santa Anita.

When I arrived there, I saw my wife and children sweeping the stable. The stable was smelly from the dung. I hated the smell there. After staying at Santa Anita for a month, we finally moved to Arkansas. It wasn't the doing of private citizens, but it was the government's doing. I will never forget this dirty affair.

MRS. TAKAE WASHIZU

After settling in the assembly center, Issei men were spreading one false rumor after another. They hid a short-wave radio in one of their beds and listened to the news from Japan. Japan announced only the battles she had won; therefore, the Issei misunderstood the situation and thought that Japan was fighting well. After we were transferred to the camp in Tule Lake, we had better facilities, such as a sewer toilet, and a separate dining place for each family. They hired teachers to teach us English, flower arrangement, *go* (a Japanese game using a checkerboard and smooth stones), and *shogi* (Japanese chess). Though some Japanese people complained about the food in the camp, I honestly appreciated the meals there. Japanese people weren't used to American food. That's why they complained. The food itself was good. When I left the camp, I expressed my appreciation.

I respected the United States because of what the government had done for us. Making a promise is one thing; carrying out one's promise is another. The United States was great, for it not only kept its word that it would protect us, but also gave us freedom to develop our interests.

MR. OSUKE TAKIZAWA AND MRS. SADAE TAKIZAWA

MR.: We went to the stable, Tanforan Assembly Center. It was terrible. The government moved the horses out and put us in. The stable stunk awfully. I felt miserable, but I couldn't do anything. It was like a prison, guards were on duty all the time, and there was barbed wire all around us. We really worried about our future. I just gave up.

MRS.: Though I was tired, I couldn't sleep because of the bad smell. It was hell. Everybody felt lonely and anxious about the future. In a word, we were confused. Deep down, we felt anger. It was a melancholy, complex feeling.

MR.: I was all mixed-up. We couldn't do anything about the orders from the U.S. government. I just lived from day to day without any purpose. I felt empty. I couldn't plan details for the following day like: Let's write a letter tomorrow. I frittered away every day. I don't remember anything much. As I told you, I just felt vacant. I didn't go out with friends, I didn't study writing, and I didn't go to church, either. We moved to Topaz in September. Before moving there, everybody, being worried, was extremely touchy.

MRS.: I composed verses expressing my feelings at Tanforan.

Inishie no Noah no kōzui Shinobu kana Dōto sakamaku Goto ki konogoro	*Translation:* I recall Noah's flood in ancient times. Angry waves were surging in these days.
Oya mo ko mo Kokoro susabi te Koe arashi Kuiru kokoro to Samishiki kokoro to	*Translation:* Both parents and children are in a rage. Their voices are harsh. Feelings of regret and loneliness exist simultaneously.
Minamina wa Izuchi ikuran Ate mo naku Tada bozen to Hibi o okuritsu	*Translation:* Nobody knows which way to go. They just pass their days vacantly.

The next poems were composed after I got to Tanforan. We lined up every meal time.

En-ento Choda no gotoku Retsu o nashi Jinpūo no naka ni Shokuji matsu mure	*Translation:* People are crowded in a long line like a snake. The crowd is waiting for a meal in the dust and wind.

"*Jinpu*" means dust and wind, the red dusty wind.

Ware mo mata Yamato omina no Hashi nareba	*Translation:* Because I am a Japanese woman, I should stand firmly at all times.

Tsuyoku zo tatame
Ikanaru toki nimo

"Toki" doesn't mean "time." It is the character for the fall season, which means an important occasion. Even in such a place . . .

Sansan to
Noboru asahi ni
Iro haete
Ran no shinme wa
Kaze ni soyogeri

Translation: The new buds of orchids are shining in the brilliant rising sun, and swinging in the breeze.

Inetsu okitsu
Shokuji ni kayoi
Ichinichi o
Koko ni sugosu ka
Hassen no hitobito

Translation: Eight thousand people spend day after day here sleeping, getting up, and coming out for meals.

Odoro odoro
Tachisawagu nari
Waga tama wa
Soko shirenu fuchi ni
Nozomishi gotoku

Translation: Standing at the edge of an abyss, my soul is deeply agitated, running in fright.

Kore wa somo
Mahiru no yume ka
Itsu no hi ni
Samen to suran
Yo no yume no gotoku

Translation: Is this a daydream? It is just like an endless dream at night. When will I wake up?

We got food without working. We were given beans or something. I didn't know what to do. Food didn't taste good, for I didn't have an appetite, leading such a life. Everybody complained and felt miserable.

WATARU ISHISAKA

Well, our hardships began from that time on. When we entered the camp, I had different ideas from most of the Issei. I never thought that Americans would hurt us or kill us. But I believe that America revealed the worst part of its political system to the whole world during the war. Though the Japanese obediently followed the orders, the government did something which was against its own Constitution. It really is a shame. There supposedly is no way possible to evacuate citizens of the USA and place them in camps without due process of law. It was one of the most shameful acts in American history. But I did not lose pride as a Japanese. There was a black attorney by the name of Michael. He really worked for the Japanese people in Colorado. The whites in the camp did everything they could for us, and I'm very grateful.

The people who suffered the most were the older Issei. They were taken to those strange places, and many of them died there. Those older Issei were already in their sixties when they entered the camps.

12

Camp Life

The WRA (War Relocation Authority) administered the ten relocation centers located throughout the United States: Gila River and Poston in Arizona, Jerome and Rohwer in Arkansas, Manzanar and Tule Lake in California, Granada (Amache) in Colorado, Minidoka in Idaho, Topaz in Utah, and Heart Mountain in Wyoming.

By June 5, 1942, all persons of Japanese descent had been removed from Military Area No. 1, which included the western half of Washington, Oregon, and California and southern Arizona. By August 5, the evacuation of Military Area No. 2, the eastern half of the Pacific Coast states and northern Arizona, had been completed. Persons of Japanese descent in other parts of the United States were not required to enter the relocation centers.

SHIZUMA TAKESHITA

The Western Defense announced two zones. The Japanese and the Japanese Americans who lived in Zone No. 1, west of Highway 99, had to evacuate first. It was thought at the time that the Japanese in Zone No. 2 might not have to evacuate. We sent our children and grandchild to a place in Zone No. 2 near Marysville, California. We were planning to join them later, but the evacuation order came to Zone No. 2 also. Our son's family had to go to the Tule Lake WRA Center, and we were evacuated to the Tanforan Assembly Center. My wife and I tried to join our sons at Tule Lake, but before our transfer procedures were completed, we were moved to the Topaz Center. From there we moved to the Tule

Lake Center in 1943. Then, later on, Tule Lake was designated as a segregated center—the center for evacuees who pledged their loyalty to Japan.

SHOICHI FUKUDA

Everyone carried as much as they could and went to the assembly center, which was located near Marysville. It was a very bad camp, because it was the last one built. The contractors must have cut corners in many ways, because the barracks were very poorly constructed. Instead of laying a foundation, they brought sand from the nearby river, placed two-by-fours on it and laid the floor directly on top of that. It was the cheapest lumber one could find. The only thing separating the interior and the outside was a very thin wall.

But we had to take those barracks, because there were no others. Within a month the floor began to warp, because it was laid right on top of the sand. When the floors dried, there were strips of space between the boards, and the grass grew out from between these spaces. These barracks did not have a ceiling. Cheap lumber was used for the roof and the walls had many holes. The mess hall was very small, so people had to wait in line. When we were late, we had to wait as long as an hour to get in. Everything was on a first come, first serve, basis. We lived there for a month, and then we were taken to Tule Lake.

Because we were latecomers, all the available jobs at the Tule Lake Camp were taken; so we had no income. After some time, I finally found a job at the warehouse. I was to take care of shipments which came in from the outside. These shipments consisted of food, furniture for white civilian workers, cement for new buildings and houses, and various other things. I worked at that job for a month and was paid fourteen dollars. Meanwhile, another job opportunity opened up for me.

Winter was coming, and the barracks were not made for cold weather. The walls had many holes and so plaster boards had to be put up to keep us warm inside. This job was done on a volunteer basis, but the things that volunteers could do were finished in a very short time. Teams of men who could do the more difficult work had to be organized; so I was hired as a manager-foreman.

I organized a twenty-man crew to do the job. In the beginning I went alone to learn the job. We were paid only fourteen dollars a month; so the crew just did not have much enthusiasm. Well, it was very difficult to be the foreman. I had to make arrangements with government officials for the next contract, and my crew would not work unless I worked ahead of them as foreman. If I was not diligent, I would not be a very good example for my children; so I did my best. Even while my crew was smoking, I would be on the phone making arrangements. Our crew put out twice as much work as the others. I did this work for a while, and then I moved on to another job.

There was a co-op store in the camp, and I worked in their warehouse. All the workers and managers there were Japanese people. Later I became the assistant buyer of the drug department. The head man's name was Hamaichi, who was a licensed pharmacist. He bought all the drugs, and I bought the toilet articles. At that time I was paid the top salary, which was nineteen dollars. The Japanese doctors, dentists, and other professional people were paid the same.

After the Tule Lake Center was designated a segregated center, many people were moved out. Those people who wanted to move as a group from Tule Lake had only one camp to go to, Jerome, Arkansas. The rumor spread that Jerome was the worst camp built, that it was in the middle of a jungle and that it was very hot. But I did not mind at all. If we were to go anyplace, I wanted to try places where I had never been. Most of the church people petitioned to move as a group, and so we were sent to Jerome. It took about a week to get there. The bus which transported us was an old one. It looked like it had not been used for ten years, and these buses were pulled out for this use only.

Jerome was very hot, with such high humidity that we were very uncomfortable. However, it was a very good place in other ways. There were fireflies, *kikyo* flowers, *ominaeshi*, and others. They were similar to the ones which grew in Japan. When we arrived in Jerome, things were much more peaceful. It was a very good place to live. Even the food was better. There was no comparison, really, with Tule Lake. The people were better, and the houses were better. People in Jerome were much more cooperative and worked harder as a whole.

The Tule Lake Camp was not organized well, and the people came from too many different backgrounds. The government did not provide good leadership or good materials. Even the things which the government did for the Japanese people in other camps were not done there. The food was very bad—frozen herring, tasteless macaroni, and hot cakes. There were lots of complaints—it was just a mess there.

By September 1942, less than seven months after President Roosevelt authorized the evacuation, the WRA was outlining a resettlement plan whereby evacuees could relocate anywhere in the U.S., except the West Coast, and expanding an already operative work-leave program. In October 1942, about ten thousand Japanese evacuees were on work-leave to help harvest crops.

In Jerome, things were quite different, but a year after we arrived there, the camp was closed because many people had left. We arrived in September, and the camp was closed in June. From there we went to the Heart Mountain Camp in Wyoming. We were there for one year. The Heart Mountain Camp was very cold. The coldest temperature which we experienced there was minus twenty-eight degrees. When one touched a doorknob, the skin would stick to the knob. We had to be very careful.

Later someone told me that there was a job in a nearby city, and they suggested that I go out there and work. It was a job in a warehouse. There were about thirty Japanese people from Sacramento and Seattle working there.

When we were working in a city near the Heart Mountain Camp, we had to go to a restaurant to eat lunch. We broke up into small groups. Our group fared well, but another group went into a restaurant which did not serve Japanese people. They wondered why they were not served while the white people who came in later were served. They could not stay there indefinitely; so they left the restaurant. Upon leaving, they saw the "No Jap" sign on the window.

There was also a large drug store in the same town which was not doing well. There was another drugstore that would do business with Japanese people and cash their checks. They were very kind to us and were very successful. Many people went there to buy things from them. Another small town in Wyoming had many stores with "No Jap" signs. All of those stores were not doing very well.

A rumor spread that we might be able to go back to Japan; but if you did not want to go back, then it was important to return to the camp, because we might not be able to get back in. If we could not get back in the camp, then we might miss the opportunity to stay in the United States. Then everybody quit their jobs and went back into the camp.

There was a so-called "bank" in the camp where people cashed checks, and the "bank" also took care of the money from the six canteens in our camp. One had to collect all these checks, count them, and take them to a bank in the city. I worked there as a manager. It was a big job. Every time I went to town, I used to bring back about thirty to forty thousand dollars in cash. Though people in the camp could not go out freely, I was able to get a permit; so I became very familiar with the town.

Meanwhile, the situation in the West eased up a little, so I was able to come back to Sacramento.[1] We had experienced so much prejudice and oppression in California that I did not want to come back here again. I even asked the administration to find a job for me elsewhere, but I finally did come back to the West Coast.

CHOICHI NITTA

The bus took us to the Marysville Assembly Center. Later we were moved to the Tule Lake WRA Center. At Tule Lake I was a ward leader, and I was to help the evacuees in the block. A block consisted of six barracks where evacuees lived, and one mess hall. I toured the block and mess hall every day. Once a week we had a movie in the mess hall. We sold tickets for five cents. The duties included lining up people at the mess hall. If anyone stayed up late and was too noisy, I had to ask them to quiet down. My salary was nineteen dollars a month, the same as doctors. Carpenters and laborers received sixteen dollars.

At Tule Lake we had some pro-Japan people. We Christians were branded as spies for America and were tormented.[2] Some were beaten up. Because of my job, I went to the office often, and a truck brought me back. Some called me a spy, but I was not physically assaulted. We were all Japanese, but some were like that.

Because our son was working in Ontario, Oregon, I requested a transfer to be near him. When Tule Lake became a segregated

[1] On December 18, 1944, the West Coast mass exclusion order against persons of Japanese descent was revoked.

[2] At the time of evacuation, a WRA survey indicated that almost fifty percent of the evacuees were Buddhist, thirty-eight percent were Christians, ten percent had no religious preference, and two percent declined to state.

center, we went to the Minidoka WRA Center in Idaho. In Idaho I was allowed outside to work with my son on an apple ranch. My wife stayed inside the center. She had a job helping visitors from outside—lending them blankets, registering them, and reporting their names to the office. Japanese evacuees who had relocated outside came in to visit relatives and friends.

Later, when I was made foreman of the apple ranch, I brought my family outside. They gave me a house and a cow and the feed for the cow. There was more milk than we could use, because there were only three of us then. (Our daughters were relocated in the East, and my oldest son was in the service.) The salary wasn't too good in those days, but they gave us a place to live.

MRS. AI MIYASAKI

First we were sent to a place called Arboga, then to Tule Lake. We were very sad. Before the evacuation, what with curfew at six P.M., and we were only women, for Miyasaki was ill with tuberculosis, packing was a terrible chore. Then the landlord, a Portuguese who lived next door, came and said that he would straighten up the place and store the rest of the things in the basement for us. So we left the rest to his kindness and went. Valuables like the piano, stove, and icebox were stored in the church.

Miyasaki wanted to go back to Weimar.[3] If he was to go to camp, he felt that he would surely die. I inquired about the Weimar hospital and the county hospital, but they would not take him because his tuberculosis was inactive. It could not be otherwise; so he went with us. We were miserable. It was pathetic. Our son was too young to be able to do anything; only the girls could help. Even to fold and bundle a blanket ... we could not do it well. But our landlord was good to us, and we somehow managed.

The relocation center at Tule Lake was not completed when we arrived. The floor had about an inch of space between the boards, wide enough for the grass under the house to grow through it. There were small insects, gnats—like mosquitoes. They got into my hair and everywhere. I really suffered. There was no closet, but there was a bed; nothing else. It was inconvenient. Lumber was available to make a closet and chairs, but since I am a woman, I could not do such work. Next to my apartment in the

[3]Weimar was a California state hospital for tubercular patients.

same barracks were two carpenters. They said that they would make chairs and things for me first, because I was quiet and had not complained. They were good to me. When people get into predicaments like that, it becomes life's showdown.

In my town in Japan was a *bakuryo* (horse trader). It so happened that his daughter was there at the same camp. Her mother had taught me *odori* (dancing) in Japan. My! To meet her again brought back memories. She was good to me. Her husband, Arao-san,* was a cook, and Mrs. was managing the kitchen. I had a sewing machine; so she asked me to do some sewing and mending for her, and this I did. Because she worked in the kitchen, she was able to take some liberties. She hid some meat under her apron and brought it to me. Well, someone saw her, "That Mrs. Arao often takes meat to Mrs. Miyasaki," they said. That became quite an incident. "It was not her meat to give, which means we have that much less to eat," they said. People at times show their worst, and it is unseemly. Mrs. Arao felt bad and I did too but I did not say anything. It was useless to say anything. When anyone confronted me about it, I would say, "Yes, I received meat once because I did some sewing for her. I did not receive it often"; but people gossiped. The toilet and shower were open in the camp; so when others came, I used to leave right away. I practically ran to avoid their gossip.

I was alone with the boy, because Mr. Miyasaki was in the hospital. Someone must have wanted to show me some kindness, for when it snowed, by morning my front doorstep was cleared. Plenty of good-sized coal was brought over to my door and neatly piled. I was troubled and told a friend that it was nice to be treated so kindly; but because the Japanese's eyes are glaring, I would suffer from that person's kindness. I did not know who it was; therefore, I told my friend, "If you notice anyone doing this kindness, inform him of my feelings." My friend must have advised him not to do it anymore because someone would be watching. Of course, someone would see. There was a child here. Kindness done and evil things said about it turns it into unkindness. Is it not a bothersome thing?

MRS. KANE KOZONO

At first I thought that there would be no food for us in the camp; but the people who lived in town were sent to camp

* A pseudonym.

through the Walerga Assembly Center in February, and they wrote us letters saying that they were being fed in the camp. In June, when we joined them in Tule Lake, they told us that when they got there, the housing wasn't quite ready. The partitions between the bathrooms and the living quarters were inadequate, but the camp facilities were pretty well set up by the time we got there. I didn't feel too inconvenienced by the housing conditions. As a matter of fact, I was a bit surprised in the camp, for there were cooks, waiters, and so forth. I didn't have to do anything. I was glad to find that, because I had never been on a vacation for even a day until that time! I had an easier life in the camp than ever before.

I made flowers day after day. An instructor of paper-flower making was there at Tule Lake with us, and a lot of people learned it. You see, there was no work I had to do. As for meals, well, when it was time to eat, someone rang the bell for the call, and we all went to the mess hall. Those who helped in the kitchen were, as I remember vaguely, getting paid. Since my son told me I didn't have to take the trouble to do any work for money, I just enjoyed my easy days there learning flower making and other interesting things.

Although we were put in camps, it wasn't such a hard time for me. My husband, with his carefree personality, was singing songs even in the camp. He found an instructor of the *biwa*-lute in the same camp, and sent a letter to our daughter in New York asking for a used *biwa*-lute. When she couldn't find one, he asked the instructor to sell him one of the two he had. "You play it very well. You must have learned it before," said the instructor. "No, I have never held anything in my hands other than hoes," so answered my husband! He was an easy-going man and used to reminisce about those days in the camp, "I had more fun during the camp than any other time in my whole life." At the time of the evacuation, we worried about the future, but after we came back from the camp, we thought we had had fun there.

MRS. RIKAE INOUYE

Toward the end, the Tule Lake Camp was infamous as a "No-No camp."[4] It wasn't like that when we were there. Our children

---

[4]This is a reference to a negative response when evacuees were later required to complete a loyalty questionnaire.

are all Americanized. While we were in Tule Lake one of my daughters became ill . . . Emmie wanted to study to be a nurse at college. Soon after we moved into the Tule Lake Camp, she received her high school diploma. Johnny, a son, hadn't started high school. In Tule Lake, a doctor told us Johnny might become blind, and Emmie couldn't work because of pleurisy. Emmie and a lot of young girls were working as nurse's aides at the camp hospital. Once they were assigned to the TB ward, but their parents prohibited them from working in that ward. Emmie was assigned there too, and she told me of her feelings. She said, "Mama, I hope to be a nurse. If I avoid the TB ward, how can I call myself a nurse in the future?" What she said was correct. Sometime later, while she was making beds, she felt a pain in her side. She consulted a doctor, and was told that she had pleurisy. My husband cried for the first time then. Entering the room . . . he said, "Johnny might go blind. Emmie has pleurisy. We might lose two children. As long as we stay in the camp, they'll ruin themselves. If the Issei are permitted to leave, we should get out of here and lead a free life, so that they may recover." My husband went to the camp office for an interview. By that time, the Issei were permitted to leave, and we went to Lawrence, Kansas.

RIICHI SATOW

We had nine children altogether by the time of the evacuation. Born in January, the baby was five months old and went to Pinedale with us. The child contracted whooping cough then. On the way to the assembly center a Pullman car was provided for pregnant women and for new mothers and their babies. My wife and our five-month-old went to Pinedale on this special car, while I took the rest of our children with me. The oldest daughter and son and the second oldest daughter were big enough to help me look after their younger brothers and sisters. That's how we went to the Pinedale Assembly Center.

You know, it was a very strained life; well, that's actually how it was throughout the wartime . . . an atmosphere of continuous tension.

I think we were relatively trouble-free while at the center. We were there about two months, for we arrived in May, and in July we left for Poston. The housing at Pinedale wasn't so bad. A large family was provided with a large house accordingly. In such re-

spects I didn't have anything to complain about. There was plenty
of food for everyone too. With regard to religious meetings, we
had no restrictions whatsoever. Having nothing else to do, we
held meetings frequently. Singing hymns, and listening to
speeches . . . that kind of life was started then.

We did not worry about the children's education or anything
then. We were more concerned with our immediate future, for we
didn't know what was going to happen at that point. For instance,
we didn't have the slightest idea where we were going to be taken
to from there. Later we learned that we were to go to Poston,
Arizona, and we went there by train. It just so happened that it
was in the middle of July, during the boiling hot summer. I tell
you it was hot!

In Poston we were met by people from Watsonville and Salinas
who arrived, we learned later, two weeks before us. There again
the air was so tense.

Mrs. Hanayo Inouye

It was awfully hot out there [Poston, Arizona]. To keep cool, I
used to soak my feet in a bucket of water—and it was just awful
standing in line at mealtime with dishes in our hands. When the
wind was a little bit too much, a terrible dust storm came along
with it. Dust was one of our biggest problems. However tight we
shut the doors and windows, the dust came in the house and all
over the inside. But we were Japanese after all; so no one spent
lazy days. Some people planted various kinds of trees in the compound, and between the trees we grew vegetables and other
things. When we first came to the camp, we all wondered what
was going to happen to us. But when we were leaving, people were
even saying that living in the camp was better than where they
had come from. The trees had grown very big by then, and we
could find nice shade under them and everything.

A lot of parents, I for one, had a problem feeding our babies as
we wanted. Generally speaking, food in the camp was pretty good,
but we couldn't get hold of our kind of baby food. Our son, Ben,
lost so much weight and turned so pale that I thought he might be
dying. It worried me a lot. After coming back from the camp, my
husband grew a lot of spinach out here for him. Until that time
the shortage of fresh produce was a big problem. Pretty soon Ben
started regaining his normal color. Now he is the tallest and
best-built in the whole family.

Like I said before, food was generally good in the camp. How-ever, there were rumors that they would refuse to give us any food when the United States was on the losing side of the war, so the women in the camp took turns by units to collect leftover bread every day. We dried what we collected each day on a piece of board under the burning sun; and because of the unbelievable heat from the desert sun, the bread became almost like well-toasted bread. We then kept it in big paper bags. That's as far as we went in precautionary steps. Anyway, four women assigned themselves to turn over the bread during the afternoon and store it in the kitchen space when it was well dried.

We had to live under the constant pressure that the food might all stop one day, and it gave me very uneasy and uncomfortable feelings to see the guards watching us from the tower. We were all fenced in. I couldn't take my eyes off my children for even a moment so that they would not go outside the fence. The guards were to shoot anyone that did.

YOSHITO FUJII

At the Minidoka Camp, housing was a big problem, and I was asked by the person in charge to help. I reluctantly agreed to become something like a housing adjuster. The barracks that were built in the camp varied in size. Some of the rooms were for three or four people, others weren't. More and more people were accommodated in the barracks. If you were lucky, you got a single room. There was a problem, especially for ladies. If several ladies were put in a four-person room, they usually had some problems. If there was only one party, no problems arose. One young woman, whose husband was in an internment camp, was put in a room with some other ladies. Being in a different situation from the others, she didn't get along with them. Later, segregation of pro-Japan and pro-American people in Tule Lake was a problem. The pro-Japan people stayed at Tule Lake, and the pro-American people were sent to other camps. When newcomers arrived from Tule Lake, we had to arrange rooms for them, and we had to share rooms equally. Six or seven people worked for me to straighten everything out.

Growing crops of our own was another problem. We had to make arrangements for farm production and other necessities. We had meetings in Salt Lake City and Chicago. Each internment camp sent its representative, and I represented our camp. I suggested that each camp should collect three or four thousand dollars in cash and we should buy seedlings and other necessary goods through a buyer. We would rotate purchasing goods with four thousand dollars in cash. My suggestion was accepted by the others. Good items were put in a freeze during the war. It was hard to get them. However, we had to have certain things in the camp, such as clothing.

I became chairman of the board in Minidoka. The camp administration in Minidoka requested that we establish a system of self-government or a community council. I suggested that we have a binary committee and that we should organize a cabinet system—a mayor, council, or board system. A board system was adopted by the camp in Minidoka. Every district sent two representatives. There were forty-two districts in the camp. In other words, we had eighty-four representatives in all. Also each block sent one person as a trustee—forty-one trustees formed the council. A board chairman was elected by general vote. I was elected and quit my other jobs because of that.

Picking up coal was another problem in camp. Japanese truck drivers were sent to pick up coal. Those truck drivers and the administrators had conflicts once in a while. Since the drivers were Japanese but the administrators were Caucasian, they had a clash of interests. The Japanese drivers got special permits to go outside of the camp on duty, but they took a longer time than they should have. Some drivers even shopped for others. They misused their privilege. The administrators established guidelines in order to eliminate the abuses. Then the drivers threatened that they would strike, and they did. It was in the midst of the cold winter season. Those who suffered most because of the strike were the camp residents, who were all Japanese. We didn't have any coal in below-zero weather, and the families with babies were miserable without a fire. The drivers didn't lose anything, but the residents suffered. Whenever such problems arose, I couldn't sleep at night. I was called out for discussions even at midnight. School, checks on resident cards . . . various problems arose one after another.

Then teachers complained that some teachers' wages were better or worse than others. The same thing occurred at the hospital. The amount of their wages was the subject. There were two sets of wages, sixteen or nineteen dollars. The difference was only three dollars. Human beings can be petty. Some people were excited about the difference and protested. Each problem was brought to me as the board chairman, and I had to solve them.

People say that they had such a hard time in the camp; however, when the United States Army decided to close the relocation camps so that we could return home, some people opposed the decision. Being used to camp life, they didn't want to leave there . . . cooks served meals regularly, et cetera. I wanted to return to my home state. Some people, who didn't feel too much of a lack for things, welcomed that kind of living environment. I couldn't think about myself only. I had to take my children into consideration. So many men, so many minds, at times.

MRS. KO TAKAKOSHI

I went directly to the Minidoka War Relocation Center in Idaho. There was nothing to do in camp, so I started to teach children how to make flowers from orange wrappings. We gathered pieces of wire and got the orange wrappings from the mess halls. When Rev. Andrews told outside friends about this, they started to send us crepe paper to make the flowers. I remember making a floral wreath out of paper flowers for a funeral because we couldn't get fresh flowers. I wasn't an expert, but friends still tell me what a fine job I did. We also made paper flowers to send to Alaska. We sent poinsettias for Christmas, lilies for Easter, and carnations for other occasions. People were very appreciative of this, and I was happy that I was able to do it.

MRS. TOME TAKATSUKI

When we finally had to evacuate, the people in the JACL (Japanese American Citizens' League)[5] made arrangements for us. We went to Walerga for a brief period. We then were transferred to Tule Lake. At that time there were many guards, and they treated us as if we were a herd of horses or cows as we lined up to board the bus. When we entered the Tule Lake Camp, nothing was built yet. There was not a thing for us to sit down on; so each of us

[5]The Japanese American Citizens' League (JACL) acted as a liaison between government officials and the evacuees during the initial phases of moving and again in the relocation camps. Their continued cooperative attitude with the American government was later to mobilize pro-Japan groups against the leaders of the JACL.

received some lumber to make our own tables and chairs. After we were settled, the people who were loyal to Japan began to agitate. Later on, the Tule Lake Camp became the place for those who were loyal to Japan, and our family was transferred to Topaz. My sister's family was in Topaz; therefore, we were sent there.

At that time my nephew was already a dentist. He said, "Those people in the Tule Lake Camp who are loyal to Japan can agitate, but I feel that America is my country, so I want to enlist in the army," and with that he volunteered. Prior to entering camp, he had wanted to enlist in the Navy and went to take the test for the Navy in San Diego. But because he was of Japanese descent, he was discriminated against. He came back disappointed, without taking the test, and entered the camp. Before we entered Topaz, he was drafted by the Army, and he happily went to Mississippi.[6] He joined the 442nd and was sent to Italy. We were extremely worried about him and hoped that he would not be bombed at sea on the way to Italy. We were much relieved to hear of his safe arrival.

In the Topaz Camp we became students under Professor Tsumori to learn calligraphy. During the day we attended English classes. At the Tule Lake Camp we studied formal flower arrangement under Professor Taizan. I remember that there was a community church in the camp, and all the various religions were combined into one.

KIYOSHI NOJI

Mrs. Noji had surgery just before the evacuation. We had difficulty going to the hospital to visit her because of the curfew regulations. The Japanese doctor did too. She was still quite weak when we evacuated.

We went to the Salinas Assembly Center and then to the Poston WRA Center in Arizona. We were in the assembly center for only a short while. It was July 1, 1942, when we entered Poston. The housing was built very poorly, so the weeds showed up between the floorboards. The food wasn't very good, but we knew it was wartime. We believed America would give us better food than any other country under the circumstances. Poston just

---

[6]Part of the loyalty oath controversy included a question to eligible men as to whether they would volunteer to be drafted. This young man indicated his loyalty, agreed to be drafted, and then was sent a draft notice.

wasn't a good camp. Some evacuees protested that the conditions were against the Geneva Conference agreement. There were some bad Caucasian employees; they were corrupt, and we couldn't get the food we were supposed to get at times.

There were demonstrations for better food. A few pro-Japanese radicals caused trouble by intimidating families that had men in the service. They assaulted Nisei who worked as leaders in the camp. They were arrested and taken to jail in Phoenix. Some of their mothers came to me for help in getting these men back. General DeWitt[7] came to visit, and things got better. The older people got used to camp life, and some hated to leave when the war ended. They knew they had to find work on the outside.

Some Caucasian church members encouraged us by saying the war would not last long. At Christmas time in the center, we received a huge number of gifts from outside Christian churches. Many sympathetic ministers came to see us. Dr. Hunter, a pacifist, said it was wrong of the United States to drop the A-bomb on Hiroshima and Nagasaki, Japan. I was waiting for President Truman to say this, but he never did.

When the war ended in 1945, most of the pastors went back to the churches from where they evacuated; but the Superintendent of our church, Dr. Chapman, did not let me go back to Salinas. He thought it was dangerous to go back there so soon. I think Dr. Chapman or his brother went to the Salinas church for a while. A vacancy occurred in the Wintersburg church in southern California, so I went there.

Kengo Tajima

Well, at Gila the housing was incomplete. I didn't take it too hard, because I had gone through a hard life; so that didn't surprise me very much. One thing that was very bad was there was no provision for family privacy. Two families would be crowded in one big room. That was a very bad thing. Even so, there were a good many matches and marriages in the camp. I would always bless the couples, and soon they would leave the camp. They could get married and stay in the camp, but they usually would go out to find jobs. They had a sort of honeymoon room in the camp.

---

[7]General DeWitt was Commanding General of the Western Defense Zone and in charge of the evacuation.

WATARU ISHISAKA

I sold some things, gave away others, and took a train from the Woodland station to the Merced Assembly Center with all my family. We were there for three or four months before we moved to the Amache Camp in Colorado.

People acted just like dumb sheep, because life was so disrupted and confused. They lost their human dignity and respect. I did not have citizenship, but I was hired as a policeman in the assembly center. I probably was the only policeman who did not have citizenship. In any case, we used to patrol the area for theft, fighting, and the like. I saw people doing all kinds of shameful things, like fooling around with other's wives, but I looked the other way. Some of the policemen said that we should punish these men and women. I said, "Leave them alone. These things have to be solved by themselves." I really fought against taking any action in those cases, and as I expected, they solved the problems by themselves. If it got more complicated, those people couldn't work it out by themselves. Other policemen took all these things down in notebooks and reported the incidents. I got really mad and said, "You fool!" Then one of them said, "What do you mean by fool?" I replied, "People's minds are confused right now. Reporting things like that isn't going to help anything." Well, the Japanese police chief really liked me because I said what I felt. He said, "You are an interesting man."

When I patrolled the area, children used to follow me, and I used to play with them. One day I saw a bunch of children looking out through the barbed-wire fence. There was a road right next to the fence and a grape vineyard beyond that. I could see ripe bunches of grapes hanging under the leaves. I could see that the children wanted to eat the grapes. I got a long pole, attached a knife to the end of it, cut the bunches down, hooked them and pulled the grapes into the fence area. The children were really happy about that; however, an MP officer passed by the fence. I had a police uniform on, so they could spot me right away. "What are you doing?" he asked. I answered, "You can see what I'm doing!" Then he said, "Do you want grapes?" I said, "Yes, of course. But it's for these children, not for me. It's natural that children want some sweet things to eat." Then he said, "I'll get some for you," and he brought a lot of grapes for the children, who were delighted. It was a kind thing to do.

One other problem which we encountered in the assembly center had to do with food. They used to feed us lots of mutton and beef tongue. One day all of us came down with diarrhea. We went to get a doctor, but those available were just too busy because of the number of patients. It was an epidemic.

It was such a terrible place. I can't even describe it, but even in that kind of atmosphere there were no serious problems or violent events.

From there we were transported to Amache, Colorado. We went by train at night, if my memory serves me correctly. All the blinds were down on the way there. When we arrived, the camp was not really ready. We made things we could grow there, and we also had pigs. There was more freedom there than in the assembly center.

In Amache, I did get involved in a demonstration about a housing problem. When we left Merced, the administration promised that family members would be able to move together and live together. However, when we arrived at the Amache Camp, the barracks were not ready yet, and we were placed in available barracks. That meant that most of the family members got split up. It was a very bad situation, so we demonstrated. Because the Japanese administrators were really afraid, they did not come out of their offices. We decided to talk to Lindley, who was the chief administrator of the Amache Camp. He said, "The camp is not ready yet. That's why we have problems. But when all the barracks are completed, everything will be arranged as promised." He was a very good man, and his statements made sense to us. So we agreed and ended the demonstration.

There was a barbed-wire fence between the administration compound (where whites lived) and our barracks. One day we went to Lindley and said, "We are not P.O.W.'s. We are here not because we want to be here, but we are forced to come here. We want you to take that barbed-wire fence down!" Then they did take it down.

You know, I give Lindley a lot of credit. (When we came back to Sacramento after the war, I was walking down the street one day. Someone tapped my shoulder. I looked back and saw it was Mr. Lindley. I said, "What are you doing here?" He said, "How are you?" I guess he remembered me. At that time he said that he was working for some water district. He said, "I'll see you again," but that was the last time I saw him.)

As I said in the beginning, they were still building barracks in the camp. They brought in lumber by train and really piled up a lot. The Japanese people went to pilfer the lumber to make shelves, storage cupboards, and furniture. The MP's used to look the other way when we went to pick up the lumber, because we told them that we were making tables, shelves, and necessary things because the government did not provide them for us.

The Japanese are a very smart, adaptable people. There was a lake close to the camp, and we went to fish there. We made nets out of onion sacks which we sewed together. Many of the nets were as much as fifty feet. Then we weighed the bottom with stones, and we caught all kinds of fish. It seemed like millions at once. We took the fish back to the camp and divided them up for those who wanted some. There were those who didn't like fish, but the people from Wakayama loved fish, and they were very good at cooking them.

There were three kinds of turtles there too. Once a man caught a turtle which was bigger than the biggest washtub. In the beginning he kept it in the public washtub and put a hundred-pound weight on it. The next day he asked me to come over and have soup. But I said, "I really don't like turtle soup." He really insisted, so I went there and drank turtle soup. We drank it for a week!

There were those who roasted rattlesnakes and ate them. They say it really gives you lots of energy. I said, "I've got lots of energy; so I don't need it." You know, there were professional snake-catchers in the camp. They were paid thirteen dollars a month. They used to always carry a long pole around with them. There was a man called Yamamoto who was a professional snake catcher. Once, he didn't tie the string tight enough and got bitten by a snake. He was in the camp hospital for two months. When I went to see him, he said, "I won't make it this time." But he got well, and I met him again after the war.

Oh, camp life was very difficult and also very interesting. We had to make a sewage plant there, and it looked like a swimming pool. Well, the *Denver Post* reported that the Japs had built a hundred thousand dollar swimming pool! It was really hilarious. We told them to come and see the pool, and the newspaper had to write a retraction. They were really looking for something to use against us.

Well, I remember lots of things. There were good things as well as bad things. There were flowers which resembled morning glories. They were a lot bigger than morning glories and really beautiful. The roots were very big, like potatoes.They said that Indians used to make wine out of those roots. Digging the roots of that plant became very popular with the Issei. They dried them and cut out the inside and made *hibachi* and things like that.

Sadly, there were those whose minds snapped in the camp, and they wandered out and died in the wilderness. There were more than several of those among the older Issei. We had to search all over for them. Sometimes those old people fell into holes and could not get out. Some of them were lucky, because we found them in time. Others died out there.

TSUGUO NAGASAWA

The camp wasn't as bad as I had feared it would be. I was afraid that heavy labor would be forced upon me and had bought a pair of shoes for menial labor. On the contrary, they didn't inflict anything like that on us at all. They assembled us and gave us food and a place to sleep. In fact I felt rather bored, though I was anxious about the future. "Would we languish for months or even for years?" I wondered. Meanwhile, there were some disturbing incidents at the Tule Lake Camp. Some Japanese people went to work for nearby farmers. The white soldiers were smaller than the Japanese. The soldiers were afraid of the Japanese, so they shot at the Japanese. About three people were killed. Pitiful! As a result, a pro-Japanese group, the *Hoshi-dan,* was formed among the Japanese people in the camp. The pro-Japanese group pledged loyalty to Japan, and the United States government decided to prosecute them. Because of that, some Japanese people hid themselves and walked on top of the barracks to escape. Some were killed and others were injured during their attempted escape. I can't say that those Japanese people were bad; on the other hand, I felt that what the WRA said might be true. The WRA said, "It's quite all right for the Japanese to sympathize with Japan and pray for her victory; however, they should pray indoors." The *Hoshi-dan* had assemblies on a field in the camp with horns. Nonmembers could also hear their ceremony; they were too conspicuous. Therefore, the WRA couldn't ignore them. That's understandable.

Mr. Masao Kaneko* was killed at Tule Lake. He had something to do with the canteen goods. The Japanese killed the Japanese. They had been fighting in Sacramento even before entering the camp. I think the killer and the victim had personal reasons for their quarrel.

I had only one bad experience with a white man. While I was taking a bath, I was pushed out because of a man in our block. The white man pointed a gun at me. He asked me where the man was and what the man was doing. I was expected to answer. Such a thing happened.

I was a manager of Block Six at first. Then I became chairman of Ward One. Toward the end, I became chairman of the entire Tule Lake Camp. The block I was in had the worst reputation. The people in the block fought a lot, and that was my biggest worry. It was the responsibility of the block manager to keep peace. Some people warned me, "This is a curse within Block Six." Toward the end, our block turned out to be a model block. Some of the causes of fighting were a continuation from the days before entering the center . . . complicated. The attitude of some young people was quite violent. They fought in the midst of block meetings and threw chairs in the block office. I didn't get hurt, but some did. After the loyal and the disloyal ones were separated, the Tule Lake Camp became the camp for disloyal people. The WRA was shrewd. The meals that were served changed a little; they turned bad. It was natural.

Anyway, the people who were put into this camp [Tule Lake] were different from the people who were satisfied with their life. Each one was rebellious. It wasn't their fault that they had been put into a camp. Washington, D.C. . . . It wasn't Japan's fault either. Nobody was to blame; however, they felt rebellious. The wages were really low, only about twenty dollars a month there. They could have earned higher wages outside. They felt desperate and rebellious. There was nobody else; so they troubled a block manager with this and that. I had to give different answers to different individuals, so that I could satisfy them. Some blocks changed their managers quite often. I asked to submit my resignation; but no matter how many elections we had, I was elected from the beginning to the end.

At one point there were two separate camps in Tule Lake. One section was a jail for the delinquent youths. The WRA didn't

*A pseudonym.

really want to keep them jailed for a long time and wanted to negotiate conditions for releasing the youths. Three people had tried before me but failed. The WRA asked me to be the fourth negotiator, and I succeeded. The WRA wanted to release everybody in the jail compound, but a responsible person had to sign for them. I persuaded the imprisoned youths and their parents to cooperate by saying, "Rather than being put in such a dark place, you should attend the *Kokumin Gakko* (People's School) run by us. If you want to go back to Japan, you should attend the *Kokumin Gakko* and learn the Japanese language so you'll be better off in Japan." The WRA office couldn't have released them even with my signature, unless their parents consented to be responsible and cooperate too. But they thought that I was a spy from the WRA and that they were being deceived by me. They thought the several people who had tried to persuade them before me were also spies, and not sincere. I said, "No, I'm not a spy. You're going back to Japan. I'm going back to Japan, too. We'll be on board the same boat." Thus I persuaded them, and the youths were released. Throughout my stay in Tule Lake, the release of those youths was the most difficult task I had.

13

On Loyalty

The loyalty question was ultimately the most confusing, tension-ridden, and emotionally painful problem that the evacuees encountered as a group in the relocation centers. Many Nisei (children of the Issei and United States citizens by birth) had volunteered their services in the armed forces of the United States. The War Department, impressed with the energy and dedication of the volunteers, prepared a loyalty questionnaire for male citizen evacuees as a preliminary to the formation of an all Japanese-American volunteer combat team. The WRA hastily used this same questionnaire to process applicants for work-leave permits and clearance in seeking resettlement outside the camps. This questionnaire was a formal registration of loyalty or disloyalty and seemed simple enough to the WRA but posed many problems for the evacuees.

Questions 27 and 28 created the "yes-yes, no-no" controversy. Question 27 asked if the evacuee were willing to serve in combat, to which many women and aged Issei replied "no." Question 28 asked if the evacuee would forswear allegiance to the Japanese emperor and the Japanese nation, to which many Issei answered "no," for to do so would leave them stateless, because they were denied naturalization in the U.S. In some situations members of families answered "no," not from conviction but to hold families together, since the evacuees were to be segregated according to their replies on the questionnaire. There were also those who answered "no" to the questions for fear that they would be forced to resettle outside the camps in a hostile and potentially dangerous anti-Japanese environment. Finally, some

Issei signed "no" because they feared the loss of their sons in combat at a time when these sons were to assume the bread-winning role in the family.[1] *Therefore, a large number of these sons signed "no" out of familial duty. There were those, of course, who signed "no" out of strong conviction and as a protest against their imprisonment. Surprisingly, they comprised less than five percent of the total number of evacuees.*

Mrs. Ai Miyasaki

At first, everyone settled in and we were healthy and happy for a while. Small shells were abundant, because that area had water long ago. We all went to gather them and made necklaces and arranged flowers. I went to school in the morning and in the afternoon went to practice some other activity. But then, signing the document regarding the loyalty oath came up, and everyone was at once excited and emotional. Rev. Kitakawa acted for the good of the Japanese people. He worked diligently as a mediator for us, but his actions were misunderstood. People began to say that the minister was a dog.[2] "He only does things the Administration wants and does not do things for our benefit," they said. Some threw garbage in front of him and said, "Dogs should eat this." He was treated badly. My married children and I wondered what we should do about the loyalty question. "Mama, what are you going to do?" my children asked. I said, "I cannot do much; so I will follow your lead." The children said that they had already signed and decided to stay here in America. "If you want to stay with us, you do the same," they said. People who signed to stay in America were discriminated against. In our block, people who chose to stay in America were called dogs, so we also became dogs. It was troublesome. I hid from people and went to sign.

I know people who were disloyal. Since they were educated, they were influential, and others listened to them.[3] And then they came back here [from camp] even after saying such bad things about America. They are back and act as though nothing hap-

[1]At the time of evacuation, the mean age of the Issei was fifty-six years.

[2]In Japanese the word is *"inu"* and is translated "dog" or "informer."

[3]Her reference is to the Kibei, who were born in the United States but had received their education in Japan and subsequently returned to the U.S. A large number of the Kibei were discouraged to find their Japanese education useless for job opportunities in this country. They tended to form the nucleus of "disloyal" groups in some relocation camps.

pened. I know a man who quit the Christian church and joined a Buddhist sect. The pressure was so strong that he quit the church. When he came back [from camp], he rejoined a Christian church.

The block managers were also under attack. They were in a difficult position. A block manager had to gather the people and explain the situation to them. While I was still in Tule Lake, I was a monitor. There were twelve blocks to a ward, and each block had a monitor. I was the only woman monitor. I did not want to be the only woman monitor, but I had to serve. I distributed the weekly news throughout the block. When I posted something on the blackboard in the mess hall, someone ripped it off right away. All were cold toward me at first. Because I was a Christian, and also being a woman, they must have felt that I was too presumptuous. There may have been some jealousy. Later on, people who were so bothersome changed and started to treat me well. In the end, they complimented me on the way I handled the matters for the block.

But finally those who refused to think that Japan could ever lose the war stayed in the Tule Lake Camp, while the rest of us were moved. When we were to leave, we were looked at very coldly. We were not served hot rice. "For dogs, cold rice is good enough," they said.

Officials said that the Colorado climate was best for Miyasaki's illness, and that was why we were sent there. After we left the Tule Lake Camp, the disloyals caused great incidents—fighting, even murder.

Mrs. Hanayo Inouye

When the loyalty question was brought up, some long-time friends fought with each other. My husband and I thought that since our children were born in the United States, we would sign "yes." Then some people accused us by saying, "What kind of fools are you to say 'yes' to a country that's treating us like this?" Oh, they were angry at us. They firmly believed that Japan would win the war and did not see why we should side with the United States. Many of our long-time friendships were broken as a result. Some of the cooks were in the so-called "No-No" group. They didn't treat us nicely. The children had snacks in the afternoon, and the children of the "Yes-Yes" group were often not served their share of snacks. Or at other times, when sugar was found missing from the kitchen, the people of the "Yes-Yes" group were charged with stealing it. Oh, a lot of those trivial things happened. Although we were all in one and the same camp, the difference between signing "yes" and "no" inevitably created friction among a lot of us.

As you might know, some people eventually chose to go back to Japan with their children.

SHIZUMA TAKESHITA

At the Tule Lake Center there were many who signed "no" to the loyalty questionnaire [not loyal to the USA] in Blocks 41 and 42, where our two sons were housed. They also signed "no." My wife and I were housed in Block 49; we signed "yes." Our second son, who was a mess hall manager, was arrested and jailed in Klamath Falls because he was thought to be an agitator. I went to the main office and made a complaint. I asked the officials to show me the warrant for his arrest, and I asked them to have a hearing for him. The hearing date was set, and they asked if he wanted an attorney. I told them that I was his stepfather, and I would act as his attorney. The hearing date was postponed, and before another date was set, they informed us that there would be no hearing. Instead, they were sending our second son to a place where they kept men who refused to go into the service— somewhere in Utah.

Meanwhile, the Tule Lake Center was designated as the center for disloyals. Our third son had even stronger ties to Japan than our second son, because he also was educated in Japan before he came to this country. He got married while in the Tule Lake Center, and his wife's parents signed "no"; therefore, he had to stay at the Tule Lake Center to care for them. My wife and I had to take our second son's wife and child and move to another center. I started to write letters in my broken English to the officer where our second son was held, and tried to have the officer persuade our son to change his loyalty statement to "yes." The officer was able to persuade my son to change his mind. He made arrangements for our son to go to the Jerome Center in Arkansas, and we joined him there later.

Many things happened in our block at Tule Lake before we left. Our block manager signed "yes" on the loyalty question, and he moved out that night. There was confusion in our block—many

meetings were held regarding the "yes" and "no" answers that we
had to answer on the loyalty questionnaire. I stood up at one of
the meetings and asked if I could express my opinion. I pleaded
with the people not to fight with each other as people were doing
in other blocks over whether they signed "yes" or "no." I told
them I felt that those who had their fathers detained in internment camps should answer "yes" if they wanted their fathers out
of there, and those who did not want to move out of Tule Lake
should answer "no." I said that regardless of what their feelings
were, anyone wanting to join their children on the outside should
answer "yes." When the block manager left, they had a meeting
and asked me to be their block manager. I told the residents not to
get upset at publicity or rumors. There was a Christian minister
in the block. I asked him to translate all communications from
the WRA office into Japanese so everyone could understand the
notices, and I told them that any communications from the
Japanese evacuees would be translated into English and brought
to the office, but not to expect that they could do everything that
we asked the officials to do. I wanted them to give a farewell party
at the mess hall whenever someone was leaving and a welcome
party when someone moved in. I also said that I was a stranger to
them, that I did not know their backgrounds, and that if I became
their block manager, I wanted to serve everyone equally. This
statement was received very well by the residents, and I served as
their block manager until I left the Tule Lake Center.

Gradually all the "no" evacuees were transferred into Tule
Lake from other centers, and most of the "yes" evacuees in Tule
Lake were transferred out to other centers. There were some, like
myself and the hospital staff, who signed "yes," still waiting to be
transferred out. Rumors started that some of the "no" newcomers
were going to get together and kill the "yes" group still there. I
went to the officials asking them to do something but was told to
wait. Meanwhile, curfews within the center went into effect, and
preparations were being made to get us out. One morning the
office notified all of us in the "yes" group to pack and get ready to
be picked up. I packed my things and went to my daughter-in-
law's quarters and packed her things. Gradually all of us were
moved out to the military quarters. That night all of us were put
on the train. When we got up in the morning, we were in Portland.

From there the train traveled to the Minidoka Center in Idaho and unloaded some who were supposed to go there. Next they separated one passenger car with people going to the Topaz, Utah, Center. Then we went through Denver, Colorado, and unloaded some people going to the Amache, Colorado, Center. The rest of us went to the Jerome, Arkansas, Center. When I got off, I learned that our passenger car was hitched on to a freight train. We spent Christmas of 1943 and the New Year of 1944 in Jerome.

KENGO TAJIMA

My first reaction was how to protect our people, what to do with our people, that was the main concern. My reaction was for our people to take this incident with a clear understanding of what the war was all about. Right or wrong, it was started; we were in this country and our children were citizens. We were not citizens, not of our own choice; but our loyalty and sympathy were with this country for our children and even for ourselves. We had lived in this country for many years. We owed what we had to this country; so our duty was to defend this country. I maintained that, and I said that which might have been rather unpopular.

There was a patriotic pro-Japanese group. These active young people would propagate pro-Japanese ideas, and if I were more outspoken, I might have angered them to do bodily harm to me. Everything went badly where I stayed.

SHOICHI FUKUDA

Meanwhile, segregation among Japanese people began on the basis of the loyalty oath. At that time, I was a block representative in our camp. I attended meetings where the loyalty question was discussed. My function was to bring back the content of these meetings. The question of loyalty or disloyalty to the United States became a very serious problem for the Tule Lake community. Some said, "We are Japanese and cannot become loyal citizens of the United States." The problem was blown out of proportion. It was poorly explained to us, and that added to the confusion. Finally, it was put to us in this way, "Are you willing to obey the law of the land?" Then it was very easy for us to answer.

The first questionnaire was confusing. That's why people were upset. People were split in groups of loyal or disloyal, and that created tremendous hurt among the people. When the issue was finally clarified, it was very easy to understand and did not create pain anymore. We were told that if we were law-abiding people, we were to transfer to any other camp we chose. Those people who could not agree to abide by the law were brought to the Tule Lake Camp.

MRS. RIYO ORITE

My son-in-law was a Nisei, who was around thirty then. He was old enough to speak before people. The people in our block complained saying, "You should take the initiative rather than us. You just keep silent." They were urging people to sign the papers for parents and children to go back to Japan. However, my son-in-law's view was that he was a Nisei, and his children were Sansei (grandchildren of the Issei, third generation). He didn't express himself, for he was afraid of the general reaction. Being pushed by them, he finally spoke up. He reluctantly said, "I'm a Nisei and my children are Sansei. I hope each family has the freedom to decide according to their situation." People who had only daughters didn't have any problem. People whose sons were in the military service were in a hard position. For those with young families . . . well it wasn't wise to go to Japan with small children who didn't know Japanese. Therefore, he desired that each family would be free to decide. Everybody stood up yelling, "Let's beat him. Let's kick him out!"

He wasn't beaten, but. . . . He didn't want to stay in the camp any longer and went to Utah. After he left, the problem of segregation arose. We had to answer "yes" or "no." Before the war, Ambassador Nomura got off the train at Sacramento on the way to New York. He made a speech before some people. The people in the Japanese association asked questions such as, "What should parents with draft-age sons do when a war breaks out?" He answered, "You should repay your debt of gratitude to the place where you've received your livelihood." I was thinking of his words at all times. So were my children.

A year after my husband's death, my son got a draft notice. He was eighteen then. Every boy had to register at a recruiting office at the age of eighteen. I didn't know what to do. I was confused and so awfully lonely. I was told to submit a request to the service for my son's draft deferment. I did, and he wasn't drafted. Later on, recruiters came to the camp and my son wanted to enlist, but being a minor, he needed his parent's signature. I didn't sign it at first in Tule Lake because of the opposition of others. My son got so mad that he didn't want to stay with me; therefore, he went to Utah. Later on, I was to move to Utah due to the problem of segregation. He must have read about it in a newspaper or something. He came to pick us up, and he came to me with his A-1 classification. I said, "Once you've got the notice, you shouldn't run away. Go in the service and fulfill your duty."

My children were born here and were taught about American life. They were willing to join the service whenever they were drafted. I couldn't do anything about it. Because my sons went into the service, people spoke ill of me. I feel I was in a position where no other choice was possible. My children said, "If we return in safety when the war is over, Mom won't have to cry any longer." I and they said, "We'll be able to smile again when the end of war comes." I felt lonely and grief stricken. However, some other people sacrificed more than I. Being a woman, I felt heartache and loneliness.

A boy who had joined the service before we came to Tule Lake told me that the Japanese-American soldiers who excelled could be promoted up to master sergeant. People in the camp spread rumors that soldiers were allowed to wear a nice uniform only when they visited their parents and that they would have their uniforms taken away after returning to their unit.

Such rumors! One woman told me that Japanese soldiers were in a pitiful state, for they had to wash dishes and do clean-up work. I found out the truth from Mr. Shibata's son when he visited his parents on leave. He said, "Mrs., just think when you sent your children to school. At school, students with high grades are praised by teachers, while those with low grades are scolded by their teachers. The military service is the same. If you do well in training, you'll be promoted."

That woman said that such fine uniforms were to be returned later. He said that once he had been given a uniform, he didn't have to return it as long as he was alive. He'd told me something completely different. He showed me his uniforms. He said that he had been given an outfit for cold weather. The service provided him with proper clothing according to the weather. That woman's son had written her that he wasn't doing anything other than washing dishes because he was just a trainee. He hadn't been in the service long enough at that time. I'd learned that every soldier washed dishes and cleaned by turns. Some soldiers who didn't keep regulations such as the curfew times were given those duties as a penalty.

Having my children in the U.S. military service, I didn't feel like declaring against the United States. If I had spoken up, people could have spread some rumors about me. I cried in the camp. Every time I went to the mess hall or to a bathhouse, I returned to my room in tears. When I went to the mess hall, I heard them saying, "Everybody in the mess hall should say 'yes' to Japan and 'no' to the United States." Three of my children were in the military service then. "I can't point a gun at Japan, and I can't abandon the Emperor either. I'll obey the United States in any other way," I said to the government officials. The officials said it was all right. I didn't have any feelings against the laws of the country. I'd obey them. Then I was transferred to Topaz from Tule Lake. However, I didn't express my feelings because I was afraid of the anti-American Japanese people.

I kept silent about my decision before the other people, but by mistake the office delivered some large boxes for packing to me only three days after my decision to say "yes" to the loyalty question. The opposing people immediately knew what it was all about. They said, "Although she's just a woman, she's something. She's going to transfer to some other camp. We told everybody at the mess hall to tell the office that we all prefer to remain at Tule Lake." When the boxes were delivered, I told the truth to the people. I was blamed by everybody, but I had no choice. Mother and children shouldn't be separated. The boxes for packing were delivered to me first. However, our move was postponed for a week. I wondered who was the next one to receive the boxes. The head of a block, who was just like a village chief in Japan, got the next. He was the one who was urging people to be anti-American at the mess hall! Only I had been made to cry because of my decision. They bullied me because I am a woman—that was typical of Japanese people. I was the third to be transferred to Topaz, Utah.

RIICHI SATOW

I maintained that we should follow whatever course this country might set and that the question of who was going to win the war should be dealt with separately. In any case, when we were confronted with the loyalty oath, my answer was naturally "yes," and I could answer without any hesitation. I heard there were some people who actually said "no" as a protest, but as I recall, a majority of the people signed "yes."

Those who signed "no" had sort of nationalistic attitudes and were determined to resist the government. It was a very small minority, but the fact was that there were some people like that.

There were problems in all camps—a lot of problems with those people. Our camp was not an exception. For example, it was in our camp that Mr. Kido was attacked. He lived in Block No. 2 and was beaten one night. The reason why they got him is not clear, but this is what I think: Being president—I think he was—of the JACL (Japanese American Citizens' League) at that time, he had to deal with the government as to what should be done about the situation. He went to Washington, D.C., and attended a board meeting of the JACL. At that meeting they decided to support the recruiting of Nisei volunteers for the Army. Of course, there was opposition to the decision. I think that was the reason behind the attack. Those who participated in it were later arrested and punished, I believed. What happened to them after that, I don't know. It wasn't just Mr. Kido in our camp, but even I was once marked by some people according to one of the rumors.[4] So my family used to sleep in the back room of our living quarters while I slept on a cot near the front door every night. I had a stick beside my bed and also a plan all worked out in my mind to drive back the attackers if they should ever come. However, they never attacked me and never took action against me. The atmosphere was so tense that anything could happen over trivial matters.

When Mr. Kido was hospitalized following the incident, I went to visit him. His hands were swollen red. He said that he had covered his head with the hands to protect himself. He also said it was lucky that they didn't hit him on the head directly. He knew that some people were about to get him; so he took some sort of precaution every night. Yet when they did attack someone, they just forcefully burst their way into the house; and by the time you'd jump out of bed to fight back, they were already on their way out, having successfully completed their attack.

[4]Besides Mr. Kido, other leaders of the JACL and supporters of the recruitment program were both verbally and physically assaulted in the camps by the pro-Japan nationalists.

There were some other incidents where the filth from a toilet was scattered in front of the houses of some Christians. There were three or four other Christian families that were maliciously harassed like that. But again, nothing like that happened to me.

Fred Kitagawa told us about a newspaper article he read while he was in a camp. There were two camps in Arkansas, one of which was Jerome, where Fred was sent. He told us that he once read a newspaper which said that I was beaten up. This group of agitators, you see, was writing letters to newspapers in other camps a few days before they were to carry out their plan to attack someone. Their letters appeared in print the same day they carried out their plans. That's how the group was doing it, according to Fred. That's how I came to know for sure that the group in our camp was planning to attack me.

If anybody tried to force me out of the camp, I had a plan. I was going to tell them to vote on it. Of course, I was convinced that if the people had a chance to vote, they were not going to vote for kicking me out. A lot of people were quiet because they were pressured by the more outspoken people. Once the quiet ones were allowed a secret ballot, I was convinced that they would vote in my favor. I knew that I had absolutely no reason to be afraid of those outspoken people, for they were in the minority when it boiled down to numbers.

At first the Nisei were not required to participate in the military because they were the children of enemy aliens, and the Army couldn't decide if they were loyal to the United States. A man from the Army by the name of McKroy or something, who was probably a Secretary of the Army, at that time branded all of us Japanese as disloyal people without having done anything to find out if his conclusion was true or not. He made us all furious, naturally, and we said that it was not right. That's when this question of volunteers came up as a test case to determine the loyalty of Japanese. Of course, there was the 100th Battalion before this, but it was in Hawaii. On the mainland they at last decided to form a special corps of Nisei, and that's how the 442nd Regiment came about. A volunteer recruitment drive was set up across the camp. At that time from camp No. 2 at Poston . . . no, maybe it was from the Poston camp as a whole, we had forty-some volunteers altogether. They were all Nisei, you know, and our oldest son was one of them. Well, my son asked me if he might volunteer when the issue came up. I told him then to wait for a while and see how the situation developed. Most of the people in our living unit were absolutely against the idea of volunteering. However, I had my own ideas about it and was not about to be influenced by others.

One night I went to the officers meeting of our church there, and that's when I learned there had been forty-some volunteers so far. When I heard about that, I kind of felt guilty because I had told my son to wait for a while. I wondered myself if it was right for me to put a stop to my son's wish to volunteer when a lot of other families decided in favor of enlisting. I made up my mind then, and when I came home from the meeting, I told him that he might go ahead and volunteer. And so he did.

YOSHITO FUJII

In the meantime, we received a "volunteer call" from Washington, D.C., and it caused a huge dispute. The majority of the Japanese people at Minidoka were against it. I, as the camp's board president, said that we'd better make it clear where we stood. We Issei are Japanese, whereas the Nisei, who were born in the United States, are American. There is a difference between parents and children. We parents should protect the Nisei's stand. I didn't believe that it was good for the Nisei to be staying in the camp and encouraged the Nisei to go to Washington, D.C., as volunteers. I encouraged the Nisei to take that action for a better future. I worked hard for them. As a result, one morning a friend of mine informed me that my grave had been dug. I said, "How fortunate I am! I'll visit my grave." There the following was written on the gravestone: "Yoshito Fujii and forty-two other people are traitors to Japan." I took the stone to my office. At that time I wasn't concerned for my life. I felt it was my fate to fight for righteousness even if I was to be murdered. I was very firm in my belief. I sent volunteers to Washington, D.C., completed my term in office, and was elected for a second term.

MRS. RIKAE INOUYE

Minoru, our son, belonged to a group of nice boys. He became acquainted with people from Washington in the camp and they volunteered for the military. Minoru wondered if he should volunteer. My husband said, "You know, this war is between Japan and the United States. Your cousins in Japan are in the military service. I feel uneasy about cousins fighting each other. You don't have to volunteer. If the United States government drafts you, you must go; but please forbear volunteering." Understanding him, Minoru didn't volunteer. When he was allowed to go outside, he went to farm.

The boys who volunteered from Tule Lake were in a pitiful situation, for their parents were condemned by other Issei in the camp. One boy, who was the manager of a block, volunteered. His mother, who was on a different block, was condemned by others. When her son was leaving, she wanted to see him off, but she was hiding far away. My friend, Mrs. Kato, and I said, "Mrs. Taniguchi,* you're to send off Robert,* aren't you? Let's go. Come on." We drew her by her hands and went to send off Mr. Robert Taniguchi. I said, "Don't be scared. You should send him off with high spirits." In those days I felt some Issei in the United States were trivial. They didn't understand things very well. They thought Japan was the greatest, which wasn't true.

JUHEI KONO

You know, in Japanese we say, "*giri.*"[5] We Japanese have that spirit. We owe a kind of *giri* to America. I told the Nisei many times that if we wanted to show the true spirit of the Japanese, we should be loyal to America, for we owe something to America, regardless of whether Japan would win or not. One time when I was in Hawaii, the FBI questioned me. I told the FBI, "Since I am Japanese, it is natural for me to want Japan to win the war. I won't deny that. But the question of loyalty is quite another thing for the Nisei. We owe something to America and the good Japanese know that. They are loyal to America, even though we are the

*A pseudonym.

[5]*Giri* is the repayment of moral debts which include obligations to persons (a liege lord, distant relatives, etc.) and obligations to one's name (to clear one's name of insult, to fulfill Japanese proprieties, etc.); however, with an act of repayment there is always the fear that the obligation has not been sufficiently repaid. A Japanese man dreads the stigma of "he does not know *giri*," for he loses respect and, in some circumstances, may be ostracized. This concept of *giri* and its antecedent *on*, the lifetime obligations a Japanese incurs, are important because they pervade every aspect of Japanese life. For a more detailed explanation, see *The Chrysanthymum and the Sword* by Ruth Benedict, Houghton Mifflin, Boston, 1946, pp. 145–176.

enemy of America in war." That loyalty usually comes from the Japanese spirit of *"giri."* And I went on, "If you don't understand this, many of us Japanese will have to suffer. If you understand this, then sooner or later you will discover Japanese loyalty and you will not doubt it." That's the statement I gave to the FBI.

Mrs. Takae Washizu

At Tule Lake we were called out one by one and questioned on loyalty. People who said "yes" were considered loyal, and those who said "no" were disloyal. I was one of those who pledged loyalty. The loyal people got a notice to leave the camp in Tule Lake and move to some other camp. There were over ten thousand "disloyal" people in all, and the camp in Tule Lake was large enough to accommodate those people. That's why we, the loyal ones, had to leave that place. We were called the "dogs of the United States" behind our back. One cook said that we dogs shouldn't use chopsticks at the table. Before I left there, I went to the cook and thanked him for his cooking. He didn't say anything. Anyway, we weren't persecuted physically. The leader and the members of a radical group of disloyals were arrested before they caused a big problem.

People who believed in Japan's victory gave up their United States citizenship. They were sent back to Japan and were never permitted to re-enter the U.S. One boy who'd abandoned his citizenship fought with his brother who'd pledged loyalty to the United States. My husband, believing that Japan would win the war, was planning to go back to Japan after the war. But I didn't want to go back to Japan. I told our three children that they should decide by themselves whether they would go back to Japan or stay here with me. All of them said they'd like to stay with me. My husband was shocked to hear that; but loving the children very much, he changed his mind and decided not to go back to Japan.

There was a couple in Tule Lake that separated due to the loyalty issue. The husband remained in the camp, but his wife and daughter left for another camp. They lived together after the war, though. Some of the Japanese people who'd abandoned their U.S. citizenship returned to Japan; others remained in this country. After the war, when they wanted to regain their citizenship, they had a hard time.[6] One American politician demanded five hundred dollars from them.

MR. OSUKE TAKIZAWA AND MRS. SADAE TAKIZAWA

MR.: We got to Topaz by train in September. It was still hot in the midst of a desert without trees. There were rebels in the camp. The Japanese people who spoke English pretty well and talked to the American officials were called dogs by the pro-Japan people. Only those Japanese who spoke English could communicate with the American officials concerning necessary matters. Ministers [who spoke English] were suspected to be spies by the pro-Japan group. They thought the ministers were pro-American. They hung dirty things and dead snakes over the table where the ministers ate meals. One minister spoke English well and talked often to the American officials. The rebels were suspicious of him and put feces in his room. His wife was scared, so finally they moved to Salt Lake City.

MRS.: There was another dispute in the camp. The argument was over whether to send sons into the military service. Some said we should, while others said we shouldn't. There was some kind of meeting held at each block. I'm not sure if Takizawa remembers, but he was appointed as chairman. We discussed whether we should pledge our loyalty to the United States or to Japan.

MR.: I wasn't really qualified to be chairman. The young Kibei suspected that I was pro-American because I was a Christian. They appointed me chairman in order to get me into trouble.

MRS.: I remember he asked everybody to speak about his opinion, one by one from the corner. Nobody said anything. After a while, somebody asked, "What's your opinion, Mr. Takizawa?"

MR.: I said, "I'm living in the United States right now, I'm alive today in the United States, I married in the United States, and our three children have gotten their education in the United States; therefore, I have benefited from this country though I was born in

[6]Recognizing that renunciation of citizenship was the result of confusion, fear of bodily harm by "disloyal" groups, and sometimes parental coercion, the federal government eventually restored citizenship to most of those renouncing their citizenship who remained in the United States after the war. Of the 1,116 adults who renounced their citizenship and went to Japan, 685 had their citizenship restored.

Japan." I couldn't say anything bold; otherwise, I could have been attacked.

MRS.: Right. The people in favor of Japan were violent. The atmosphere became tense. The people in favor of Japan were happy to hear any statement in favor of Japan. We had a feeling of gratitude toward Japan. It wasn't fair to be kept in a camp. However, if we had been in Russia, we could have been killed. Though we had a lot of complaints about the camp, we couldn't hate this country wholeheartedly. We just hoped that Japan and the United States would draw the war to a close as soon as possible. Since Takizawa's statement wasn't all for Japan, the atmosphere turned sour.

MR.: I forgot his name, but a man stood up yelling, "I don't agree with you!" A lot of people applauded.

MRS.: The man was close to Takizawa and visited us often. Even *he* didn't agree with Takizawa. Though he wasn't the type of person who considers things deeply, he loved Japan very much. I don't remember how we passed a resolution, but the meeting ended in peace.

There were four young people in the camp who were about to graduate from college, including one of our sons. They pledged loyalty, but the majority of people did not. One day when our son was sitting in the bathroom, he was attacked by seven or eight young people. Later, we found he was attacked because he was going to get out of the camp for his schooling.

MR.: The violent youngsters complained that college kids stuck together and didn't associate with others.

MRS.: Our son was obliged to quit college before graduating because of the evacuation. He felt angry at being put in such a place in spite of his being a citizen. At first he wasn't willing to go back to school. We advised him to concentrate on completing his college work for a while. Later, we kept silent, for he resented our advice. We didn't know what to do about him. He seemed touchy and impatient in the camp. One day he went to the employment office in camp and found a job he wanted on the list. When he asked for it, he was told that he had to have a college degree to be qualified for the job. He told us about the incident. He realized that he should work on his degree. Then he decided to get out of the camp. At that time, many youngsters felt frustrated at being put in such a place.

MR.: The Issei, considering themselves Japanese, could take it. However, the Nisei, considering themselves American, couldn't stand it.

MINEJIRO SHIBATA

The Japanese people from Japan felt loyalty toward Japan. I don't know how their children who were born here felt. . . . Quite a few children born on Terminal Island were sympathetic to Japan, for they went to a Japanese school on the island and received a Japanese-style education. They didn't speak English even at school. When they spoke English, they were thought to be saucy by their friends. My daughter, who is in her fifties, doesn't pronounce English well even now; instead, she speaks Japanese well. Though I have American citizenship now, I couldn't forget about Japan then.

TSUGUO NAGASAWA

When the question of loyalty or disloyalty came up, I was really perplexed about what to do. I didn't know how to answer. Everybody was put in a different position according to his family circumstance. As I've told you, my elder brother who was in Japan had died. His wife sent me telegrams through the Red Cross. My elder brother was Koichi Nagasawa. He graduated from Waseda University and the University of Chicago. He was a scholar and wrote quite a few books. During the war he was employed by the Mitsubishi Company in Japan. He was killed by a bomb dropped by the United States. My brother did not believe that Japan could win the war against the United States. He, who didn't like the war, was killed by a United States bomb . . . Koichi Nagasawa. When I returned to Japan, I visited his house. . . . There was a hole in the books . . . this much. . . . It was awful. Half of his body was blasted away. Though I should have been loyal to the United States, I joined the disloyal group. Unless I was in the disloyal group, I couldn't go back to Japan to take care of family affairs. I told my wife to stay here with our children, but she wouldn't listen to me. I took everybody with me and went to Japan. Once we'd gone, we didn't come back here for ten years. It took ten years.

Out of some 120,000 evacuees detained in the ten relocation centers, 4,724 eventually returned to Japan after the war: 1,659 were aliens, 1,949 were American citizens, of whom all but 100 were children under twenty years of age accompanying parents, and 1,116 were adults who had renounced their American citizenship.

PART V:
THE RETURN

14

Repayment

SHOICHI FUKUDA

One week before I knew that I was coming back to California, an attorney in Florin sent a message to me and said that the fifteen acres of land which I had put up for sale went for three thousand two hundred dollars. There was a house and a well on it, but it still sold for less than thirty-five hundred. I actually received less than three thousand because of attorney's fees and other incidentals. After I came back, I went to see the realtor. He said, "It went cheap, but we could not help it. There is a vacant lot about five blocks further back in the countryside. It is about one mile behind your old place and has a small house. It's about twelve hundred dollars." It was unworkable land, so we could not use it immediately. Well, I went to WRA and talked to them about it. But they said, "You received money, so there is nothing we can do about it."

RIICHI SATOW

Our things were all gone by the time we got back home. Nothing was left . . . everything had been stolen. I had a big bookcase stacked full, but none of the books was left. Probably someone sold the books to a junkman, for even wastepapers at that time were valuable and salable.

HANAYO INOUYE

When we had to evacuate, we left a stove and a lot of other things at the Japanese school. When we came back from the camp, we believed that everything, including Emiko's piano, would be there. Nothing was left. Someone had set a fire to the school as the "Japs were coming back."

CHOICHI NITTA

When I returned to Loomis, I didn't have too many difficulties. I went to a meat market and they told me that I didn't have to pay cash, that I could pay the bill monthly like before. There was one store that didn't like Japanese. They had a "No Jap" sign. And there was a shoe store that didn't like Japanese. One Red Cross chairman in Loomis wouldn't help us when we asked for assistance. We didn't feel good about that. After her, Mrs. Nixon became the chairman. She was friendly toward us Japanese. Her husband was the head of the Fruit Growers Association, and they were both good to us.

As for our house, the contract was for the tenants to vacate on one month's notice, but they were still there when we returned. We moved into the upstairs rooms. They didn't like us taking the beds and our refrigerator back, but they weren't paying rent—I guess they hated to leave. When we wrote them before our return, they wrote back saying the atmosphere around there was not so good and for us not to return.

I left the fruit ranch in the care of the Fruit Growers Association, and they managed it. I heard that fruit prices were good during those years, but I didn't receive much money from them. When we returned, the farm tools and many things were gone, and we didn't know who took them. Just some dishes were left.

SADAME INOUYE

Since we did not have anything expensive, we decided not to sell. We knew a high school teacher who had a big basement in his home; so he let us store personal things in his basement. We left the farm as it was and later took proceedings for what we left. However, we got only about ten percent of the value. It was April or May when we left. We were about to harvest cabbages and strawberries, but we had to give them up. We asked for compensation later but we hardly got anything.

The Evacuation Claims Act of 1948 and a 1951 amendment resulted in limited payments of most claims without lengthy litigation for loss of real or personal property. When the final claim was paid in 1965, it brought the total paid by the government to thirty-eight million dollars, less than ten cents on the dollar, according to the San Francisco Federal Reserve Bank's 1942 estimate of Japanese property losses.

15

Relocation: Picking Up the Pieces

Tsuguo Nagasawa

When I learned that Japan had been defeated, I didn't believe that it could be so devastating. I couldn't believe everything broadcast by the American news media, for being Japanese, I was prejudiced in favor of Japan. After the war, most people [interned Japanese] got out of camp right away. The people who were to return to Japan waited for eight months before the boat's arrival. About four hundred and fifty people returned to Japan on our boat. We took a night train from the Tule Lake Camp to San Pedro Harbor. By the time we got to San Pedro, the original number of people had decreased. By the time we boarded the boat at San Pedro, they couldn't escape; so they went to Japan. But others were allowed to get off. Nobody tried to stop them, even though they had promised to return to Japan. I was ready with my luggage and everything else. I couldn't change my mind because I had a big family . . . five children, seven people in all.

The sailing was rough. We were on an American military boat. As we began our approach . . . landing in Japan, the powerful leaders of the *Hoshi-dan* became silent. Seeing the actual conditions in Japan . . . nobody had imagined that Japan had been defeated so badly! Those leaders who had been tough and boastful in camp and had troubled the WRA a lot, became silent and looked disheartened. I was so shaken by the scene as to feel my tears.

We arrived at a center in Kurihama in Kanagawa Ken. The place used to be a naval school. They served humble meals there. In Japan if you could get a breakfast of *miso* (soybean paste) soup, pickles, and rice, you should have appreciated it. The meals weren't good in comparison to those in the United States, but it was as much as Japan could provide, for she had surrendered. The girls in charge knew that we had returned from abroad. They gave us these words, "It's been hard work for you for a long time." The people from nearby areas such as Kanagawa and Tokyo got out of the center earlier. The people from remote areas such as Kagoshima and other Kyushu areas got out later, depending on family conditions. We were one of the early families to get out.

We had food difficulties, for we were used to the American way. We quickly ate up one cabbage, but should have rationed it to last a week. We realized that later. The rice ration wasn't enough either, for we were used to a luxurious way. Luckily, it wasn't far to Yamanashi Ken, where my mother lived. She shared her extra rice with us. Having five growing children, we never had enough rice. We also bought rice on the black market.

When we first arrived in Japan, the United States customs office warned me that I wouldn't have any other place to exchange dollars if I didn't do so in Kurihama, so I exchanged dollars at a rate of sixteen yen. Later on, I heard that the rate was raised up to two hundred and fifty or three hundred yen! And I had exchanged everything, even the silver coins.

Luckily, we had a lot of job offers from the Japanese side because we knew English. Concerning employment, we were popular in the prefectural offices, Foreign Affairs Department, and with the occupation forces. I said, "Give me a week's rest in my hometown. I'll visit my ancestral grave and will come back." I promised to work in Kanagawa Ken and left my family, the children and my wife, in the countryside. It was dangerous and costly to live in the city, because it was still chaotic there. The conditions of defeat were awful. The Omori, Otaku, and Kamata areas of Tokyo were burned to ashes.

I worked for the United States Provost Court in Yokohama and helped the Japanese people. There were some pitiful cases. The Japanese people thought it was all right to buy American goods if they paid money, but American law was different. It prohibited receiving, picking up, buying, or stealing American goods. One girl bought a blanket at a store in Yokohama. She thought her mother in Hokkaido must be freezing. She bought the American blanket at a Japanese store and mailed it. There was mail inspection at that time, and she was arrested and brought to court.

Reading her letter, I felt sorry for her. Filial piety. She thought she was guilt-free because she paid money for the blanket. My job was to write a petition. I translated her letter into English. I felt sorry for the dutiful girl. I worked hard to prove her innocence and did succeed in getting her released. United States law was such. There were shortages of everything then. No sheets of paper . . . don't pick up or receive. . . . Soldiers of the occupational forces threw up their hats in celebration. Then people picked them up and wore them. Wasn't it natural? I felt they were innocent. Don't pick up or receive. . . . Soldiers gave out their hats and jackets. Due to the shortage of goods, receiving gifts shouldn't have been a crime.

I heard that the leader of the *Hoshi-dan* had a good job, but I didn't get in touch with him. Most of the *Hoshi-dan* members didn't have good jobs. A few of them weren't allowed to come back to the United States. I planned to return to the States after three or four years. The major I was worki g for asked me if I was satisfied with my job. He said he would help me return to the United States if I wanted to do so. It was fun to be in Japan in those days. I was able to have things done by showing my name card. I answered that I was satisfied. If I had returned then. . . . When the Korean War broke out, I was given a job assignment which involved deciding whether items taken from Korea should be repaired in Japan or in the United States—radios and teletype machines mostly. The Yokohama base was a signal depot. There's a signal depot in Sacramento too. My job was to assess which way would be cheaper.

Our children were small in the beginning. As time passed, they reached their maturity. Being United States citizens, they received notices from the United States embassy and were given the choice of returning to the United States or staying in Japan. The embassy said that their United States citizenship would be terminated if they decided to stay in Japan. Our older children decided to return. Then I and my wife, with our ten-year-old daughter, returned two years later. Returning to Japan was a big mistake. I made a big mistake. All of the children had difficulties with English after returning to the United States. Everything was my fault.

I do gardening work now. Since I started old, I work only part-time. My wife does gardening with our oldest son. Being old, I feel too tired to work with young people. I'm almost eighty.

*Less than a year after the evacuation, various work-leave pro-
grams had been established, and thousands of evacuees gradually left the relocation camps to resettle in all areas of the United
States, except the West Coast, where "military necessity" was
still given as the formal reason for continuing the exclusion pol-
icy. Ironically, many evacuees found employment in defense
plants in other parts of the United States. Finally, in December
1944, the Western Defense Command announced the termina-
tion of the exclusion, effective on January 2, 1945; yet when the
war ended in August 1945, more than one-third of the evacuees
remained in the camps. The threat of returning to a sometimes
violently hostile community kept many in the camps. Their
economic situation held others, especially some aged Issei, in the
security of the camps, where at least meals and a place to sleep
were guaranteed. The returning evacuees had no specific
employment opportunities, no guarantees of housing, and no
funding until jobs could be found, and most alien Issei were still
not eligible for New Deal programs of economic reconstruction.
In late winter of 1946, the evacuees who remained in the camps
were simply given train fare to the point of evacuation, and the
camps were closed. The Issei began their struggle to adapt and
survive once again.*

Nisuke Mitsumori

I had heard of trouble before coming back. It concerned the
question of whether those who had been relocated should be allowed to go back to where they came from. People were allowed
to leave the camp after January, 1945. They gave us identification
cards and told us that the government would give us official permission to return if we brought these identification cards to
them. Our photographs and fingerprints were on these cards. It
was the government's decision, but we were still called "Japs" by
others. When the first Japanese family went back to Pasadena, the
people who received this Japanese family were harassed.[1] Somebody wrote some unpleasant things on their garage door. . . . At
that time the church became a major force for accepting returning
Japanese. The church accommodated them, helped them to find

[1]In 1945 there were thirty-six authenticated acts of violence against returning
Japanese in California.

jobs and housing, but white neighbors still looked angrily at families who accepted the Japanese.

MRS. RIYO ORITE

Since I was leaving the camp, my daughter also wanted to leave. Though she'd asked her block manager for cooperation, she couldn't get any help from him. I was concerned for her and asked my block manager to help. He sympathized and agreed to help her. Her husband had already left the camp by then, and, having five children, she wanted to leave with me.

My daughter said I was lucky because all of my children were grown up, and they didn't cause me any hardships. (She was struggling with her small children in the camp.) We cried together. When we finally left the camp, we got up at three or four in the morning and woke up the children. We asked to kindle a fire, then we ate breakfast and got on a train. I couldn't even see where my luggage was. I asked for a flashlight and looked for it. At that time one grandchild was only three months old—just a suckling. It was hard. I pitied the parents with babies. I and my grandchild got on a sleeping car, and the young adults got on a separate coach.

We returned to Richmond in the darkness. We went to a special housing area there and were given rooms according to the number of people in each family.

MINEJIRO SHIBATA

When we returned, nobody was living on Terminal Island. The houses had been broken down and replaced with warehouses for the canning company. The government claims that they have compensated us for our loss, but the compensation wasn't enough for us to regain our property.

I, my wife, and children were in Los Angeles. At one time, we stayed at my cousin's place for a week or so.

Though I worked, I didn't make too much money. Some people lived on religious organizations or something. I don't like to live on others, so I clench my teeth and bear a certain amount of hardship.

Masao Hirata

In 1946 everyone was allowed to return to California; so we moved back here. When we got out of the camp, they gave each of us only twenty-five dollars per person. I experienced unspeakable hardships to support all my family. I will never forget it. When we returned to California, we didn't have a place to live. One of my friends leased me this small house. The next problem was that I couldn't start my work. I didn't have a car or anything. My farm had not been touched for five years, and I didn't even have any tools to cut down the tall weeds on the land. But I had to work to support my family; so I borrowed old tools and worked on my farm. Every Japanese person had to start again from the beginning. Because we were all not living in our old neighborhoods, we couldn't ask for help from anybody.

When I was looking for a house for my family, one of my friends offered a house to rent. The rent was seventy-five dollars a month, and I had to pay three months in advance. Then I went back to camp and brought my family here. Unfortunately, the baggage we had sent didn't arrive here for over a month. We had great difficulty without beds, cooking tools, and so on. We suffered a lot for that month, although I bought some necessary things little by little. How can I describe the hardships we experienced to begin living again after the war? I had to use an old truck which I had to push from behind to start the engine. I had to finance my six children through school. I think what made me overcome all these hardships were my youth and strong will.

Shoichi Fukuda

By April we were able to return to the West Coast. I came back to California in May. Everybody was afraid of being attacked by the white people. The war was still going on at that time, and prejudice and oppression were very severe. The first problem was that I could not find a home to live in. The homes which were formerly occupied by Japanese people were occupied by many black families. When houses were found, they were shared by four or five families. Sheets were hung in the rooms to divide them into smaller units. I had a very difficult time finding a place to live. When I finally found a house, it was small and dirty. The owner did not honor his agreement, so we had no light. We lived by candlelight for about a month.

For the first month, I helped in Mr. Osuga's hostel, which was located in the Sunday School classrooms of the Japanese Pioneer Methodist Church. I paid for my own room and board and also helped him. A small number of Japanese people used to come back to Sacramento every time a train came in; so I would go to the station to pick them up.

My son, Joseph, came back to Sacramento by himself, and in July my other son came to live with us.

I continued looking for a job. Some Chinese were farming in south Sacramento; so I went there to work. Then some Japanese people began to farm in the northern part of Sacramento; so I went to work for them. I wanted to work in the city, but I could not find anything at all. The C.P.C. cannery would not hire Japanese at that time. Finally I went to the C.I.O. union and asked them about a job. They asked, "What kind of job do you want?" I answered, "Anything I can get." They told me that when they found something, they would let me know. A few days later they told me that there was a job at a Safeway store working in a warehouse during the night. "If you don't mind working at night, the job is yours." My friend and I were looking for a job at the same time; so we both got a job at the same place in the produce department. My job was to place orders in a truck in time for a driver to deliver the produce early in the morning.

Some interesting things happened while I was working at the warehouse. During the watermelon season, we would get lots of them at once. Our foreman told us that we could each take one home, so I put a nice big one in a potato sack and carried it on my back. It was about two A.M. A police car followed me and finally stopped me. One of the policemen asked what I was doing and what was in that potato sack. I explained that I worked for Safeway and that I had permission to take the watermelon home. If boxes were broken at the warehouse and the contents were no longer salable, we were allowed to take the items home. I was stopped by the police many times.

In August, the war came to an end. The night before the end of the war, we workers had lunch together. We talked about everything, including politics and war. The others said that they felt sorry for me, because Japan was not doing so well and might be conquered any day. We had quite an argument, because I felt that Japan would never be conquered.

The next day factories were blowing their sirens and cars were honking their horns. They said, "Japan is conquered! Japan is conquered!" I was very shocked and felt *nasakenai* (it's a shameful situation). I just did not want to talk to anyone, but I could not take a day off. Tears were rolling down my face. I did not want to see anybody at work, and I did not want to talk to my wife either. I walked to the warehouse and worked silently. I was very grateful to the people there. I had argued vigorously that Japan was not going to lose the war, but these people did not even mention the war at all. Those union people were very sympathetic toward me. I was very surprised, and at the same time I respected their sensitivity. One of my co-workers said, "Sorry," to me. I was really impressed by him. The next day I felt much better, because these people seemed to understand me very well.

During the war there was a ration system. Everything was purchased with coupons. Now that the war had ended, people were free to buy anything they wanted and in any amount, so everyone tore up their coupons and threw them out of car windows as they passed in the streets. We had accumulated quite a lot of coupons to buy meat and sugar, but when the war ended, these coupons were no longer necessary. We laughed at ourselves, for if we had known this, we could have bought lots of meat and sugar.

Even in those days there were quite a number of "No Jap" signs. It was very strange and interesting that those stores which had those signs posted never were popular or successful. The other places which did business with Japanese people were very popular and successful. Many of the stores with "No Jap" signs closed after the war.

At that time they paid seventy-five cents an hour at the cannery; but I was paid about eighty-nine cents an hour plus any overtime at the warehouse, and I thought it was the best job I ever held. I was very happy about that; so I worked very hard. However, I still wanted to have my own store. I went to the McClatchy Realty, and they found a small store for me. It did not have anything in it, not even shelves; so I had to make them by myself. Lumber was not available at that time. Fortunately, I found a store which was going out of business, and I bought shelves from them. I wanted to begin a dry goods store there, but I could not find any material to sell. I bought anything I could lay my hands on, such as paint, hardware, et cetera. As it was shortly after the war, the wholesale stores did not have an abundance of material, and being Japanese added to my difficulty. I bought anything I could get and put them on the shelves. Later I located a wholesale store through which, if I bought many other little items, I could buy a dozen handkerchiefs. Another wholesale store permitted me to buy a dozen towels if I purchased other items in less demand. So I was compelled to purchase all these extra items. Fortunately, all the things which I brought home sold very well. In time, I was able to get more dry goods, and I began to cut out other items which I did not want to sell.

Yardage was very difficult to find, and flannel was a particularly rare item. There was one salesman who said that he could get some flannel for me. It was factory made, so it was not the best quality material, but he got me one bolt which was one thousand yards. When the flannel came, it was too bulky to put inside the store, so I put it outside, right on the sidewalk. Well, customers came and asked me to cut five or ten yards at a time for them. That one thousand yards of flannel sold in three days.

Meanwhile, we were allowed to send parcels to Japan. We decided to make parcels and send them back to Japan according to the orders we got. We made that service free as long as customers bought things from us. We became very, very busy with this parcel business.

From morning till night customers came in continuously. In the daytime we took orders, put materials in boxes, and wrote down the forwarding addresses. In the evenings after we closed the store, we made up parcels. We bought lots of sugar. And our customers bought it and asked us to send it to relatives in Japan. We worked from very early morning till very late at night. Sometimes it was three-thirty in the morning before we could get to bed. However, lots of taxes were put on the parcels afterwards, so this parcel business began to decline. We were there in our stores for over ten years.

We kept two stores open for a while, but the Japanese moved out of that area; so we closed the small store. Finally, the redevelopment agency started working in that area, and we had to move out. Well, actually, people moved out of the place first because of the redevelopment; so we closed the store and retired.

We then took a tour of Japan and Europe and came back to the States. I did not do anything for two years. It was very boring, so I opened a variety store on Broadway. I had it for five years, but it was not successful, so I closed it at the end of the lease. I retired again and have been taking it easy since then.

JUHEI KONO

"*Sho-ri-to*" means groups of people who thought Japan had won the war when, in fact, she had lost. They could not admit that Japan had lost. Once I was invited to speak especially to explain to the *sho-ri-to* people that Japan had lost the war. "All right, I understand, I understand," those people said, but in their hearts they did not want to believe me. So I told them, "You don't want to admit that Japan lost the war, even though she was defeated. Remember, as long as she comes back again, it's all right. Therefore, you must have hope in the future." I told the *sho-ri-to*, "If you really love Japan, you must change your mind and hope that Japan will survive and develop again. But if you don't love Japan, you can continue the way you feel, and then you will be disloyal Japanese instead of loyal Japanese."

At that time I was trying to decide whether to go back to Japan or back to the mainland from Hawaii. I finally came to the mainland in 1947 because of the problem of educating our children. The oldest daughter had just finished grammar school, and she had to prepare for high school. Of course, we had good high schools over there too. But, after all, Hawaii is a small place. In order to give her a broader education, I thought that we should go back to Japan or to the mainland. My wife didn't want to go to Japan; so I sacrificed my own desires. The children were all happy about that.

Oh, the housing situation was terrible during that time. I came ahead of my family to try to find some place to live. But in San Francisco, Los Angeles, or wherever, there was no housing. After looking for a month, I finally decided to buy a used car and look with my family as soon as they arrived in San Francisco. We had to stay somewhere with the four children. Even at hotels during that time you couldn't get two rooms. When they arrived, I started traveling with them and decided to stop wherever we could find a house.

Before we left the Bay area, I asked the government housing authorities in Richmond to let me know if they had any vacancies. At first they didn't allow us to use their housing unless I had some connection with the military. I am a minister; so I asked them for special consideration. I left a request and then went out. In West Los Angeles there was no housing—in Los Angeles, no housing. We went to Riverside, and from Riverside we went to Arizona—then on to Salt Lake City, no housing—Denver, oh, no housing. In Denver we couldn't even stay in a hotel, because there was no room for six people. Finally we went to Chicago through Omaha. We found the same situation in Chicago. It was a difficult time. When we got to Chicago, I received a letter from one of my minister friends in California. It said that his wife had had serious surgery. He asked me to come to California and help him for a little while. I thought I must help him somehow. Instead of going on to Washington or to New York, we stopped right there and came back. When we arrived in Richmond, there was news about a government house, just one room, but it was open.

SHIZUMA TAKESHITA

The Western Defense lifted the ban on Japanese around the end of January or the first of February, 1945. My wife and I came back in March. We wanted to rent a house, but there were no vacancies at that time, because so many black people moved into Oakland during the war to work for Kaiser.

I put an advertisement in the newspaper for a place to rent. I got a call back from someone saying, "We don't want you Japs; so go somewhere else." I said to him in my broken English that we came back at the orders of the government. Then we got a call from the parents of the mayor of Piedmont asking us to go there. We both did domestic work for them. I was almost seventy years old and learned to do chores from my wife. World War II ended while we were working there. We listened to the Emperor of Japan proclaim defeat. We declared our loyalty to the U.S.A., but when we heard that the country of our birth was defeated, we cried.

We worked for Mr. and Mrs. Dinsmoor for about a year, and we liked it because we didn't have to worry about food or a place to live. When the Ogawas, who had worked for them before the war, returned, they asked us to find another place. We worked at several places after that. The last place we worked before we took a trip to Japan was Senator Knowland's father's place. He was the owner of the *Oakland Tribune.* We worked for him for two years. Mrs. Knowland suffered a stroke about three weeks after we started to work there, and she died on the third day of her illness.

Senator Knowland came back from Washington, D.C., for the funeral. Mrs. Knowland was his stepmother, but he was very attached to her. His real mother had passed away when he was still young, and his stepmother was very good to him. Before the Senator returned to Washington, D.C., he made arrangements to have his eldest daughter and her husband come to live with his father, and he asked us to look after his father and daughter. We worked for them for two years, but had to quit because I started to have heart trouble and was advised by the doctor to rest. My condition improved after I rested, and we decided to take a trip to Japan to see our eldest son and his family.

When World War II broke out, this son was required to serve in the Japanese Army because he was living in Japan. He thought he would not get out alive; so he sent us a letter with some of his hair for us to keep. I did not show this letter to my wife, as it came while she was at work. If and when he died, I was going to show it to her. Later, through the Red Cross and return postcards, we found out that he was safe.

We took a cargo ship to Japan in 1952 for a visit. We met our daughter-in-law and two grandchildren for the first time. Our son's family was living in Fukushima Ken, and he was working for the Shoyei Seishi Company. While we were there, my first wife's niece came to see us all the way from Nagano Ken. Then we took a trip to Nagano Ken and visited relatives. We traveled to my birthplace, Iki-no-shima, in Nagasaki Ken and visited friends whom we had known in this country and had moved back to Japan. We spent seven months in Japan, and after our return we started to do domestic work again.

Then we tried to get our eldest son to come and live in the United States, but he had lost his U.S. citizenship when he served in the Japanese Army. We arranged to have him come on a three-months' visitor's visa. On the third day after he arrived, he said he didn't want to return to Japan; so we decided to find out if he could stay here permanently. I mentioned this to Senator Knowland's daughter. She got in touch with her father, and he introduced a bill for our son. The immigration office heard this, and they got upset. They wanted to deport him. My wife told them in her broken English that she lost her first husband when the boys were very young, and that she had to take them to Japan to have their grandparents raise them, because she couldn't support them. She pleaded with the officers and told them that her eldest son had to serve in the Japanese Army against his will because he was living in Japan at the time. The officer instructed us to send in affidavits. We hired an attorney and sent in the proper documents. At the first hearing we won. But the district attorney wasn't satisfied; so he set another hearing, and we won this also. Then the district attorney referred the case to Washington, D.C. We asked the Japanese American Citizens League's attorney to help us, and the judgment in Washington, D.C., was advantageous to us. They ruled that our son did not lose his citizenship; therefore, he was able to remain in this country. It took three years to get the case settled.

We bought a three-bedroom house in East Oakland and lived together. About three years later, we made arrangements to have my stepson's wife and two sons come and join him. Our grandsons were nine and eleven years old at the time. Now the older grandson is studying at the University of California in Berkeley and will be graduating before long. The younger one was student body president at Oakland High School. He received a recommendation to the Air Force Academy, and he graduated from there. He is a second lieutenant and stationed at Taizau now. Our daughter-in-law went to an adult education school for three years. She passed her citizenship examination in English.[2] Since both parents became citizens, the children became U.S. citizens automatically. We have six votes in our family now.

RIICHI SATOW

I began to worry about the education of my children as the days went by, and I decided it was not good to keep them in camp any longer. Another thing that made me think that the time was ripe for us to get out of the camp was that a lot of people started making trouble in the camp over nothing. That really made me worry, "Japan is winning some battles now, and they are like this. What's going to happen if Japan starts losing the war?" I didn't want to be around when the news of Japan's defeat reached our camp, because anything could happen. Of course, the rumor that someone was out to get me in the camp had been worrying me. But mainly I was so worried about a possible uproar on the day of Japan's defeat that I decided it was best to leave the camp as early as possible; so that I wouldn't be forced by circumstances to get

[2]In 1952 the Immigration and Nationality Act, which provided that all races were eligible for citizenship, was passed.

involved in the riot in any way. I completed the necessary paper-
work to get my family out. Fortunately, Mr. and Mrs. Kodama in
Colorado had a job for me out there.

We settled in a small community called Keenesburg, which was
about twenty-five miles from Denver. Radishes and other vegetables grew very well out there; so we settled down to grow vegetables. There our children started a normal school schedule again.
Hannah graduated from Keenesburg High School, but the other
children didn't, because before their graduation we all came back
to California. We were there about three and a half years.

It was a very peaceful life there, and we didn't have any problems. The Japanese were very industrious people and the community liked us for that. Germans had settled that community.
Since Germany was also one of the enemy countries, the Germans there were very friendly toward us Japanese. My landowner
used to tell me that it was all right for me to tell him my true
feelings about the war. I thought to myself at that time, "I am by
far more loyal to America than this man." Talking about this
man, and about the Germans in general. . . . He was originally
from Germany and came to the States at the age of seven or so.
His wife finished school here. Anyhow, both of them were of
German ancestry. Although the land which they worked used to
be utterly barren, they cultivated and developed it into beautiful
farmland. Those Germans I came to know had acquired very little
formal education themselves, and they were not so enthusiastic
about sending their kids to school either. However, when it came
to the business of farming, they did a superb job. They were also
very industrious people and worked hard. That's why most of
them were successful in this country. It was funny, though, when
their children happened to go to high school, the parents thought
they had some kind of great scholars born in their family; but
hardly anybody went to college from that community, whereas
most of the Nisei were at least high school graduates, and some
even had college degrees. Therefore, the Nisei were treated like
noble scholars there.

In Keenesburg there was a Dr. Foot, a Baptist and a long-time
missionary in Japan; he helped us a lot. On many occasions I
asked for his assistance, and on other occasions he counted on
mine. In a town called Brighton there was a Baptist church where
two of my boys, Osami and Satoru, and two of my brother's,
received baptism. Since the war was still going on at that time,
none of the local church members showed up at the ceremony.

So, it was Dr. Fischer, Dr. Foot, an old minister of the church by the name of Rev. Worthley,* and two families that came to witness the four boys' baptism. Rev. Worthley officiated at the ceremony, and Dr. Fischer and Dr. Foot sang hymns. Now, concerning this occasion, there arose a problem . . . even though it was not originally a problem to us at all. There was a newspaper called the *Christian Science Monitor,* or something like that, and it scooped the news about our boys' baptism. The story's criticism later hurt Rev. Worthley's position in the church.

The paper questioned whether it was right for a Christian church to discriminate against certain people, and said that what took place in regards to our boys' baptismal ceremony posed a big question. I don't know who gave them the information about it, but anyhow the paper wrote the story, and put Rev. Worthley in hot water as a consequence. He succumbed to the anti-Japanese pressure of some members of the church, whereas Dr. Foot maintained all the way that no one should ever give in to such pressure. However, the fact of it was that it really didn't matter to us whether or not our sons were officially recognized as members of that particular church at all, since we were planning to go back to California sooner or later anyhow. But during the war, even Christians tended to have hostile feelings against us to some degree, so it might have been just a natural reaction. It was a time when people were extremely hostile towards the ministers who showed understanding or favorable attitudes toward the Japanese. Yes, there used to be such times.

After a while I decided that Colorado was not a good place for me to send my children to colleges. There was a college in Fort Collins, and a university in Boulder, but whatever college they might choose, a tuition of four hundred dollars was required. I had too many children for that. I would not have to worry about any tuition fees if we went back to California. And besides, I knew there was a college near our house in Sacramento. My wife and children had wanted to come home here long before that. I remember they kept telling me that they did. I had to have more than just a desire to come back here. I required of myself some sort of goal to a degree. Having been president of the Strawberry Association, I left some of my responsibilities unfulfilled because of the sudden outbreak of the war. None was my personal responsibility, but because of the law, I, the president, had to eventually

*A pseudonym.

assume them . . . some of which were pretty heavy for anyone to carry out. Then I consulted my wife. . . . She said that whatever I decided was fine with her. We immediately started packing up our belongings. . . . I had a truck then for my job. It was a pretty big one, and on it we piled up as much as possible. Rumor had it that there still were shortages of many things, furniture for one, because it was right after the war. That's why we decided to bring whatever we had along with us to California. We had all kinds of junk on the truck.

I was probably close to fifty years old then and was still healthy and strong. I drove a passenger car and traveled with my wife and the little ones. My oldest son was in the service and stationed somewhere in Europe, the oldest daughter was married and living in Boston, and the second oldest daughter was in a nursing school. We had still six other children to look after. Hannah was the oldest of the six then. She had just finished high school. The next oldest was Satoru—now they call him Bill—and he was around sixteen or so. I let him drive the truck with Hannah sitting next to him. I told them to follow me in the truck, while I drove the passenger car with the rest of my family. It was winter, still the early part of January. Crossing the Rockies was a little bit danger-ous because of the icy conditions of the road; so we decided to take the southern route and headed for Albuquerque, New Mexico. Passing through Arizona on Route 66, we made it to Bakersfield, and then from there we came all the way up here. Oh, it took us around six days in all. We never stayed on the road till dark. Every day around three o'clock, we were already on the way to a hotel for the night. You see, we had children traveling with us; therefore, we took it slow. The youngest was about four years old.

At a place called Flagstaff on our way through Arizona, the truck had engine trouble. You see, Satoru was supposed to follow us in the truck with Hannah, and we lost sight of them for a while. It was snowing then. It kind of worried me; so I pulled over to the side of the road and waited for them. Well, in a short while, there they were, driving very slowly. When I looked at poor Sat-oru, oh, his face was pale and he was almost half-crying! Then we found out that one of the parts was broken, and it was impossible to drive the truck any longer. We knew we could easily fix it as long as we could get hold of the right spare part. Anyhow, we got to a nearby garage. Luckily, they had the right kind of part we needed, and also they gave us very courteous service. We spent a few hours in Flagstaff waiting for the truck to be fixed and then moved on. This was in January 1947. By the time we got back here, our house was unoccupied, so we moved right back in. When we left for the camp, we asked a real estate company to take care of our house for us. We put them in charge of it and left. They had rented our house to a white family. This family had disappeared with three or four months rent unpaid.

When we got back, everybody was busy trying to earn a living. You see, we lost just about everything. Those who owned land were at least able to keep their land, but most of us were economically destroyed, completely uprooted. Therefore, we were all busy trying to recover from our losses. In California I grew strawberries again until 1950 or 1951.

MRS. KO TAKAKOSHI

After the war we came back to Seattle and stayed at the Baptist Women's Home until we found a place to live. Miss McCullough and Miss Ramsey, who had moved from Seattle to Twin Falls, Idaho, to be near us in the Minidoka Camp, were already back in Seattle. They waited for our return and helped us in many ways. There must have been twenty to twenty-five people staying at the Home at one time. Some families sent one member out to find a place before the rest of the family came out from the camp. Because of these friends, we were able to live without much fear, even in adverse circumstances. We were very fortunate.

YOSHITO FUJII

On the first of January, the ban against Japanese people was lifted on the Pacific Coast. If you wanted to, you could return. I wondered how American society as a whole would accept us. I knew I could force myself to return and hire somebody to take care of my business. I came back to Seattle in April to see what was going on and to take a look at the actual conditions. I've been living here since then.

We were not abused when we returned. People couldn't distinguish us from the Chinese who ran the businesses before. The people in the area to which I'd returned trusted us. The Caucasians here were kinder than the Caucasians in California. The majority of the people here are Norwegians. They are gentle people from northern Europe. Japanese people ran hotels, and Norwegians stayed there. They relied on the middle-aged Japanese maids, and the maids' services were good.

My family joined me around September. We took care of the N.P. Hotel, and we hired a stubborn old Caucasian gentleman to manage it. The Filipinos were prejudiced against the Japanese then, for the Japanese soldiers had treated the Filipinos cruelly. Some Filipinos were dangerous. The Caucasian old man whom we hired was tough enough to handle the Filipinos. That's why nothing dangerous happened to us.

When Japan surrendered, I was at the N.P. Hotel. There were five or six people gathered there. I thought the war itself was foolish. I could tell that it was a hopeless war for Japan from the beginning, but we cried. All of us were Issei.

As I said, I ran the N.P. Hotel, which my parents-in-law owned. I got a notice whenever somebody was leaving the camp, and I would arrange a room. I gave up my bottling company. That was because all of the Japanese grocery stores had been closed down. There used to be a lot of small Japanese groceries here, but they were taken over by chain stores after the war. Such small businesses couldn't have competed with a large chain-store business. The change, of course, was good for me. I later opened the Harold Hotel. Then I opened my two other businesses. I own apartments now. I'm supposed to be semi-retired, but I can't seem to take it easy.

TOKUSHIGA KIZUKA

I had an American friend in Watsonsville who owned a summer house. He wrote me saying that they had the house ready for us; so we came back and went straight to their summer house without having to stay in the hostel like some other people did. Our American friend was so nice. He even had food in the freezer. My own family and my wife's relatives all moved in together. The American friend even had a car for us to use. We stayed there for about a week until we rented our own place.

In 1947 after I returned to Watsonville, I first went to see Mr. Hutson, who was a lawyer. I told him that I was back, but I had no money and didn't know what to do. He told me not to worry about money, that I'd get a loan. I used to grow tomatoes and sugar beets, but he suggested that I start to grow strawberries, since there was a demand and I had a lot of helping hands. I started to look for land to lease, but no one wanted to lease to a Japanese. I finally went to see an old acquaintance from before the war. His name was Mr. Toni Osbild,[3] a Portuguese descendant, who lived in Elkhorn. He owned about five hundred acres of land. I told him the situation I was in and of not being able to lease land anywhere. I asked if he would lease me some of his land. He offered to lease a hundred and twenty-five acres along the Salinas Road and even offered to dig a well for water. That is how I got started on my strawberry farming in 1947. We were the second group of people (Japanese) to start in Watsonville after the war, but we were the only people who continued on, because the other people quit after the first harvest. With a partner, Mr. Takiyoshi, we worked about a hundred acres.

We did not have a house in the field; so we had to build one. At that time there was a big shortage of lumber and nails, so we bought an old barn and disassembled it very carefully piece by piece. With that lumber we built a shed and a house, but there was not enough lumber. About that time they had some old Army barracks for sale at Fort Ord, but they were sold only to soldiers. Luckily, my partner's brother was a soldier, so he bought six barracks for us. Then we all took turns to buy nails, because we could only buy five pounds of nails per person. We finally finished building the house, but it was not easy. It all turned out well, and I retired early. Because I remained in the United States, I was able to live comfortably. This is my greatest joy.

Mrs. Takae Washizu

The war was over on the fifteenth of August, and I came back to California in October. My husband had left the camp in June before the war was over. I and my two daughters came back to California together. My husband went to the house of one of his old friends, and we went to Rev. Nakamura's church in Sacramento. Quite a few people were there. Rev. Nakamura had four children. There was no parsonage; so he slept on the balcony in the church and provided a room for the sick. We were given a separate place too. He also arranged for Japanese people to work as domestic helpers for white families so that some of us could get

[3]The name is spelled according to Mr. Kizuka's pronunciation.

employment. Mrs. Nakamura's parents were in charge of the cooking. Others cleaned the place and washed dishes and were paid a dollar and thirty-five cents a day.

As soon as Rev. Nakamura returned to California in June, he opened up his place for people in need. He closed it in February of the following year. Not only Christians but also Buddhists came into his place. He decided to close it down because of some idle people. There were quite a few people there who just relied on Rev. Nakamura's kindness and didn't take their own initiative in finding their means of living. Rev. Nakamura wanted them to make their best efforts out in society without his help.

There wasn't enough housing available for the Japanese people. I knew one couple with children who rented somebody's basement and slept there like dogs. It was a pitiful period. Soon after Rev. Nakamura closed down his facilities, a Buddhist church opened up the same kind of accommodations. Gradually, one house after another appeared to be available for Japanese people. Our daughters worked as schoolgirls for one white family, and I worked as a domestic helper for another white family. My husband and son worked on a farm. In other words, we lived separately. By the time I quit my job, we could afford a house of our own.

WATARU ISHISAKA

The Issei really helped each other after the war, but the younger generation, the Nisei, became so individualistic and selfish that those who left camp to survey the situation in Sacramento went back to the camp and brought only bad news about living conditions and such. However, I thought what they said was very unreasonable, and I just couldn't accept it, so I decided to take a look myself. A friend and I came back to California together. When we came back and saw our old friends, we were greatly welcomed. I was really mad about the incorrect news which was brought back by the others. I went right back to the camp and said, "Damn you! What you said was all lies. We should all go back to California. What are you going to do about your children's education?" Well, some wouldn't believe me. Some even ridiculed me, but those who came won out. They all benefited from coming back to California. I was really mad at those who had brought bad news about California. Those people got financially ahead of others who came back later. I still tell them, "You told others not to go back to Sacramento, but you came back here first and tried to get ahead." Well, one of them said, "Don't talk about that any more. It's in the past." This man [a Nisei] is a big shot in this town now, but I always remind him of this fact. I really think that there are tremendous differences between the Issei and the younger generation Japanese—their humanity, their relationships with one another are poor. I'm very sorry about that.

I returned to Sacramento again to look for a house for my family, and I met Mr. Fukuda. He was very troubled, because he couldn't find a house or a job. One day Mr. Fukuda said, "Mr. Ishisaka, I've got to find a job. I can't go on like this." So the next day we went to look for jobs. We walked down to "M" Street where there was a sign which said, "C.I.O." So I said, "Well, let's try this." But Mr. Fukuda said, "But this is a union, and they will not give us a job." I said, "You don't know unless you try." I was a lot more aggressive than he, and told him to follow me. I said to a clerk, "I need a job. I've got no money." He said, "What kind of job do you want?" I replied, "Anything." Then he said, "Can you work tonight?" Well, I was sure surprised. I looked at Mr. Fukuda and said, "How about that? They want us to work from this evening!" So, both of us went to work that night. The job was in a Safeway warehouse. We received union wages and made good money there, but my main purpose was to find a house so that my wife and children could come back and start their schooling.

Well, one day I met Fumi-chan of the Kozono family. She said that her brother was in the Army; so she had to come back and help her father farm, since there was no one who could help them. She asked me to come. I knew they really needed help; so I quit working at the warehouse though that job paid much better. I helped them through the peach season. After that, she helped me to find a house.

My philosophy of life is that we should not fight against the flow of time. If you see a man in need, you must help him. You see, I sure didn't make money working at the Kozonos', but Mr. Kozono had a car and helped me to find a house. They also helped me move in too. I was finally able to move my family out of the camp and into a house in Sacramento. I found some houses in the Pocket Area in Sacramento and housed many people who returned from the camps. I called my family back. My parents, my older brother and his family, my friend and his family—they all came to live with us, more than ten people altogether. Those people did not have the pioneering spirit; so I had to carry them until they could stand on their own feet. Well, it's all a matter of individual determination. The man who owned the land where we lived decided to sell, and we then moved to Woodland. I took all my family and friends there. By that time my friends had accumulated some money, and they were able to become independent farmers.

At that time many Japanese people were coming back from camps and also from the East, but there were very few places for them to stay. It was miserable for everyone at that time. People lived in small rooms divided by blankets or sheets. People like me who came here first and found housing for their families were lucky. We didn't have to suffer as much, but my wife really went through a lot with so many people in our household.

Later we moved to a ranch down below Galt. They had about ten thousand acres there, and I raised tomatoes and beans. I leased from eight hundred to two thousand acres at various times. I had to have at least five men full time on the ranch, because we used heavy equipment. Most of the harvesting was done by machines. I used to drive at least a hundred and fifty miles a day. I had to go back and forth, and I had to fix machines and buy parts. I was very busy.

I had to be on the field by seven to supervise the workers. At that time we didn't have enough help; so we used to have winos and convicts. Some of those men were strong, and they were good workers too. If we had to keep them past five, we had to feed them dinner, because the prison mess hall closed at five. Then I had to take them to a restaurant. By the time I took them back to their road camp and came home, it was one or two in the morning. It was a good-paying job, but I worked too hard and wrecked my health. At that time my twins, Woody and Howard, were in grammar school. It was the first time that the school had Japanese students in classes. They were in the eighth grade when we moved to Elk Grove. We stayed there for twenty years.

Then I got sick, a heart attack, and I didn't have any salary. I had to pay the children's school expenses out of my savings. Anthony, the youngest one, was in the eighth grade. My wife went to work for the first time. She's really had a hard life. She had to work and had to take care of me. She is a good woman. I got well, and I started working, until five years ago when I began to have heart trouble again. Now I'm retired. However, I would like to work if I could. A man is happier that way.

My father lived with us for thirty years, and I really respected my father. He was a real human being. He loved nature, especially birds and animals. When we moved to Galt, I told him not to work anymore. He loved to play with our children, who enjoyed watching Grandpa trap foxes. Every day he went out and trapped foxes. He caught over thirty of them and kept them in a huge cage. Foxes cannot be tamed easily, but he patiently fed them and tried to tame them. Feed for foxes was very expensive, but it was his pleasure; so I didn't complain. When he was in Japan, he had many white-eyed birds and Japanese hunting birds. He had over fifty at one time or another. My grandmother used to say that feeding those birds was a big job. Father was very carefree and had no greed about money, but my mother suffered a lot because of that. For that matter, I'm just like him, and my wife suffered a lot financially. But our children are well educated. Two have their doctorates, and two have their bachelor degrees.

Mrs. Kane Kozono

I know some people had a lot of trouble when they returned. I heard that some found their homes burned down when they came back. We were in the camp only for three years, and we were also lucky that a boss whom we knew very well at the cannery here was a kind man. Ard, my son, said to him, "I am going into the Army. My folks are going to Amache. Will you please look after my father while I'm gone?" The boss then answered him, "All right. Don't worry about your parents. I will do my best to take care of your mama and papa."

Most of my white neighbors in West Sacramento were kind and good to us. A white woman right across the street was a very good neighbor. When we were evacuated, I asked her to keep a strongbox for us. At the bottom of the box were receipts and some papers to prove that my husband loaned money to different people. When I came back here from the camp, she visited me and said, "Mrs. Kozono, here it is. I brought your box back." I opened it, and found everything in there just as I put it: the papers, the documents, and all the other valuable things. Nothing was missing. Prior to the evacuation she told me, "If the time should come when you have to go to a camp, don't hesitate to let me know whatever you need. I'll be glad to send it to you." It was very nice of her. In fact, I asked her one time from the camp to send me an umbrella. She kindly did so.

When I learned that we were getting out of the camp, it kind of worried me how we would be received back in our old neighborhood; so I wrote to my neighbor about it. She answered, "I asked a lot of neighbors here about your concern. Everybody said, 'Why should we dislike the Kozonos at all? It would be so nice to have them back here again.' That's what we all think." That was her answer. When we did come back to West Sacramento, one of our neighbors visited us right away with a lot of vegetables from their family garden. Everybody welcomed us back.

When we Japanese were evacuated, some of the people, thinking that cash would be needed in the camp, sold their land and other property that they owned, along with the tools they had; whereas my husband and I thought that having cash wouldn't do any good because we did not know what was about to happen to us. We also thought that no one would steal our property . . . well, rather, we didn't care if someone did. So, instead of selling what we owned, we decided to leave it all, including the land. We put the tools and farming equipment in the garage. By removing some of the floor-tiles, we put our beds and mattresses in the basement, together with our locked car.

While we were still in the camp, the cannery wanted to borrow some of the stuff we left. We didn't feel we could refuse, because we left our ranch under the care of the cannery. We let the boss at the cannery know about the arrangement of our basement. They didn't touch our car, but instead they used our tractor, for they had a huge ranch. They gave it back to us when we returned, though it was pretty worn out by then.

There was a Mexican family that was working for us at evacuation time. When we left for the camp, we gave them the rice and all the other groceries that were left in our house and asked them to live in our house and take care of it for us. They were a very nice Mexican couple with a lot of children. They took very good care of our house, as a matter of fact. We informed them from the camp when we were coming home. When I came home, I found just about everything in pretty good shape. The icebox was still there as we left it. The interior of the house was kind of messy but other than that, it was fine. We were glad that nothing was missing.

On our ranch, which was in front of our house, we had about forty acres of boysenberries. When they were about ready to be picked—it was June 5—that was when we had to go to camp. It was also in June that we came back from camp. Again, it was the harvest time of boysenberries.

When we were about to restart our life here, we were told that we had accumulated a debt of two thousand dollars to the cannery in the three years of our absence, and the boss wanted us to sell the boysenberries that year so as to pay back the debt. You see, before we went to the camp, we had some peach trees and walnut trees in addition to the boysenberries which were ready to be harvested. We left all that under the care of someone. Now I don't know how much the workers made off of it nor how much they were actually paid. Some of them might have reported more hours than they actually worked. I don't think the boss at the cannery made any dishonest money himself, but it was the workers who did so, I suppose. Anyhow, we found ourselves with a two thousand dollar debt to pay.

The boysenberry harvest of that year was picked by those who had no houses to go back to upon their return from the camp. A lot of them came and helped us on the ranch. One day when we brought the boysenberries into the cannery, the workers there were on strike, and we were told we'd have to dump all the berries. Our daughter was driving the truck. She was staying with us that season, having come back from Washington, D.C. When she returned from the cannery, she told us about the strike and what she was told to do. I told her that we couldn't possibly dump any of it, since we had paid the workers to pick it. I told her to ask the boss to let us use the cannery's icebox for a while, and, as it turned out, the boss let us do so.

The next buyer we had was a pie factory in town. They bought as much as we harvested. We asked them if we could continue to bring in a lot more from our ranch, and they agreed. For quite a while we sold it to them at eleven cents a pound. When the strike at the cannery was finally over, the boss said he could buy from us at the same price. At that point we shifted back to the cannery again. I am glad about the way it worked out. Without any great trouble, we were able to pay back the two thousand dollars quickly.

It's not a big ranch we have here, and therefore whatever problems we had about our ranch were not big either. Just little by little each year we made a profit on our ranch with the help of our son, Ard. My son is a quiet, gentle man. When my husband was around eighty, he decided ranch work was too much for him to continue any longer and wanted to work in town instead. Luckily, some TV station was newly built not too far from where we live. Since he needed some pocket money himself, he went there and asked if they needed a janitor. Being near to the place, he and our son, the two of them, became janitors at the TV building.

My husband's mother was still living in Japan at that time. She was a hundred years old then and wanted to have a birthday anniversary. My husband went back to Japan to celebrate her anniversary, since she wanted him to very badly. He stayed in Japan for a long time, nearly ten years. And all that time he was not doing anything over there except drinking. I told him to come home, since it had been almost ten years by then. When he did, he had a paralysis problem. It's been six years since he died. After he came back from Japan, he was bedridden until he died.

MRS. HANAYO INOUYE

When we left camp, we received thirty dollars apiece, including the children, to cover whatever expenses that might occur in the short period of time to follow. We came straight back to Sacramento.

We were invited to come back and work for the Robinsons near Marysville again. However, my husband thought that the time had come for our children to continue their schooling. Some of them were already of high school age, and eventually the question of going to college came up. If we stayed in Sacramento, we knew our children could go to colleges of their choosing; so my husband was not quite willing to go back to the Robinsons. That was when Mr. Sato invited us to stay with his family. He is truly a kind man. You see, he had nine children of his own. Who would do the same as he did for us? At that time Kanji was working at the Christian Center, and Takaji had received a scholarship upon graduating from high school. He used to go to school half-heartedly, saying that because of the war, anything could happen and so what was the use of studying. He would find a lot of excuses not to take school seriously. But in the end he straightened himself out and studied very hard. I'm proud of him. One thing that troubled us was that because of the kind of scholarship he was granted, he could not go to a college here. It meant a loss to us during the harvest seasons. Takaji went to college in Detroit, and his older brother also went there. Although he had only a high school diploma, he worked for some pepper company. Out of the savings he made while working for the company, he put himself through a school of electrical engineering.

When Takaji turned eighteen, he was going to be drafted. Again and again, my husband proved his smartness in handling the matter. At that time there was a funeral service almost every day for those who were killed in action overseas. Therefore, I was very much reluctant to see Takaji go in to the service at that particular time. I knew he had to go one way or another, but the question was when. The Army then was looking for people who could speak Japanese to be interpreters; so my husband told Takaji to volunteer for it, which meant that he had to further study the language for several months. That's how my husband went around buying extra time for our son. About the time Japan surrendered, Takaji was assigned to Japan; so he really didn't have to fight in any actual combat situations.

We stayed at the Satos' for nearly two years, and in the meantime my husband went to work from there. When we Japanese people came back from the camp, most of us didn't have houses to return to. Some people took shelter in leaky barns and slept on haystacks. The situation was that bad. Mr. Robinson wanted us to go back and work for him. While we knew that if we accepted his offer we were guaranteed a comfortable living unlike other people, we decided at that time not to go back. People laughed at us for refusing such a nice offer and said that we must be out of our minds.

Yet we stayed with the Satos and from there my husband went to work, and at the same time we looked for a new place to live. After checking a number of places, we found one that we almost decided to buy. Then, out of nowhere, we heard of this fifty acres of land. We liked it very much at first sight.

I am so grateful to our two oldest sons; I can't praise them enough. I know of some young people who didn't like their large families and went to work somewhere and never returned. The ones that were left home were the old and the very little ones. Our oldest son had a good job, but yet he came back here. Being an experienced electrician, he found a job when he came home and worked from three to twelve at night. Then in the mornings he used to get up early and help us in the fields. I used to find the lights on in his room until late at night after he came back from work. One night I peeked into his room, for the lights never went off that night again. He was reading a book. The younger son finished high school, but he was not able to go to college. I remember he was ordering a lot of books, and he was studying at home. Later he went to Washington and was licensed as an engineer. He deserves what he has now. He really worked hard. When Takaji came back from military service, he saw what his brother was doing and said to me, "I'll help you work in the field for one year." At that time I thought that after getting out of the service, he might have lost his interest in school. Anyhow, he stayed home and helped us for one year. With the savings he made during that year, he went back to school in Berkeley.

When he started his schooling again, he used to tell me that however hard he studied, he could not comprehend as well as he used to. He made it in the end though. On Friday nights he came back here from the University in Berkeley, and on the following Saturdays and Sundays he worked in the strawberry fields. Then on Sunday evening he went back to Berkeley on a six o'clock bus. All my children worked hard like that one way or another.

It was in 1952 that they bought me air tickets to Japan. I wasn't quite ready to go at that time, but they said, "Mama, you've had enough hardships. Why don't you visit your parents in Japan while they are still alive?" So I did. It had been thirty years since I had left Japan.

○ ○ ○ ○ ○ ○ ○ ○ ○ ○ ○ ○ ○ ○ ○

Well, I still work this land. It took my husband a lot of pain and toil to buy this land; so I don't think it's right just to let it stand idle.

PART VI:
THE LEGACY

16

The Foundation Is Laid

NISUKE MITSUMORI

I am embarrassed to say this, but I have no hobbies. I have always worked. I don't like to brag about myself, but I struggled with great difficulties. I was sick for a while and poor. Another reason why I kind of avoided having a hobby was my fear that I might die any day, and I felt that to use my energy and time for my own recreation and pleasure was not excusable. . . . I know how to play *go,* but I don't play it. I don't fish either. My children say that I should have some kind of hobby. I could not play with them, and for that I feel sorry for them.

If young people learned a little more about the difficulties in the Issei's life struggle, their ideas might change somewhat. It is important for them to know that they can be as they are today because of their grandparents. I am afraid that they are not interested in learning this. I think the Nisei, too, suffered with us Issei. Some Issei farmers had a hard time, and sometimes the cost of producing was higher than what they could earn by selling their products. The children of those farmers, the Nisei, did not even have a pair of shoes to wear to go to church. The Sansei (third generation, grandchildren of the Issei) do not know much about these experiences. That's why I feel they take everything for granted.

A banker I know says that if it is a Japanese signature, there's no problem. I have had a lot of dealings with the Bank of California and the First Security National Bank. Those who work in loan departments at these banks know very well that Japanese always others—Japanese and blacks, blacks and whites, whites and Japanese—we can create a spirit of understanding; and then we can expect a truly harmonized world. If the Japanese hate to be Japanese or try not to talk about it, then that's an abnormal state. Soon it will give birth to something very strange. But it appears to me that people [Nisei and Sansei] these days have a tendency to put a little bit too much emphasis on distinctive Japanese views. If Japanese people insist on pushing forward what is good only for the Japanese, then other ethnic groups will step back unwillingly. There is no truly harmonized life in that approach. Then you have to face the rising antagonism. We should live our lives for the good of the whole world.

MRS. TOME TAKATSUKI

We, the Issei, felt that to be a burden to someone else or to receive grants from the government was a shame. When we came from Japan, we came only with the bare necessities, and we all worked hard. Eventually people opened businesses or worked on farms. The young mothers did not go out to work until the children were old enough. They stayed at home and helped take care of their businesses and waited for the children to come home from school. They economized on clothes and food, and strived to remain economically independent. This is characteristic of the Japanese people: they worked hard and saved money.

MRS. HANAYO INOUYE

I believe it's best to be honest, just, and to study hard, to not be insolent and conceited. When you think that you are wiser than others, you are very likely to go wrong. They say in Japan, "The lower the wisterias hang down their heads, the more upwardly people look to them." The more humble you are, the more you will be looked up to.

We Issei have gone through tremendous toil and hardships, and most of us tried our best to even look after our parents back in Japan. People in this country don't take care of their parents to that extent. The Japanese of the Meiji era were taught in school to honor "filial piety to parents, fraternity among brothers and sisters, harmony between husband and wife." Times have changed.

Mrs. Kane Kozono

Buddhist teachings make us walk straight and in the right direction. Buddhist wisdom also teaches us to be straightforward and to know our place in life. "In weaving, a string has to follow its own line on a given cog. If it moves out of its place and stands in another string's way, it snaps short. It has to stay where it is set and follow the straight line." My mother taught me that. I have always kept it in mind so that I could live an honest, straightforward life. Since I've raised my children with that same idea, they are very honest.

Riichi Satow

If the Japanese could remain simply part of the human race, it would be just ideal. However, that is not possible in the light of the international situation we have today. Arabs have their own identity, Israelis have their own, and Europeans may think they are the best race of people in the world. How about Japanese? And how about black people? In my opinion the Japanese are, despite many shortcomings, an outstanding group of people. By that I mean we do have something other ethnic groups don't have. We should try to preserve the good aspects of our culture and possibly develop them. I don't believe in making a big fuss about one's ethnicity on everything; however, I do believe that no one should ever forget one's ethnic identity. It's impossible to forget it completely. On a political level, we are, of course, committed to the American system. But on a cultural level, we can introduce our cultural heritage and contribute our cultural wisdom to American society.

Following Columbus, the Pilgrim Fathers came all the way from Europe to America. Many came and immigrated to this country. The American continent must have seemed, when seen from Europe, truly both the New Heaven and the New Earth. Also to the people of the Middle East, America must have seemed that way . . . a wonderful land. The morality in this country is decaying to a certain degree; yet America has not lost her way totally. She is still a country of great hope and promise. In a very short period of history, she grew to be such a great country and is still "the land of milk and honey."

For the last hundred years the Japanese people have immigrated to America, and as seen from Japan, it was the New Heaven and the New Earth. It's a marvelous thing to leave this for our children to succeed in. We are all responsible for keeping this beautiful land for our Sansei and Yonsei (fourth generation, great grandchildren of the Issei), and for many more generations of ours to come. We shouldn't ever ruin this land in any way; instead, we must hold ourselves responsible for making this land as it should be.

Minejiro Shibata

No, I don't miss those old days. Thinking back, I wouldn't call it a humane life. People drank, gambled, and fought. Being broke, they robbed, deceived others and their wives. There were too many problems in those days. I like my present life, for I can live like a human being should live. People today own a house and a car. . . . Of course, we couldn't afford a car then.

I don't want to go back to Japan to live. I'm used to living here. Though I've been here for fifty years, I don't speak English well. My Japanese isn't good, either. I'm just in-between. Since my children were raised here, it's best for us to live in this country. I don't have too many friends and acquaintances in Japan. Besides that, having been taken over by the next generation, the house where I was born and raised doesn't have a place for me. I'd be just a hanger-on there. Having established my life here for fifty years, I feel that this is my home.

Now I don't want to catch fish anymore; I just want to see the sea. I retired about fifteen years ago. I had a whiskey business for ten years after that, but it was a dangerous, bad business.

Three years ago, my mother died at the age of ninety-nine in Japan. She felt terribly bored all the time. She was too old to listen to the radio or to watch TV. It's a Japanese family custom to celebrate one's hundredth-year birthday at the age of ninety-nine. I went to Japan to celebrate my mother's hundredth birthday. Seeing her well, I came back here without any worries, but she became sick a few months later. Outsiders say she was happy to live such a long time, but I'm not sure if she was really happy.

As I've turned old, I don't have anything to say. Observing young people today, I daresay that the Nisei and Sansei are more reliable than the young people in Japan who are spineless. Some compare them to bean sprouts, which is true. They shouldn't be that weak-minded. Japanese movie stars and singers are spoiling the society. Our young people are much more serious.

There aren't too many Issei fishermen left. In my bachelorhood, my acquaintances drank, gambled, and fought. Some died; others returned to Japan. Having been irresponsible in their young days, the single Issei in Japan are living alone in misery. They have neither family nor savings. They say it's better not to have any burdens. As for me, a life without a family isn't a true life. You'll be at a loss after you get old. The government doesn't take care of you completely. In the first place, you shouldn't rely on others. I always tell my children not to rely on others. Japanese people complain that the Japanese social security system doesn't pay enough. They just think of getting money for free. The social welfare system in Sweden is given as a good example, but we shouldn't forget that Swedish workers have half of their income deducted for social security. When I visited Japan, people said to me, "We envy you because the social security system in the United States pays you well." I said, "We work and pay a premium for it." They think we get our social security for free. What I've done isn't good enough for me to advise young people. I admire them. . . .

17

Children and Grandchildren

YOSHITO FUJII

I brought our family genealogy back when I made a trip to Japan. I showed it to my children and grandchildren. They were deeply impressed by it. I showed them when our family line started, and they were amazed. At one time I advocated the following: What about making a genealogy of the Issei, Nisei, and Sansei? We Japanese didn't appear in the United States by accident. It would be interesting in the future. People who have family records should offer them for studies. If we donate reports on Japanese Americans to schools, students may get interested in us. It may not be valuable to the Nisei and Sansei at present; however, it may be valuable ten generations later or something.

The Nisei, who observed their fathers as youngsters, still don't realize how hard their fathers struggled. They are too subjective to realize what the Issei actually have done. The Sansei are amazed at how great their grandfathers were. The Sansei question themselves about whether they could do the same things that their grandfathers had in the past, and they come to the realization that what their grandfathers had done wasn't easy. The old people were great! They've started to appreciate the Issei.

When I traveled to Japan, the principal of my old high school asked me to give a speech at a high school in Hiroshima. I talked about my personal history—how, many years ago, I had graduated from high school and when I had left for America. I gave the speech while student riots were going on in the United States. I said to them, "Don't imitate such foolishness. You should study and learn. Science is advancing rapidly. Those students who can't catch up with their studies cause riots. They feel discouraged with study. I have learned something new every day since my graduation from college about fifty years ago. I consider study a lifelong task." I told the students about a TV program which I had seen in San Diego. The theme was: every living thing has feelings. It made me think. After I returned home, I took a look at the plants in the yard. I also checked the carp in the pond. I decided not to forget to feed the fish. Eventually, the fish learned to anticipate my footsteps. One Sunday one of my grandchildren, who kept his fish in my pond, came over to see the fish with his friend. He named the fish "Mikan" or something. The pond was full of water lilies, and they couldn't see the fish well. They stirred the water with a stick. I told them not to do such a thing but to copy what his grandpa would do. I said, "Come on, come on," gently. Then all of the fish came up. I said, "Every living thing has feelings. You should be nice to them next time." Your heart communicates with other living things. You shouldn't waste even a minute. I still have new things to learn. The Sansei and Yonsei's future can be bright, depending on their way of thinking.

MASAO HIRATA

My present wife and I were not going to have children. But as time passed, she wanted our own children. She felt lonely in America, because she didn't understand English nor have a friend here. I was perplexed at the unexpected request from her. I already had six children and was fifty-six years old when I married her. But I understood her and decided to have our child. First, we had decided to have only one child, but two years later, we had another daughter. Then a boy was born.

Last year, on May 20, which was the birthday of my eldest son and my second son, I visited the hospital where they were born to take pictures. Then I went to the place where I was working on a strawberry farm when my eldest daughter was born. My father died after she was born. When he was dying, he said to me, "I really regret that I was not able to send you beyond junior high school." Now an elementary school stands on the very place where he died. Someone planted a pine tree there, and I brought the tree back here. All my children and grandchildren got together. We had dinner together and had a celebration party at my third daughter's house.

Sometimes my eldest son invites me to go out golfing, and we play together. Since I was not rich, bringing up six children was difficult, but they helped me a lot. One day they asked me to get a car for them, but it was not easy for me to buy it. I got the car for them on the condition that they help me work after school so that I could work extra to pay for it. As soon as they came back from school, they changed their clothes, ate some cake or fruit, and worked a few hours every day. I think it's important to give children what they want, even though you may be poor.

We have always helped one another in my family; therefore, the relationship between my older children and myself is close. Some people are surprised because the first wife and I are divorced. Even my present wife is surprised, too. As soon as something goes wrong with my health, two sons come over to visit me, saying, "How do you feel, Papa? Are you all right?" So I feel strong. Although we don't live together, our hearts are always one. My eldest daughter brought her daughter here yesterday. "Hi, Grandpa!" she said. I said, "Oh, Cathy, welcome here!" I am happy with these grandchildren. I have ten of them. My second son's son is now going to college. He is receiving a scholarship from the state. He told me that all he had to pay was for the books he needed. That's a good thing, so I told my younger children to get scholarships. Then one said, "Daddy, I got five A's and only one B." "Oh, you had better get all A's," I said. "Oh, that's too hard!" This is a happy conversation to have with my children.

I think that money should be for bringing up and educating children. There is no value in money saved that isn't used for the children's education. In my opinion, it is our responsibility to bring up and educate our children so that they may become independent from other people.

When my son's friend visited my house, he said to my eldest son Takeo, "Hey, Tak, your papa isn't papa-like. He looks like your brother, doesn't he?" When I talk with people, I consider myself to be the same age as they are. I never talk as a senior to them. How could we communicate with each other without being together in our hearts? The three children I have now also think of me as their friend and say, "Daddy, let's go someplace. Give me a ride." And we go golfing together. I have golf clubs for all three children, share the balls in a bucket, and enjoy shooting.

Parents and children should play or do something together. This way they can understand one another better. Usually parents don't want to be bothered by their children, but that is not right. Children are happy to do something together with their parents. My wife also seems this way; she avoids playing with them. So I always say to her that it is not good. I say to her, "They cannot wash dishes as well as you since they are young, but do it together." It is natural that children can't accomplish things as well as we adults. When we worked together on a farm, I gave the children a small part of it to take care of themselves, showed them how to seed watermelons, and let them do it themselves. How happy and excited they were to find the sprouts from the place they had seeded. For them it was a great discovery. "Papa! Flowers came out! We got watermelons!" they reported excitedly. We can't educate children by just telling them; we have to show them through actions and doing things together with them.

I hear that the fathers in Japan, in spite of their being important executives, earning a lot of money and financing their children through schools, come home late at night when the children are asleep, go to work after the children have already left for school, and don't have any chance to see the children or talk to them. They have no communication nor contact with one another. The only relationship they have is that they are of the same blood. This is very sad. Parents should teach their children so that the children can talk about anything to their parents without hesitation. My children used to bring their friends to my house to introduce them to me. I used to tell them that everyone hid their bad points and only showed good points, and that the only way to judge the friend was to see the mother and father. The child will become like the parent in later years.

When my sons were in the military in Europe, I wrote them long letters every week about golfing events here and other topics. I kept all the letters which they wrote to me, and when they returned home, they asked me what I was going to do with that huge number of letters. I told them that I was going to keep them as a memory, and they laughed with pleasure. We are always together at heart even if we live far apart.

The Issei worked very very hard to support their families and to send their children to school. Since the Issei didn't know English, they worked on farms and brought up many children. But the children have become Americans who don't know Japanese. In

Japan there is a saying, "Be dutiful to your parents, be faithful to your country," but in America, the philosophy is not the same. In America they don't teach filial piety. The Issei don't like the attitude of their children and say that the children aren't grateful. In my opinion, this is not true. The Nisei know it, but because of the language problem, they cannot communicate their feelings to their parents and other Issei people. I say to the Issei people, "I think that we Issei are responsible for this fact, because the Nisei didn't come from the sky but were brought up and educated by us. If my children are bad, I am the one who is responsible."

We Japanese people here are also citizens in this country and have the same rights as the others. But the color of our face and of our hair has not changed even after a hundred years. As long as we have the blood of the Japanese, we have inherited many good aspects that the Japanese possess.

Kiyoshi Noji

I think the Japanese Issei are a quiet and peaceful people, and I think their education and upbringing in Japan contributed to this. They do not like to fight. They are grateful for the kindnesses they receive, and they like to reciprocate.

One good characteristic of the Sansei is that they are broad in their thinking, like the Americans. The Issei were raised in a small country and their thinking is not broad. I think the Sansei can contribute more to this country by knowing more about Japan. The Japanese tradition of "loyalty" is a strong point. Another good point is *reigi* (etiquette). We are too busy these days, but we should apply what we can to our daily lives. And another thing is "delicacy." Mrs. Noji's group is in a poetry class today. There is beauty and delicacy in such art. We do need "masculinity," but we also need "tenderness."

Mr. Osuke Takizawa and Mrs. Sadae Takizawa

Mr.: (looking at a photo) These people were from my neighborhood and from the same village as mine. This man is dead, this man is dead, and this man was the owner of an inn. He was thrown off a horse and died. I'm the only survivor among these people.

Mrs.: It is a joy to live for eighty-eight years. However, you can't help feeling lonely after all of your friends have died.

Mr.: I believe children and grandchildren must know the way their grandparents walked. The Sansei and the Yonsei should know their grandparents' history. One thing for sure is that the Issei in the United States were all diligent and did their best. All of the Issei wish that the Sansei and the Yonsei learn and appreciate our history. That is greater filial piety than building a large monument or holding a special celebration for us.

You are a homeless dog without your identity. Though we are U.S. citizens, we are Japanese. The color of our faces and so on. . . . Losing identity is the same as losing money: you lose your way of life.

Even if a person becomes rich or gets a high position in the federal government, you can't retain your greatness with a rotten life. Take Nixon, for example. He was famous once; however, such shameful deeds have arisen around him. You can hide only so much. Even Nixon, who was the president of one of the great nations in the world, couldn't hide the facts. I believe our God judged him.

Mrs.: I believe so too. The President of the U.S. doesn't have to come from among the Sansei or the Yonsei. All I desire is that people with great thoughts who lead others spiritually should come from among them. That is my wish.

Wataru Ishisaka

I was a little different from most Issei. I really didn't like those Japanese organizations. However, I was one of the persons responsible for creating a Japanese youth organization in Courtland, because the youth organization had the definite and useful purpose of education.

The other day one of those Japanese *kenjinkai* clubs had a celebration for one of its older members. Well, that's fine, but the guests donate between ten and one hundred dollars for that event. If they have money like that, then they should start a scholarship fund or something for the sake of educating the youth. That's my opinion. We must look at things in the long run. If you create a scholarship, then a student can use it for one semester's fees or books. But they don't understand that. Sometimes those people have heads like acorns!

One of the mistakes that the Issei made was that they all came to America by themselves. All other European immigrants came as families. That's why it seems to me that the Europeans were more successful than the Issei. The Europeans came here with the idea of settling here, while the Issei came here to make money and go home. It was the biggest mistake that the Issei made.

But the Japanese are honest people, and they work very hard. If the Sansei continue the same tradition of honesty and hard work, they can establish strong roots in this country. However, I hope that they learn to see things with a long-range view, instead of just earning money for tomorrow. The Japanese must become intimate with the land and learn to deal in big business. If you are an office worker, your life is very stable because you get a monthly income; however, your life style is set forever. You must really think about these things. A farmer's life is very hard, but there is a great deal of freedom and also greater possibilities. But young people don't like to get their hands dirty. They want to buy big houses and big cars. These are just for outside looks only. They don't give you real roots. One should pour his whole life into anything he does.

It's our responsibility to teach the youth about being Japanese, about our traditions and having pride in being Japanese. I do think that the feeling of not bringing shame to the Japanese race is very important.

They say that this period is very different from the past, but I feel there were periods like this before. There were always those people who used dope and alcohol. It all depends on the leadership of the community and government. They say children now are very bad, but it is all their parents' fault. There is no family education. I think if young people learn to respect grandparents and older people, they have a great future. But if they don't, they will not be any good. These things have to be taught. The most important thing for a human being is to have an education. It's very important not to produce children who are half baked. Some say, "You had children at a convenient time." But I say there is no such thing as a good period or a convenient time. Each period has its own problems. One must always be aware of them.

But first is education. With education, respect and courtesy come too. The youth who do not have respect have nothing.

People who do not have courtesy and respect are just like dogs and cats. It's really true. Something will work out. I couldn't send all my children to the University of California in Berkeley, but they were all able to graduate from colleges. The twins went to a state college, and one got his doctorate. Anthony, the youngest, was able to go to Berkeley and get his doctorate there. Two children have doctorates, and two have bachelor degrees.

I wanted to send all my sons to the University of California in Berkeley, but I had a heart attack, and I had to spend all my savings on the hospital and doctor bills. My mother was ill too, and we spent our money for her as well. However, I think a man can make it somehow, just like the poem which says: "When a man puts his name on the line, he does his best."

KENGO TAJIMA

A man should have historical faith. That is not only the history of the old people, but particularly the history of our various backgrounds, the culture that is behind us.

SADAKUSU ENOMOTO

After the war I turned over the nursery business to my eldest son, who is nearly sixty. He is in the nursery business in Redwood City, and my second son is running the import business within the nursery now. We have ten acres in Half Moon Bay and a new 10,000-square-foot nursery in Redwood City. Once I was asked to march in a parade as a pioneer in Redwood City.

PART VII:
APPENDIXES

Biographical Sketches

ENOMOTO, SADAKUSU was ninety-four years old when he was interviewed in San Francisco, California. He was born in 1880 and emigrated to the United States in 1899. He worked as a houseboy while acquiring some facility in English and eventually attended a business college. Before and after World War II, Mr. Enomoto was a successful nurseryman with acreage in the South San Francisco Bay area.

FUJII, YOSHITO is the second son of a farmer who traveled to the United States, returned to Japan, and subsequently encouraged the emigration of several hundred Japanese. Yoshito Fujii was born in Hiroshima Ken and emigrated in 1919 at the age of nineteen. He finished high school in Seattle, Washington, and continued his education but stopped just short of receiving his master's in sociology. Mr. Fujii became a successful businessman and owned a bottling company and other rental property before his internment in a North Dakota camp after the outbreak of World War II. He was reunited with his family at the Puyallup Assembly Center and then transferred to the Minidoka Relocation Center in Idaho. After the war, Mr. Fujii returned to Seattle and reestablished himself in the hotel business. He was seventy-three years old and semi-retired when he was interviewed.

FUKUDA, SHOICHI, the son of a Tokyo merchant, was born on January 3, 1901, in Kumamoto Ken. His father had emigrated to the United States alone, leaving his son in the care of his wife and grandmother, both of whom died before Mr. Fukuda was eleven years old. His early years, which were lonely and difficult, were spent in various apprenticeships. When Mr. Fukuda was seventeen, his father made arrangements for his emigration. Mr. Fukuda worked as a traveling dry goods salesman, a small grocery store owner, and a farmer in Broderick, California.

HAYASHI, KAZUKO (MINEJIMA) was the daughter of a samurai who became a Shinto priest. Even after her father's death, when the family's wealth was diminished, Mrs. Hayashi was treated as a person with rank and social position. In 1909 she married Mr. Minejima and emigrated to a Japanese Christian farming colony in Livingston, California, where Mr. Minejima was the equivalent of a village chief in Japan. Mr. Minejima died in 1911, when his wife was pregnant with their first child. She married Mr. Hayashi in 1914. Mrs. Hayashi helped her husband farm in the Salinas area. He died suddenly in 1925, when she was pregnant with their youngest son. With help from Mr. Hayashi's two brothers, Mrs. Hayashi managed to raise seven children. During the war her family was evacuated to Arizona, and she then relocated in the Midwest. She returned to California in 1960.

HIRATA, MASAO was born in Kumamoto Ken in 1903. He graduated from elementary school and was then forced to work hard for his room and board, since his mother had died and his father had emigrated. In 1920 he met his father for the first time in the United States. They both worked as farm laborers. Mr. Hirata later bought land to farm for himself. He was interned in Roseburg, New Mexico, while his wife and six children were evacuated to the Poston Relocation Camp. The Hiratas returned to California in 1946. They were divorced in 1953, and Mr. Hirata remarried in 1959. He became a father again at fifty-six and raised three more children. He was seventy-one when he was interviewed in Los Angeles, California.

IGARASHI, TOSHIKO, born in 1894 in Chiba Ken, is the daughter of a Christian medical doctor. Mrs. Igarashi completed elementary school, four years in a women's school, and then became a certificated midwife and registered nurse. After she and Mr. Igarashi were married, they came to the United States and settled in Sacramento, California. She helped her husband in their grocery business while he studied to become a minister. After the war, the Igarashis set up a hostel in their church to receive families returning from relocation camps.

INOUYE, HANAYO was born in 1902, the second daughter in a somewhat privileged middle-class farming family in Hiroshima Ken. Mrs. Inouye completed six years of elementary school and two years of high school. When she was twenty-one years old, she married Mr. Inouye, who was visiting Japan from the United States, and she returned with him to California. Before the war, the Inouyes managed a ranch in the Marysville, California, area. After the war, the Inouyes refused a generous job offer to return to Marysville because they felt that educational opportunities in Sacramento were much better for their children. All three Inouye sons eventually obtained a college education. Mrs. Inouye was seventy-two and still working the family farm when she was interviewed in Elk Grove, California.

INOUYE, RIKAE, born in Ehime Ken in 1897, was the daughter of a farmer who was also a village official. She came to the United States after her marriage to Mr. Inouye, who was farming rented land north of Seattle, Washington. The Inouyes later moved to California to farm, and Mrs. Inouye helped her husband by selling their produce in a flea market until the war began. The Inouyes spent a year in the Tule Lake Relocation Center, where two of their children became ill. They left the camp and resettled in Kansas until the end of the war, when they returned to California. Mrs. Inouye found work in a cannery and retired in 1962.

INOUYE, SADAME was born on December 3, 1888, in Takata Ken. He was the eldest son in a family of farmers and stonecutters. Mr. Inouye emigrated in 1906 to earn money to pay off family debts. He worked as a farm laborer and returned to Japan for a family visit and to marry in 1917. In 1919 Mr. Inouye joined a Japanese farm colony in Merced, California, but the colony eventually failed, and he moved to Sacramento, California, to farm. After the war, Mr. Inouye returned to the Sacramento area to resume farming.

ISHISAKA, WATARU was born in 1906 in Kumamoto Ken. He emigrated in 1923 and married a Nisei (second-generation Japanese

American). He spent his entire life farming in the United States and was the proud father of four children, including a set of twins. He spent the war years in the Amache, Colorado, Relocation Camp. An incredibly energetic man, Mr. Ishisaka helped support several families upon his return to the Sacramento, California, farming area after the war. Mr. Ishisaka died in the spring of 1978.

ITANO, MASAO was born in Okayama Ken in 1889. He emigrated to the United States in 1906 and became a domestic worker until he saved enough money to begin high school. He eventually graduated from a university in 1917 with a major in agriculture and farmed in California until 1920. He worked as an insurance agent until the war. During the war years, Mr. Itano was interned in Bismarck, North Dakota, and Santa Fe, New Mexico, but later joined his family in the Tule Lake Relocation Center. Each of Mr. Itano's four children left various relocation camps to obtain a university education. After the war, Mr. Itano returned to California.

KIZUKA, TOKUSHIGA was born on May 22, 1901, in Fukuoka Ken. When he was six, his parents left him in Japan and emigrated to the United States. He was seventeen years old before his father summoned him to make the trip. He worked as a farm laborer and eventually farmed his own land around Watsonville, California, until the war. Mr. Kizuka was active in the Japanese community and as a result was interned for seven months in Bismarck, North Dakota, and then in New Mexico for more than two years. His family was evacuated to the Poston, Arizona, Relocation Camp, where he finally joined them. During the war, Mr. Kizuka's eldest son joined the Army. Mr. Kizuka returned to Watsonville after the war and resumed farming with the help of both Caucasian and Japanese friends in the community. He was interviewed in Watsonville in October, 1973.

KONO, JUHEI was seventy-six years old at the time he was interviewed in Seattle, Washington. He was born in Hiroshima Ken on January 9, 1898, and emigrated in 1911, after graduating from elementary school. He attended the College of Puget Sound and received his M.A. from the Pacific School of Religion in Berkeley, California. Mr. Kono was living in Hawaii when Pearl Harbor was bombed. He comments extensively on the social and moral climate within the Japanese community as a whole and on his work as a minister in specific areas.

Kozono, Kane was born on September 11, 1880, in Fukuoka Ken. She attended grammar school only sporadically and did not learn how to write. She sailed to the United States in 1907 to meet her husband, who was working as a gardener in Alameda, California. Mrs. Kozono worked as a housemaid and then as a farm laborer when her husband moved to the Sacramento area. In addition to helping her husband in the fields, Mrs. Kozono raised six children. The Kozonos were evacuated to the Tule Lake and Amache relocation camps during the war, but returned to the Sacramento area after the war.

Miyasaki, Ai is the daughter of a progressive-thinking farmer-pawnbroker, who insisted that all his children attend school. Mrs. Miyasaki completed high school before she came to the United States in 1916 from Kumamoto Ken, where she was born in 1892. Mrs. Miyasaki, an independent and outspoken woman, was careful in her choice of a husband. She suffered severe culture shock when she followed her new husband into the restaurant business near Reno, Nevada, where life was lonely, because very few people spoke Japanese in that area. She almost returned to Japan but decided to stay with her husband when they moved to the Sacramento area. The Miyasakis ran a boarding house and restaurant until the war. They resettled in the Sacramento area, but because Mr. Miyasaki continued to suffer from tuberculosis and its complications, Mrs. Miyasaki found work as a housekeeper. She is now retired.

Mitsumori, Nisuke, the son of a farmer, was born in Yamaguchi Ken on February 15, 1888. After emigrating in 1905, his first job in the United States was setting type at a Japanese weekly newspaper, the *Nichi Bei Shimbun.* He worked briefly as a cabin boy on a small ship and as a farm laborer before joining the United States Army during World War I. In 1936 Mr. Mitsumori finished college and became an accountant. During World War II, he spent only a few months in the Manzanar Relocation Center and then went to the University of Michigan to teach Japanese to American military personnel. Mr. Mit-sumori was eighty-four when he was interviewed in Pasadena, California.

NAGASAWA, TSUGUO was born on December 29, 1896, in Yamanashi Ken, the son of a bookkeeper. His parents had emi-grated, and Mr. Nagasawa spent many lonely and unhappy years as a child raised by relatives. In 1915 he joined his father in the United States and worked at various jobs along the West Coast. He finally settled in Portland, Oregon. There he experienced business failures that left him with bitter feelings about Cauca-sians and Christianity. Mr. Nagasawa spent most of the war years in the Tule Lake Relocation Center and identified himself with Japanese sympathizers during the war. After the war, he returned to Japan, where he lived for ten years before he fol-lowed his children back to the United States. When he was interviewed, Mr. Nagasawa was seventy-eight years old and still working four days a week as a gardener.

NITTA, CHOICHI was born on March 17, 1887, in Yamaguchi Ken. He emigrated at the age of sixteen and spent most of his years farming. He was eighty-six years old when he was interviewed in Loomis, California.

NOJI, KIYOSHI was born in 1899 in Miyagi Ken, the second son in a farming family of six. A well-educated man, he attended a Christian mission school in Sendai, Japan, and completed four years of college before coming to the United States. He emi-grated in 1927 and continued his education at the Pacific School of Religion and then received his master's degree from Prince-ton. He has served as a minister in various Japanese Christian churches along the West Coast. He was interviewed in Seattle, Washington.

ORITE, RIYO, born in Hiroshima Ken in 1895, was the daughter of a farmer and acupuncturist. Her childhood was generally a happy one, and her father hired a variety of special teachers to school her in flower arranging, music, and sewing. She came to the United States in June, 1914, after her marriage to Mr. Orite. She spent many lonely years as a housewife and mother in Wyoming, where her husband worked for a railroad company.

In 1927 the Orites moved to Sacramento in order to school their children in the Japanese language. Mrs. Orite enjoyed the companionship of other Japanese when her family was evacuated to the Tule Lake Relocation Center, but she also had many misfortunes during the war years. Her husband died, and her son was drafted into the military. She was seventy-nine when she was interviewed in Sacramento, California.

OSAKI, TOMI was born in 1890 in Wakayama Ken. She entered Kyoritsu University for women after completing elementary school and prepared herself for a teaching career. She taught in a girls' high school and became a proctor. She married Mr. Osaki in 1920 when he had returned to Japan for a visit. Once in the United States, Mrs. Osaki helped her husband on his pear ranch and raised three children. After the war, Mrs. Osaki began a Japanese language school and her husband became a gardener. She was interviewed in San Francisco, California.

SATOW, RIICHI was the son of a landed farmer who emigrated to the United States to recoup his financial losses in Japan. Mr. Satow was born on April 29, 1895, in Chiba Ken and came to the United States at the age of seventeen. He spent most of his early years as a farm laborer but eventually became an independent strawberry farmer. Mr. Satow, his wife, and nine children spent most of the war years in the Poston, Arizona, Relocation Center. He relocated in Colorado, but eventually returned to California, where he felt economic and educational opportunities were more favorable for his family. Mr. Satow was seventy-nine when he was interviewed in Sacramento, California.

SHIBATA, MINEJIRO was born the son of a poor farmer in Shizuoka Ken in 1902. He emigrated to the United States in 1919 at the age of seventeen and spent his most active years as a fisherman working out of Terminal Island. He was separated from his family when he was interned in Bismarck, North Dakota, after the outbreak of World War II. After seven months, he joined his family at an assembly center, the Santa Anita Race Track. The Shibatas were eventually assigned to the Jerome, Arkansas, Relocation Center. When he was interviewed, Mr. Shibata was seventy-one years old and living in Los Angeles, California.

TAJIMA, KENGO was ninety-one years old when he was interviewed in San Anselmo, California. He was born in 1884, the
son of a poor farmer in Gumma Ken. His family was Christian,
unusual in Japan in those times. Mr. Tajima came to the United
States as a theological student and became a minister. He has
served in Salt Lake City, Utah; Cincinnati, Ohio; and Pasadena,
California.

TAKAHASHI, KAMECHIYO was born in Wakayama Ken in 1889.
After completing elementary school, Mrs. Takahashi obtained
a license to teach sewing. When she was nineteen, she met and
married Mr. Takahashi, who was also a teacher in a nearby
town. Her husband emigrated in 1913, but Mrs. Takahashi was
pregnant with her second child and remained in Japan until
1916. During the three years before her emigration, she became
a certified midwife, and she set up a clinic in San Francisco
soon after her arrival in the United States. After being
evacuated to the Topaz Relocation Center, Mr. Takahashi died.
Mrs. Takahashi was eighty-one years old when she was interviewed in San Mateo, California.

TAKAKOSHI, KO was born in 1903 in Fukushima Ken. She emigrated to the United States in 1918 and soon married. Her contacts with Caucasians in the state of Washington centered
around a Baptist church, and she remembered being treated
with respect and kindness. When her family was evacuated to
the Minidoka Relocation Camp, Caucasian members of her
church were helpful during the war years, as well as during the
resettlement period. Unlike those of most other Issei, Mrs.
Takakoshi's Caucasian contacts were gratifying. Mrs.
Takakoshi was seventy-one when she was interviewed in
Seattle, Washington.

TAKATSUKI, TOME was a school teacher who was born on June 4,
1891, in Ehime Ken. She taught in a Japanese language school in
Sacramento, California, and her husband was a produce jobber.
Though they eventually purchased a house, they encountered
discrimination in the real estate market in 1920. The Taka-
tsukis spent the war years in the Tule Lake and Topaz relocation camps. Since they had no children, Mrs. Takatsuki gave
financial assistance to a niece and nephew to complete their

college educations. Mrs. Takatsuki was seventy-eight when she was interviewed in Sacramento, California.

TAKESHITA, SHIZUMA was born in Nagasaki Ken on September 10, 1880. He ran away from home at the age of seventeen to become an apprentice lawyer in Tokyo. His plans were thwarted, but his sponsor helped Mr. Takeshita secure passage to the United States in 1921. Mr. Takeshita worked for the *Nichi Bei Shimbun* in the San Francisco Bay area, and then became an insurance salesman until he retired in 1937. He spent the war years in the Topaz, Tule Lake, Jerome, and Heart Mountain relocation camps. Upon his release at the age of sixty-four, he began learning to do housework as an occupation and also spent much of his time and energies regaining citizenship status for his stepson, who had been forced into the Japanese Army during the war. He was interviewed in Oakland, California.

TAKIZAWA, OSUKE was born in 1886, the second son of a village official in Nagano Ken. He was a farm laborer in the United States and clerked in his future in-laws' grocery store before his marriage. He also helped his in-laws in their noodle factory. Mr. Takizawa was employed in an import-export firm when the war began. The Takizawas relocated in Minneapolis after the war, but eventually returned to Oakland, California, in 1951. When he was interviewed, Mr. Takizawa was eighty-eight.

TAKIZAWA, SADAE was born in 1889 in Nagano Ken. Although her father was originally a farmer, he was a descendant of a samurai family. She graduated from a girls' high school before she and her family joined her father in the United States in 1907. Her father ran a noodle factory and a grocery store, where Mr. Osuke Takizawa worked. She married Mr. Takizawa in 1919 at the age of twenty-seven. The Takizawas were evacuated to the Tanforan Assembly Center and then to the Topaz Relocation Center, where Mrs. Takizawa spent her time raising her three children occasionally writing some poetry, and reading. Mrs. Takizawa was eighty-three when she was interviewed.

WASHIZU, TAKAE was born in January, 1900, in Aichi Prefecture. Her father was a poor tenant farmer, and Mrs. Washizu felt that she was mistreated in school and in her village because of her poverty. She emigrated to rebel against a village that had treated her with disdain. She was twenty-one and her husband was forty-three when she married and followed him to the United States in 1921. Throughout her life she worked hard as a farm laborer, raised three children, and felt that she and her husband did not have much in common. But she continued to work hard for her family, because she had no alternatives and believed that all would eventually benefit from staying together. After their return from the Amache, Colorado, Relocation Camp, the family split up in order to find employment and housing. The Washizus eventually found a house and resumed their lives together.

YAMAMOTO, ZENTASO was born in Wakayama Ken in August, 1886. He emigrated in 1907 and first worked on a railroad but spent most of his years farming. Two of his sons served in the United States military while Mr. Yamamoto remained in the Poston, Arizona, Relocation Center. Mr. Yamamoto was eighty-eight when he was interviewed in Watsonville, California.

Index